TOUR DE OZ

TOUR DE OZ

BRET HARRIS

HarperCollins*Publishers*

HarperCollins*Publishers*
First published in Australia in 2017
by HarperCollins*Publishers* Australia Pty Limited
ABN 36 009 913 517
harpercollins.com.au

HarperCollins*Publishers*
Level 13, 201 Elizabeth Street, Sydney NSW 2000, Australia
Unit D1, 63 Apollo Drive, Rosedale, Auckland 0632, New Zealand
A 53, Sector 57, Noida, UP, India
1 London Bridge Street, London, SE1 9GF, United Kingdom
2 Bloor Street East, 20th floor, Toronto, Ontario M4W 1A8, Canada
195 Broadway, New York NY 10007, USA

National Library of Australia Cataloguing-in-Publication data:

Harris, Bret, author.
Tour de Oz / Bret Harris.
ISBN: 978 1 4607 5177 0 (paperback)
ISBN: 978 1 4607 0665 7 (ebook)
Richardson, Arthur, 1872-1939—Travel.
White, Frank—Travel.
White, Alex—Travel.
Mackay, Donald, 1870-1958—Travel.
Cyclists—Australia.
Cycling—Australia—19th century.
Bicycle touring—Australia—19th century.

Cover design by Hazel Lam, HarperCollins Design Studio
Cover images: Donald Mackay courtesy of the Museum of Applied Arts and
Sciences; Arthur Richardson on bicycle, 1897, courtesy of the State Library of
Western Australia (000739D); all other images by shutterstock.com
Typeset in Perpetua Regular by Kirby Jones
Printed and bound in Australia by Griffin Press
The papers used by HarperCollins in the manufacture of this book are a natural,
recyclable product made from wood grown in sustainable plantation forests.
The fibre source and manufacturing processes meet recognised international
environmental standards, and carry certification.

CONTENTS

Author's Note

IT was fate that led me to write this story about the first bicycle race around Australia. When publisher Helen Littleton approached me with the idea I was fascinated. A lone cyclist riding around this vast island continent in 1899– 1900. And all the while being pursued by a rival party of three cyclists riding in the opposite direction. What a yarn! During my research I discovered that it was Helen's distant relative, the Toowoomba bicycle manufacturer Thomas Alfred Trevethan, who first suggested to Arthur Richardson that he should attempt to become the first to ride a bicycle around Australia. Helen had no idea of her family connection to the historic ride, yet she instinctively knew it was a great Australian story. Fate, perhaps.

I am indebted to Helen for her encouragement and support, but my gratitude certainly does not end with her. I was warned there was not sufficient information on the two competing rides to put together a book, but I managed to glean material from several largely untapped sources.

I owe special thanks to the News Corp librarian Lurline Campbell, who has assisted me with almost all of my books, for teaching me how to use Trove, an Australian online library service. The rides were extensively covered by newspapers of the day, principally the *West Australian*, providing a wealth of valuable information.

I acquired a copy of *The Story of a Remarkable Ride* from the National Library in Canberra. This was Arthur Richardson's own account of his ride as told to 'Pedal', the *West Australian*'s cycling writer. I found a tattered second-hand copy of Frank Clune's excellent biography of Donald Mackay, *Last of the Explorers*, in the iconic Gould's bookstore in Newtown, Sydney. And two pioneering books — *The Bicycle and the Bush* and *Wheeling Matilda* — by the pre-eminent cycling historian Jim Fitzpatrick provided great background.

I desperately needed more information to flesh out the story, but I was unsure where to find it. Then, fortuitously, I found some of the cyclists' descendants, who were incredibly supportive and helpful. Once I contacted these relatives the emails just kept coming and I was able to include never-before-published material in the book.

It is important to note that the overlanders used outdated language which would be offensive today, but was common practice in the less politically correct times of the late nineteenth century and early twentieth century.

A researcher, Robyn Horner, put me in contact with one of Arthur's descendants, June Bagley, who referred me to another relative, Bruce Cameron, whose wife, Jasmine, was Arthur's great-niece. Bruce was a tremendous source of information, particularly in relation to Arthur's character, family background and military career. Without Bruce's tremendous input, it would have been difficult to create a complete picture of Arthur.

Details of the lives of the White brothers, Frank and Alex, were sketchy. There was very little to be found about their backgrounds or what happened to them after the ride. Then I happened upon an article in the *Listening Post*, the journal of the Western Australian branch of the RSL, about the experiences of Fred White, the younger brother of Frank and Alex, in World War I. Fred's granddaughter May Hayes-Thompson was quoted in the article and I tracked her down in the West Australian Wheatbelt region. A charming lady, May could not have been more helpful, sending me wonderful information about the White family's history.

There was more pure luck — or was it fate once again? While I was talking to the around Australia record-holder, Peter Heal, in his home in Canberra, he happened to mention that he had been interviewed by an ABC broadcaster who told him she was related to Donald Mackay. I contacted Genevieve Jacobs at the ABC in Canberra and she invited me to visit Wallendbeen, the historic Mackay family pastoral property, where she lives with her husband, David Baldry, who is Donald Mackay's great-nephew.

Wallendbeen is a special place. Genevieve and David live in the original station manager's cottage, which has had some modern extensions. David showed me around the beautiful property and we were joined at dinner by Mike Baldry, the family's historian. It was great listening to the three of them talk about Donald and the Mackay family history. After dinner, Mike gave me a bundle of yellowed newspaper articles written by Donald for the *Cootamundra Herald* about his ride around Australia, which proved a fantastic addition to the source material.

I suspect the tremendous support I received from the descendants had little to do with me, but was more a desire on their part to see the historic achievements of their cycling ancestors rightfully acknowledged. I hope I have not disappointed them.

I do not pretend to be a cycling expert, but as the nineteenth-century British prime minister Benjamin Disraeli once said, 'The best way to become acquainted with a subject is to write about it.' I consulted the above-mentioned cycling historian Jim Fitzpatrick, while my friend and occasional colleague Rupert Guinness, the doyen of Australian cycling journalists, was generous with his knowledge. Another old colleague Peter Cunningham also offered valuable advice. I learned a lot from Daniel Oakman, a senior curator at the National Museum in Canberra, who had developed a superb exhibition called 'Freewheeling: Cycling in Australia'. Similarly, Margaret Simpson, a curator at the Powerhouse Museum in Sydney, had created an exhibition on Donald Mackay and was very helpful. I would also like to acknowledge the efforts of librarians at the National Library in Canberra, the Mitchell Library in Sydney, the State Library of Western Australia and the Battye Library in Perth.

With my research complete, I started to piece together this amazing story, but I could not have done it without the guidance of one of HarperCollins' senior editors, Scott Forbes, who is the most thorough editor I have ever worked with. The most important thing I learned from Scott was to see the story through the eyes of the reader. Unfortunately, Scott suffered severe illness during the editing process, but still managed to read the manuscript in his hospital bed. That's the spirit of the overlanders! While Scott was recuperating, we were fortunate to secure the services of brilliant editor Amanda O'Connell to complete the project. My thanks also go to Madeleine James for co-ordinating the final edit and chasing photographs.

Last, but not least, I need to acknowledge the love, support and patience of my wife, Jenny, and our daughters, Sophie and Rachel, who lost our dining-room table for eighteen months while I used it as a desk.

This remarkable story centres on four main characters — Arthur Richardson, Donald Mackay and the White brothers, Frank and Alex. But there is a fifth character: Australia. While writing about the overlanders and their incredible rides, I realised I was also drawing a profile of an ancient, yet young, country on the verge of nationhood. And what an enormously satisfying experience that was. From the rapidly growing cities of the south-east to the rugged wilderness of the North West, I could feel the growing sense of Australianness as the cyclists raced each other around the island continent at the turn of the century. If you want to fall in love with your country, write (or read) a book about someone riding a bike around it.

Bret Harris, 2017

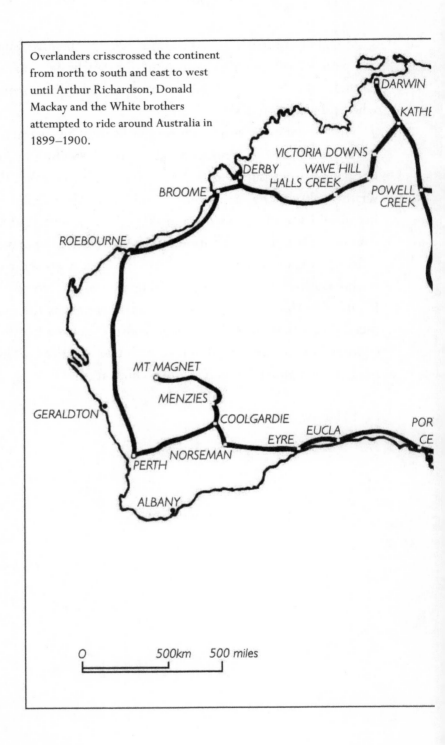

Overlanders crisscrossed the continent
from north to south and east to west
until Arthur Richardson, Donald
Mackay and the White brothers
attempted to ride around Australia in
1899–1900.

DARWIN

KATHE

VICTORIA DOWNS

DERBY   WAVE HILL

HALLS CREEK

POWELL
CREEK

BROOME

ROEBOURNE

MT MAGNET

MENZIES

GERALDTON

COOLGARDIE

POR

EUCLA

CE

EYRE

NORSEMAN

PERTH

ALBANY

O   500km   500 miles

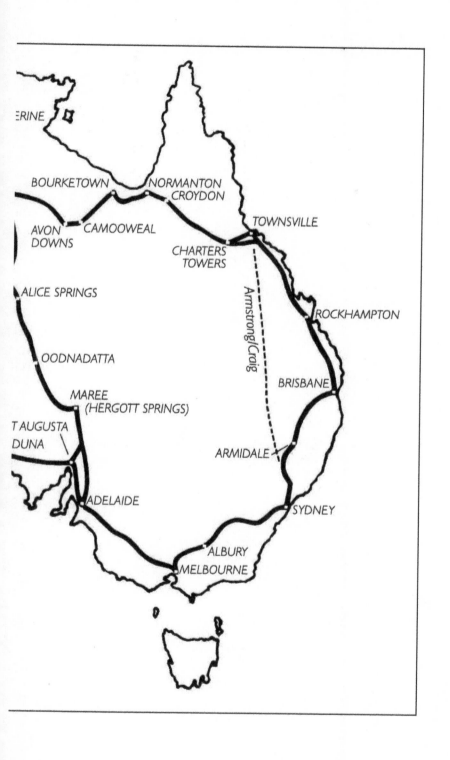

ERINE

BOURKETOWN

NORMANTON
CROYDON

AVON
DOWNS

CAMOOWEAL

TOWNSVILLE

CHARTERS
TOWERS

ALICE SPRINGS

Armstrong/Craig

ROCKHAMPTON

OODNADATTA

MAREE
(HERGOTT SPRINGS)

BRISBANE

T AUGUSTA
DUNA

ARMIDALE

ADELAIDE

SYDNEY

ALBURY
MELBOURNE

Prologue

The Dream of
the Overlander

Before mounting his bicycle he scans the vast blue horizon. Endless flat plains shimmer in the scorching heat. Squat saltbush scrub offers no shade from the blazing sun.

Wiping the sweat from his forehead, Arthur Richardson picks up a faint track in the shifting sands. He knows these tracks can disappear without trace. Even worse, a cyclist can be confronted by tracks leading in different directions. Take the wrong one and the cyclist might end up who knows where, hundreds of kilometres out of his way. If he runs out of food and water, which is a real danger if he loses his bearings, he might perish. It might be weeks or even months before anyone finds his body, mummified by the hot desert wind and sand – if they ever do.

But Arthur is not one to entertain such negative thoughts. An unlikely looking adventurer, he is thin and mild in manner. Just twenty-four years old, he seems to belong behind a desk in a city office rather than on a bicycle, inching across the harshest terrain on the Australian continent. But he is tough, resourceful and apparently fearless. After seven years prospecting for gold around Coolgardie in Western Australia's eastern goldfields, he knows how to survive in the outback. Astonishingly, he only began riding a bicycle a few months before embarking on this journey across an alien landscape, the Nullarbor Plain, which the explorer John Eyre described as 'a hideous anomaly, a blot on the face of nature, the sort of place one gets into in bad dreams'.

Arthur is one of the new breed of cyclists known as the overlanders, most of whom have emerged from the sandy tracks of the Western Australian goldfields of the 1890s. They are hardy, courageous, independent-minded, adventurous and maybe even a touch mad. Crisscrossing the continent from north to south and east to west, they have blazed trails from coastal cities to the wild frontier, traversing rivers, mountains, deserts and plains. With a cycling craze sweeping the world, the overlanders' exploits excite the public and the press, who follow their every move, not to mention bicycle and tyre companies keen to capitalise on their amazing feats. But to achieve fame, if not fortune, an overlander must be the first to navigate a route or be the fastest. So they race each other and chase records, all the while proving the utility of this revolutionary machine, the bicycle.

Although he was warned not to do something as foolhardy as ride across the Nullarbor, particularly on his own, Arthur was determined to make this pioneering trip. The more than 2000-kilometre journey he is attempting is by far the longest since Percy Armstrong's first transcontinental ride from the Gulf of Carpentaria to Melbourne three years earlier. Many overlanders have contemplated crossing the Nullarbor, but none before Arthur has dared – the fearsome wasteland is just too dangerous. That has not deterred Arthur; in fact, it may well be what is spurring him on.

Arthur, carrying only a small repair kit and water bag, has a great capacity to endure hardship, the constant companion of the overlander. On this ride alone he has already slogged through the worst sandhills in Australia, baked in temperatures '1000 degrees in the shade', travelled more than 350 kilometres without seeing another human being and been blinded by sandstorms. He is sunburned, saddle-sore and exhausted, his wrists aching from the strain of holding the handlebars. There is still much hard riding ahead of him, but he is just past the halfway mark with about 1200 kilometres to go. It is now Wednesday, 9 December 1896, and he has been riding for sixteen days. By his calculations he should reach Adelaide by Christmas.

While a rider less accustomed to privation might be envisioning the warm welcome he would be likely to receive at the end of his ride, not to mention the comfortable bed and satisfying meal, Arthur is already thinking of a new adventure. Something bigger, much bigger. If he can conquer the Nullarbor, why not go all the way and ride right around Australia? Make a complete circuit of the colossal island continent. This is a big dream, but it is within reach. The amazing new technology of the bicycle, which has tamed the arid wasteland of the Nullarbor, can carry him — even if not always easily or quickly — over any terrain anywhere. As long as he keeps pedalling, the bike will take him wherever he wants to go, even if he has to occasionally dismount to push the machine through patches of soft sand or carry it over his head while wading through a river.

Yet the idea seems insane, something thought up by a madman. The Nullarbor, hideous as it is, is one thing, but the wild far north of Australia is another altogether. This is one of the most dangerous places on earth, particularly for a lone cyclist. Arthur would have to contend not only with thirst and hunger while riding across a sandy desert, but would face dangers from flooding rivers, untamed wilderness, hungry crocodiles, poisonous snakes and Aboriginal warriors resisting European intrusion. And if he was not drowned, eaten, poisoned or speared, he might well perish of exhaustion or some exotic disease.

Arthur is intelligent, if somewhat strong-willed and stubborn. He knows the risks are real and the challenge great. But how else do you test yourself? Against other overlanders, against other bicycles and against the country itself. Is that not what being an overlander is all about? After what he has been through, he feels he can tackle just about anything.

The first to ride around Australia. The idea has grabbed hold of him. He cannot stop thinking about it. But he cannot afford to get too far ahead of himself. He still has to finish this ride. He takes a swig of precious water from his water bag and stows it. Swinging a leg over the saddle, he shifts his weight onto the upper pedal and pushes down. The wheels begin to turn and he rides towards a new horizon, the dream of the overlander beckoning.

* * *

The dream of the overlander begins to unfold a few years later on Monday, 5 June 1899. On a cool, crisp morning, thousands of onlookers throng St Georges Terrace, Perth's main street, which is lined with elaborate multi-storeyed buildings, a legacy of the gold boom. Rarely has Perth experienced such excitement. Chosen as the starting point for this historic bicycle ride around Australia, the young town is bursting with civic pride. It seems as if the whole population has come out, waving and cheering wildly. The governor of Western Australia, Sir Gerard Smith, sporting an elegantly waxed moustache and white goatee, adds a touch of pomp and circumstance to the momentous occasion, while sponsors of the ride gleefully calculate the anticipated increase in sales of bicycles and tyres.

In the middle of this hubbub stands Arthur Richardson, stern-faced and steely-eyed, wondering what all the fuss is about. A centre of calm amid the chaos surrounding him, his expression does not betray any emotion, certainly not fear. If anything, he is mildly irritated that he should have to tolerate the overbearing well-wishers, the pompous bigwigs keen to bask in his reflected glory and the nosy reporters with their interminable questions.

Arthur's pioneering conquest of the Nullarbor Plain is well known to the crowd. As he predicted, he reached Adelaide in time for Christmas, thirty-one days after setting out, after riding approximately 2100 kilometres over primitive roads and sandy tracks in temperatures that soared to 52 degrees. The longest stretch of the journey without seeing another human being, black or white, was 354 kilometres, while the furthest waterless stage was 128 kilometres. Arthur had a 'rough time of it', but he enjoyed the ride, which inspired a spate of long-distance cycle journeys. From 1896 to 1900 about two dozen cyclists undertook overland rides across the harshest and most isolated parts of the continent. And now he has inspired something even more thrilling.

For the tremendous excitement is due not just to Arthur's ride, but because it is now clear that he is engaged in a race. A rival team of three overlanders has decided to compete with

Arthur to be the first to ride around Australia. It will not be a traditional race in that the competitors are not setting off at the same time or even from the same place. In fact, they will be riding in opposite directions and departing a month apart. But the trio will be trying to beat Arthur around the continent or, at the very least, lower his time. They also aim to better the world long-distance record held by the British cyclist Robert Louis Jefferson, who rode 16,000 kilometres from London to Irkutsk and back, the capital of Eastern Siberia, in 1896.

Arthur is fully aware of his rivals' plans, but he is unfazed. He has met one of the opposing team, Frank White, and knows of his remarkable achievements. They shared an oyster dinner a few nights earlier, swapped tales of epic rides, compared their routes and preparations, took each other's measure and agreed to dine together again if they survive. He may not admit it, but deep down Arthur knows the trio will benefit from mutual support and camaraderie. But he has faith in his skills and stamina. Unlike his rivals, he is not afraid to ride alone.

The questions from the press, however, are exhausting, much more so than a hard ride across harsh terrain. He would rather push his bike across a sandhill than be interrogated. He is repeatedly quizzed on the likelihood of failure, a lonely death on some godforsaken plain. Heaving a deep sigh, he responds as he always does: 'I have anticipated the journey which I am about to undertake for the past two or three years. I fully appreciate the difficulties and dangers attending it, but being fond of adventure and quite inured to hardships, I have little fear of failing.' He cannot wait to leave.

At last the time has arrived. Sir Gerard solemnly signs Arthur's time-sheet at 10.45am and wishes him good luck, possibly not fully realising just how much he will need it. The crowd strains to catch a glimpse of the overlander as he sets off from the General Post Office with an escort of cyclists, who show their respect by accompanying him for several kilometres along a bad road. As Perth vanishes in the distance behind them, the last of the riders wave cheerily, yell farewell and turn around. Alone at last, striking a steady rhythm, Arthur feels his heart lift and his spirits soar. He is free.

* * *

There are similar scenes one month later in Melbourne when the rival overlanders depart on the cold, windy Wednesday afternoon of 5 July. Melbourne is the centre of Australian cycling and there is a real buzz in the city. If anything, the excitement and anticipation surrounding the race have increased. 'The movements of these riders will be watched with interest as it is practically a race around the continent and the first attempt of its kind,' the *Leader* reported.

Two men stand by their bikes in front of the grand General Post Office, the brothers Frank and Alex White. They do not look at all alike. Frank is tall and thin with a prominent nose and weak chin; Alex is handsome and broad-chested with a square jaw. While he is seven years younger, Alex looks the older of the two brothers. More importantly, both appear to be in excellent condition and their brand new machines glisten in the winter sun.

Frank learned to ride in Coolgardie, Arthur's home for so many years, where the brothers, too, went in search of gold. He later became a member of the Metropolitan Cycling Club, the leading club in Perth. He has been riding for three years as he prepares to set out around Australia and is already something of a national hero, having undertaken a record-breaking ride from Perth to Rockhampton and back again the previous year. He completed the 14,500-kilometre ride in five months, taking 152 days. He also became the first to ride across the Nullarbor east to west.

Alex, however, is an unproven rider, drafted by his older brother at the last minute. Learning to ride on the old French-manufactured Gladiator bicycle Frank rode from Perth to Rockhampton, he has only been cycling since the previous October. 'Don't think he is a novice, though,' Frank tells the press. 'He is a big strapping fellow and can plug all day.'

The third member of the team is nowhere to be seen. The wealthy pastoralist and amateur cyclist Donald Mackay has had to postpone his departure due to business commitments, but it is anticipated he will join the others in Brisbane. 'Frank White, the overlander, or cirumcontinentaler, will be accompanied by Donald Mackay, the well-known squatter of Wallendbeen, New South Wales,' the *Launceston Examiner* reported. 'Mackay is a true sport and cycles for the love of it. He has cash galore and his friends say that if he likes the country through which he passes he will buy it as a few million acres more or less are nothing to him.'

Melbourne is an appropriate starting point for the White brothers' ride. Approaching the turn of the century, it is one of the largest and wealthiest cities in the world, its population exploding to around 490,000 during the gold rush of the 1850s, leading to the construction of palatial mansions, stately public buildings and beautiful wide boulevards. It will become Australia's first capital when the six colonies federate in 1901. The cycle race is symbolic of a growing sense of nationhood, fulfilling a need for new heroes in an isolated land yearning for identity and ripe for myth-making, its European settlement little more than one hundred years old. A large crowd of several hundred, principally cyclists, throngs the corner of Bourke and Elizabeth streets to give the brothers a big cheer as they ride off at a quarter past one, leaving the comforts of the most civilised city in the land for god knows what lies beyond the far horizon. The race around Australia is on.

The steely determination is evident in Arthur Richardson's eyes in this studio portrait of the overlander on his bicycle.

Stage One

A Restless Soul

Arthur
Perth to Roebourne
5 June to 2 July 1899

WHEN asked why he wanted to ride around Australia, Arthur would say that 'a love of adventure and pioneering work' were what drove him. While he did not regard himself as an explorer, he was curious about what was over the horizon, particularly the last frontier that was Australia's wild north. 'During my life on the goldfields I had met several men who had roughed it in western Queensland and on the Kimberley and I always had a yearning to see the country, which, to the vast majority, even in Australia, is still a closed book,' Arthur recalled. 'I had, during 1896, been across to the South Australian border from the Coolgardie fields, and I wanted to traverse the continent higher up.'

The prospect of financial reward was also a motivating factor. Bicycle manufacturers and tyre companies provided bikes and tyres, and also offered lucrative cash incentives – but the overlanders, particularly unproven riders, usually had to complete the course to receive payment.

When Arthur initially approached the Dunlop Tyre Company for support, the managers laughed in his face, saying the journey around Australia was far too dangerous. Dunlop would not have wanted to be associated with a failed ride, particularly if it ended tragically, but Arthur, drawing on his Nullarbor experience, managed to convince them he was capable of completing it and secured their backing. If Arthur somehow managed to succeed, Dunlop would not want to miss the opportunity to exploit his ride commercially. It was a gamble, but one that the company considered worth taking. It was certainly minuscule compared with the risk Arthur would face.

Arthur was provided with a Beeston Humber path-racer, the aristocrat among bicycles, a diamond-framed design reminiscent of today's modern bicycle. But it had just one gear and no auxillary brakes, and its steel frame was heavy, making for a slow ride compared with today's carbon-fibre bikes. But the old-fashioned bikes ridden by the overlanders had their advantages. Their ride was smoother, particularly over rugged terrain. The steel frame absorbed the imperfections of rough roads and tracks and could be repaired almost anywhere with the exception of the remote outback because every town had a blacksmith. Arthur's path-racer was fitted with newly invented brazeless joints, which could be completed without brazing, or soldering at high temperatures, and provided a joint which was 'at once light, rigid and strong without exercising undue strain on the tubes or other parts and whereby the parts can be readily detached when so desired', according to English inventor James Twigwell. His bike also had multiflex Dunlop pneumatic tyres of the latest pattern, duplex forks and side stays, and 88-gear

Bicycle messengers played a key role in the development of the Western Australian goldfields by providing fast and reliable communication.

and 6-and-a-half-inch cranks, which is near the top of the range of a modern multi-gear bicycle.

Percy Armstrong, Australia's first transcontinental cyclist in 1893, the founder of Coolgardie's 'Special Bicycle Express' messenger service and owner of the largest bicycle sales agency in Western Australia, also arranged for reports of Arthur's progress to be printed in the *West Australian* newspaper, for which the overlander received payment. Whenever Arthur arrived at a telegraph station he was required to send a telegram to the newspaper for publication to keep the public informed of his ride, although he did not always meet his deadlines.

There were conflicting reports about how much money Arthur was to receive from his sponsors. The *Eastern Districts Chronicle* in York, Western Australia, quoting an English cycling newspaper, claimed he received £500, the equivalent today of $72,000, an average annual salary. This was disputed by the *Kapunda Herald* on 18 May 1900: 'According to one English

cycling paper, Arthur Richardson, the Westralian cyclist ...
received the sum of £500 ... Needless to state, the amount
is greatly exaggerated, and we think that £150 [$21,000 in
today's money] would be nearer the mark.'

But the driving force behind Arthur's epic ride was his
burning ambition to become the first to cycle around Australia.
This was the dream he was chasing.

* * *

Arthur was a restless soul, which was perhaps not surprising
given his somewhat exotic background. He was born on 23
February 1872 in Recife, the capital of the state of Pernambuco
and a city known as the Venice of Brazil for its many rivers, small
islands and bridges. He was one of ten children of Dr Arthur
Richardson, an Englishman who was in charge of the British
hospital in Recife, and his wife, Isabella (née Merrifield).
Arthur was the second child and first son. A Richardson
family tradition was naming the first son Arthur, but he was
affectionately known as 'Artie' to family and friends.

Dr Richardson was descended from a long-established
Yorkshire family. He received his professional education at
Victoria University in Manchester and obtained his diplomas
in England, Scotland and Belgium. When Arthur was a young
boy the family moved back to England where Dr Richardson
occupied for some time the position of honorary surgeon to the
Manchester Dispensary.

In 1880 the Richardsons migrated to Queensland and lived
in Townsville before moving to Auckland, New Zealand, the
following year where Dr Richardson was honorary surgeon
to the Auckland Hospital. Arthur completed his primary

schooling in Auckland and started high school at Auckland Grammar School, which later produced mountain climber and explorer Sir Edmund Hillary, but the Richardsons moved back to Australia, to Adelaide, in 1885 and after spending his formative years in the City of Churches, Arthur became 'practically a South Australian'. He attended Whinham College in North Adelaide and later Adelaide Collegiate School. Interestingly, the aims of Whinham College were 'to develop moral training, physical training and mental training' in that order, which would have been a solid grounding for his ride around Australia.

Arthur studied engineering at the Adelaide School of Mines and served his time as a mechanical engineer at the Glanville Way and Works Yard. Afterwards he worked as a miner and station hand in the outback and was in the South Australian Militia Rifle Company. When gold was discovered at Coolgardie in 1892 he was among the first hundred prospectors to join in the rush, leaving Albany, a port on the southern coast of Western Australia, with three 'brumbies' and a pack. It was one of the few times he used horses because he did not seem to get along with them.

For seven years Arthur prospected in and around Coolgardie, gaining valuable experience and skills as a bushman. It was in Coolgardie that Arthur and his brothers learned to ride bicycles. They joined a bicycle club and competed in races.

Arthur capitalised on the fame and recognition he earned with his ride across the Nullarbor by opening a cycle shop with his brother Frank in Kalgoorlie, in the heart of Western Australia's eastern goldfields. Richardson Bros Cycle Mechanics ('Accessories, Repairs, Highest Grade Workmanship') became a successful business.

His father also moved to Kalgoorlie to practise as a physician and became a 'prominent and popular' local identity. When Dr Richardson died of 'heart trouble' in 1927 at eighty-four years of age, the *Western Argus* eulogised him as a 'notable goldfields identity': 'Dr Arthur Richardson, one of the most prominent figures in the history of Kalgoorlie, dating back to the early years of these goldfields, passed away on Wednesday. The late Dr Richardson retained possession of his mental faculties to a remarkable degree for a man who had gone much beyond the allotted span of life. He was a great believer in walking as an exercise for the preservation of health, and his daily habit was to walk for many miles in visiting his patients or in taking part in social functions. He was a wonderfully well preserved man of upright carriage and distinguished presence.'

It would seem that Arthur inherited some of his father's traits. Arthur did not drink or smoke and he was also a strong believer in the benefits of walking. Arthur would take a 'little stroll' from Bullabulling to Coolgardie, a distance of twenty-eight kilometres, to have tea with his friend Harry Sparrow and stroll back again. On one occasion he walked eighty-three kilometres without food or water after breaking the front forks of his bicycle in rough country. His long walks would have been a good preparation for his ride, which involved a lot of tramping over unrideable terrain.

Arthur was described in contemporary newspaper reports as being of medium height and having a slight, wiry frame. More than one questioned whether he had the physical capacity to endure such an arduous and dangerous journey as a cycle ride around Australia, especially on his own. Maybe the press expected to see some powerful athlete rather than a slightly built, average-looking fellow. But cycling is more forgiving

Arthur capitalised on his fame by opening a cycle shop in Kalgoorlie with his brothers Frank and Herbert, Richardson Bros Cycle Mechanics. It is believed the bicycle in the window was the one Arthur rode around Australia.

of height and weight than other sports. Unlike runners and swimmers, cyclists do not have an ideal body type. Training and experience are more important in cycling than a specific physique and Arthur was well qualified in both of those areas.

Even so, Arthur's physique did not seem to inspire much confidence. There is a photograph of him on his bicycle in which he is wearing a jacket, knickerbockers and a cap with a pom-pom on top, which was typical cycling attire for the time. A rucksack is tied to his handlebars. He hunches forward slightly, staring straight at the camera. The expression on his face is enigmatic, his lips curved in a half smile like the Mona Lisa's. He looks like he is setting off for a picnic in a park rather than a death-defying adventure around an intimidating continent.

But appearances can be deceiving. Arthur was as hard as iron. A quiet, unassuming character, he was also highly independent, determined and almost fearless. And like all the overlanders who were prepared to risk their lives riding across remote, uninhabited places, he had boundless self-confidence. He had to have a healthy ego to believe he would be able to survive such a dangerous and difficult journey. A young man, Arthur would also have had a certain youthful sense of invincibility, at least when he set off – for riding around Australia on his own would remind him of his mortality and the fragility of life.

* * *

Arthur had to decide where he would start his ride and in which direction he would travel. He had a close association with Adelaide and was a member of the North Adelaide Bicycle Club, while Melbourne was the epicentre of Australian cycling. But given his time in the eastern goldfields of Western Australia there was an argument for him to leave from Perth, also a noted cycling town and home to Percy Armstrong's Cycling Agency, the sole Western Australian depot for the Beeston Humber path-racer. And Arthur had another practical reason for choosing Perth. It would be the beginning of winter when he set out and weather conditions and the availability of water influenced his thinking about the course he should take.

'Because of enquiries which I had prosecuted I was of the opinion that I would get through what might be termed the bad country under the most favourable weather conditions of the year,' Arthur recalled. 'Taking the rainfall and astronomical conditions of the past few years as a guide, by starting in June and going north through the Murchison, the tropical rains would be over, the most temperate weather would be prevalent about the time that I expected to be crossing from Derby to Queensland, and water would then also be more easily obtainable than at any other time of the year.' So from Perth he would cycle clockwise around the continent.

To work out the details of his route, Arthur, in his typically meticulous manner, contacted a range of experts, including the surveyor-general of Western Australia. 'Of late I have been gathering information from miners and others on the goldfields who are acquainted with the different portions of the country through which I shall pass and they are not nearly as fearful as I at first supposed,' Arthur said. 'Mr Johnson, the surveyor-general, has been very helpful to me in supplying information regarding the tracks, and is having a plan prepared for my use.'

A large map of Arthur's intended route was erected above Armstrong's Cycle Agency in Hay Street in Perth to allow the public to follow his progress, but he did not always travel quite according to plan. His original idea was to ride via Dongara to Geraldton, keeping as close to the coast as possible, continue north to Carnarvon and Roebourne and then follow the telegraph line to Derby. He would then go down the Fitzroy River to the police camp at Fitzroy Crossing and strike out along the telegraph line to Halls Creek at the edge of the Great Sandy Desert. This way he would avoid the tall red sand dunes of Australia's second-biggest desert, although patches of it would have to be traversed.

Water would be plentiful during the winter months and the distance between places where Arthur would be able to obtain provisions would not exceed 300 kilometres. From Halls Creek he would pass similar country until he struck Port Darwin where he would touch the coast for the first time since leaving Derby. From Port Darwin he would follow the Overland Telegraph

Line down to Powell Creek. From there he anticipated fairly flat country with black soil plains and rivers right on to Normanton in the Gulf Country of north-west Queensland. It was on this stage that Arthur expected to face the most danger from hostile Aboriginal groups. 'I will need to camp well away from water and avoid them as much as possible,' he said.

Once he entered Queensland's pastoral country, Arthur considered his difficulties would be at an end. From Croydon it would be relatively easy riding down through Charters Towers, Rockhampton, Brisbane, Sydney, Melbourne, Adelaide and Port Augusta. He would then have to traverse once more the greatest obstacle he had ever encountered in his riding career, Eyres Sand Patch on the Nullarbor Plain, but as he had crossed it before, and others had done so since, he was confident of succeeding again.

The route did not include the island colony of Tasmania, probably because interrupting the journey by crossing Bass Strait in a steamer would mean that the overlander could not claim the world record for the longest continuous ride.

Arthur had full confidence in his bicycle and estimated that the whole trip would take him no more than five or six months. His load was light, weighing no more than 11.4 kilograms. He took a repair kit, some duplicate parts, a water bag, a camera and an oil-sheet, but no blanket or rug. He did not think it necessary to carry a substantial supply of provisions as he could obtain food at cattle and sheep stations, which would last him until he again reached civilisation. 'Should my machine fail me (of which I have no fear) I will be able to fix it up again, as I have served my time as a mechanical engineer and know all about a bicycle,' Arthur said, not as a boast, but as a statement of fact.

That Arthur anticipated completing the circuit of Australia in five or six months indicated just how much he underestimated the enormousness of the task.

Despite Arthur's confident predictions, many people, according to the *West Australian*'s cycling writer, 'Pedal', were 'dubious to his chances of success'. The *Launceston Examiner* expressed grave reservations about whether 'wiry-looking' Arthur would be able to 'endure such a journey'.

There were even fears that Arthur would simply disappear somewhere in the great emptiness between Perth and Port Darwin and never be heard of again. 'During the journey along the West Australian coast to Port Darwin in the Northern Territory he will cover the most difficult and dangerous part of his course,' the *Evening News* in Sydney reported on 13 July 1899. 'Much of the country he will have to traverse is unsettled and without roads or tracks and a large portion of it is infested with uncivilised natives or the more dangerous half-civilised class. Locally, Richardson is regarded as having a considerable chance of disappearing on the journey to Port Darwin. If he reach that port safely, his future course will be comparatively easy.'

Newspaper talk did not worry Arthur. He had heard the same prophecies of doom before and proved them wrong. He was confident he would do so again. 'When I bought a machine in 1896 and learned to ride it and three weeks later expressed my intention of doing what no other cyclist had done before – riding across, via Eucla and Port Augusta, to Adelaide – those who heard of it called me foolhardy and, after vainly endeavouring to dissuade me from making the attempt, predicted that I would not succeed,' Arthur recalled. 'Succeed I did, however.

'There were the same prophets of disaster to the fore when it became known that I was starting for a ride around the continent, who looked upon the undertaking as a foolhardy one. [But] I had made up my mind to lead the way in riding round Australia on the wheel.'

* * *

The roads around Perth were bad so Arthur had a rough departure, but he soon took advantage of the smoother railway tracks of the Midland Railway Line running from Midland Junction, sixteen kilometres north-east of Perth, through the Wheatbelt to Walkaway, a small town thirty kilometres south-east of Geraldton. In the late nineteenth century, Australia had a little-developed road network. The condition of roads

Dr Arthur Richardson, father of the overlander, stands on the balcony of his house in Kalgoorlie with members of his family. Richardson senior was a highly respected member of the community.

had declined in the 1880s following the introduction of the railways, which became the dominant form of transport for the next fifty years. City roads were relatively good, but most roads outside country towns, particularly roads leading to other colonies, were rough and unsealed. There was no track or trail that stretched along the entirety of the Australian coast. Arthur, like other overlanders, would be following dirt tracks, railway lines and cattle and camel pads formed by the passage of stock and wild animals, and in the trackless wilderness of the outback he would be guided by a compass or stars in the night sky.

With rain falling in torrents, Arthur camped at a farm near Bindoon, eighty-four kilometres from Perth, soaking wet. In the morning he pushed on to Walebing, about 178 kilometres north-east of Perth, riding across a fifty-kilometre sand plain, the last twenty-five kilometres in the dark, narrowly avoiding a serious accident. 'Riding down a steep grade I suddenly struck a high bridge over a creek, and bumping over the first few sleepers swerved and struck the combing on the edge, skidded, balanced for the fraction of a second, and then over I went – not into the creek, but into the railway,' Arthur recalled. 'I walked over the next bridge.'

Arthur was treated well at Walebing sheep station, which had been established in 1847 by an Irishman, Anthony O'Grady Lefroy, a nephew of the chief justice of Ireland, Thomas Langlois Lefroy, who was the novelist Jane Austen's youthful love. Lefroy, who was also the colonial treasurer of Western Australia for thirty years, retired from Walebing Station in 1873, handing it over to his sons, one of whom, Henry Lefroy, would become premier of Western Australia. While at Walebing, Arthur observed 'one thousand fat sheep' leaving for shipment to the Perth butchers Holmes Bros & Co. Living on meagre rations, he would have wondered how long it would be before he could enjoy a fat lamb chop or two.

On the morning of Thursday, 8 June 1899, Arthur, still following the railway line, telegraphed from Carnamah, stating that he intended travelling towards Mullewa, a town in the saltbush plains and mulga country of the Mid West region of Western Australia, 470 kilometres north of Perth, on the Geraldton–Cue railway line, which had only opened in 1897. His original intention had been to travel northwards via Geraldton, but the red sand plains between Dongara, located at the mouth of the Irwin River, and Champion Bay had proved too heavy. Altering his plan, he pursued a course further inland, keeping Geraldton on his left.

The Murchison Gascoyne area of Western Australia's Mid West is characterised by endless kilometres of rich red earth and rugged rock formations. It has a semi-arid tropical climate with predominantly winter rainfall and that is precisely what Arthur encountered as the vast blue sky darkened and he was drenched by heavy storms. This stretch turned out to be one of the hardest of his journey with the rivers in flood and the rain-splattered red earth turning into a morass, which made cycling an impossibility.

A daily pattern emerged. Each morning Arthur would set out on a tramp for several kilometres through mud so thick and sticky that occasionally the bike chain became clogged and he was forced to take it off altogether. On many occasions he waded through swollen rivers with the bike above his head and water up to his armpits. This would continue until the sun began to set, at which point, bone-tired, he would camp for the night, often in the scrub, wet and miserable.

The road to Mullewa, ninety-eight kilometres north-east of Geraldton, was so poor that even after he reached firmer ground Arthur could not risk riding in the dark for the country was all cut up with watercourses after heavy rain and he broke two chains in thick mud. 'You can fancy almost dead flat country (saltbush) with a surface like cement and looks for all the world like a dry salt lake with bushes on it,' Arthur recalled.

> There had been heavy rains and very little traffic on it for years, as it is a back track; the whole country is cut up with watercourses, or breakaways as we call them on the fields. There is in some cases a sheer drop of twenty feet, and as all the ground looks alike, especially at night, it is rather exciting work riding a bike, and I went very near breaking both my bike and neck several times. It makes one sweat to suddenly ride onto a dark shadow, and realising in an instant what it is, you spring off the back of the machine just in time to grab it as it glides into space – space with a hard bottom, too.

Unable to see the track in the dark, Arthur camped on a wet sandhill in the scrub all night. He had no shelter other than his bike leaning against a stump. Wood was scarce so he lit four or five sticks at one end and tried to warm one side of his body at a time as heavy frost covered the ground. Cold, wet and hungry, he was in a bad mood as he prayed for daylight.

Arthur had arrived too early to see the spectacular wild flowers that carpet the plains from August to September as he continued towards Mullewa, which takes its name from an Aboriginal word meaning 'place of fog'. He arrived in the town at nine o'clock on the morning of Saturday, 10 June, having ridden 466 kilometres from Perth.

Mullewa marked the finishing point of the little-known De Grey–Mullewa stock route, pioneered by explorer E.T. Hooley in 1866, which at around 1800 kilometres equals the famous Canning Stock Route in length. The route, commencing at the mouth of the De Grey River in the Pilbara, was vital to Western Australia's early stock movement and provided Arthur with something vaguely resembling a road to ride on.

Arthur left Mullewa two days later and followed the stock route to Murgoo, a sheep station 175 kilometres north-east. Nothing was heard of him again until he arrived at Boolardy, a sheep station fifty-six kilometres further to the north. Arthur set off immediately from Boolardy for the long stage to Cossack, an abandoned pearling town 1480 kilometres north of Perth on Butchers Inlet at the mouth of the Harding River in the Pilbara region. As the crow flies the distance from Boolardy to Cossack is about 720 kilometres, but along the stock route, heading north, it increased by 160 kilometres or more.

From Boolardy, Arthur rode to Manfred Station, seventy-nine kilometres further north, on roads made heavy by the recent rain. It poured again that night and the next day the road to Milly Milly Station, whose homestead was situated alongside the Murchison River, was even worse, but the manager, Mr Daly, made his stay comfortable.

Upon his departure for a lambing camp, Arthur was caught in heavy rain and had to spell all day before crossing the Dividing Range and reaching the Gascoyne River, at 865 kilometres the longest in Western Australia. The Gascoyne is an 'upside-down river': it flows on the surface for about one-third of the year and below the dry river bed for the remainder. It was flowing as Arthur pulled up on its bank, conscious of the need to make up time lost on the rain-drenched tracks. Ironically, he made better progress as he moved into the steep hill country, racing up and down rocky gorges as if on a hair-raising ride in one of the amusement parks that had begun to spring up in the major cities in the 1890s.

'It was in the hilly country that the fastest progress was made, though I would not have cared to have been seen by either the manufacturers of my machine or the makers of the tyres dashing down through some of the rocky gorges, with the machine leaping and bounding in all directions over rocks and across ruts,' Arthur recalled. 'Though such treatment was unfair to the machine it was the only way to get over the ground. You had to let your machine go down the hills to make up time and counteract the continual tramp, tramp through the boggy country.'

It continued to be 'very wild, rough, auriferous country' along the Gascoyne River and Arthur was again caught in the rain and had to take off the chain and drag the bicycle until he reached Mount Clere sheep station. The manager, Mr W. Ritchard, helped him across the Gascoyne River with horses. 'I also crossed it twice afterwards that day, having to strip off and carry the bike overhead, with the river running very strong,' Arthur recalled.

After arriving at the Thomas River police camp, Arthur rode along 'almost impassable' roads by moonlight to Bangemall, an almost deserted mining centre on the Lyons River. There were about twenty men working the gold reefs and there was a small Tremain flour mill, but it was not operating. The incessant rain was not only a hindrance to the overlander, but it caused the cancellation of a horse-racing carnival at Bangemall as the country had become very boggy.

At Bangemall, Arthur rode down a plunging gorge which the miners told him was considered dangerous even for pack horses. He already regarded his successful navigation of the hill country as proof of the triumph of the bicycle over the horse. 'On all of the stations through this Nor'-West country I found that the cycle had to a large extent superseded the horse, and machines are to be found at nearly all the homesteads,' Arthur recalled.

He rode next to Lyons River homestead, situated in an elevated position commanding panoramic views of the ancient eroded Kennedy Ranges in the west and the Lyons River in the east. After a good feed he started out once more, intending to ride by moonlight, but it was the night of a lunar eclipse and he had to camp on the river in total darkness in damp conditions. Lying on the wet ground, he regretted sending his oil-sheet back to Perth. 'Nice camping this! Wet clothes, wet ground, and no blankets,' he complained.

The next day Arthur pushed on to Towera Station in the Pilbara, the large, dry region of red earth in the north of Western Australia, which has some of the world's most ancient natural landscapes, dating back two billion years. The explorer Francis Gregory had reported seeing iron ore in the Pilbara in 1861, but mining was not economically viable at that time. As he pushed on through the desert, Arthur, the mining engineer, might have wondered how to extract the rich mineral beneath his wheels.

After riding over slate hills where a small alluvial patch had been worked, Arthur camped beside a well in the scrub. Visited by a group of Aboriginal people, he became the surprising object of desire:

They were quite friendly, though I kept my eye on them. They were on the tramp, and had camped at the well for a time. All night long they kept their fires going, and till midnight sang in their weird, wild fashion, which gave me the bluey creeps. A long, low wail, and then short, broken yelps in a high key by an old black gin, with the deeper guttural notes of the men, produce a peculiar discord, which in the dark stilly night becomes weirdly monotonous. The gins came to my camp and asked for bacca, but I had none. For two hours one of them, a lean, skinny creature, about twenty years of age, sat opposite me and gazed at me without uttering a sound. Then she suddenly disappeared in the darkness, and when I left in the morning an old gin told me that her man had discovered her there, and taking her off had asserted his conjugal rights by administering a sound thrashing and forbidding her to set eyes on the white fellah again.

Arthur's use of 'gin' showed just how politically incorrect language was in those days.

The next stage was to McCarthy's sheep station, now known as Uaroo Station, 130 kilometres south of Onslow, a coastal town in the Pilbara. The spell at McCarthy's gave Arthur a chance to mend his shoes, which were coming apart because of the wet conditions and rough terrain. An overlander had to be resourceful. Arthur obtained some rivets from an old boot and used them to hold his shoes together. He was rather pleased with his handiwork. 'I made a fair job,' he said.

From McCarthy's, Arthur rode to Nanutarra Station on the Ashburton River, 108 kilometres south of Onslow, which had recently been visited by bushrangers who were now 'camping at government expense after a very short reign'. The river at the station was running a banker and Arthur had to 'negotiate a difficult crossing'. Beyond Mount Stuart the track led to Red

Hill Station and then Yarraloola Station, along the Robe River, where Arthur camped for the night.

Arthur reached Mardie Station, near the mouth of the Fortescue River, the next day for lunch. Pushing on, he camped on a creek for the night before encountering very bad roads and strong headwinds on the way to where Karratha is now located.

Then, on Sunday afternoon, 2 July, Arthur rode into Roebourne, a gold-rush town on the Harding River with a population of 300, which at the time was the largest settlement between Perth and Port Darwin and regarded as the capital of the North West.

'Richardson, the cyclist, who is attempting to ride round Australia, arrived at Roebourne at four o'clock on Sunday afternoon,' the *Western Argus* reported. 'When he reached Roebourne his cyclometer showed that 1155 miles had been traversed. Richardson looks none the worse for his journey and he speaks in very hopeful terms of being the first man to cycle round Australia. He expected to reach Perth about the end of November.'

His machine and tyres were 'in perfect order' and he was pleased with the cottered joints (pins which fixed the crank to its crankshaft), which had been questioned. 'When I left Perth doubt was expressed about the reliability of the cottered joints in the Humber, but these are a great success, the frame being as stiff as ever.'

In Roebourne, Arthur received a telegram from Percy Armstrong, which revealed the strong connection between the cycle agent and the overlander.

```
Dear Arthur, I am very pleased to get yours
of the 10th inst. I thought that you must be
```

having a bad time with the rain and you seem
to have got the full benefit of it. It was a
mistake to throw away your oilskin which by
the bye has not been returned to us. I was
surprised to hear that you had broken the
chain, and can only suppose that it was through
the mud jamming it. I am sending on tomorrow
by the S.S. *Albany* two chains, one an Abingdon
and the other a Garrard. Now I must insist
that you take both these with you, or if you
like you can post one to Darwin and take one
of them. I am also sending a pair of C.B. cups
[hub cups] and some assd [sic] balls [assorted
ball bearings] and chain links and a parcel of
tyres etc. from the Dunlop Tyre Coy. These will
all go on to Derby. If your tyres are doubtful
you had better put on the new ones and a wire
will get you a new pair to Darwin. If there is
anything that you want on the road further on,
be sure and wire me and I will see that it is
sent.

I have not heard anything further about
White, but will wire you if any news comes to
hand. Am wiring you to Cossack advising the
goods to Derby. Hoping that you are keeping
the working parts of the machine as clean as
possible, and wishing you the best of luck.

Yours sincerely, P.W. Armstrong.

Clearly, Arthur and his backers were keeping a close eye on the
rival overlanders.

Until Arthur arrived in Roebourne, 'uneasiness' was felt about his welfare because of the 'dearth of tidings' regarding his progress. 'The overlander left Perth over a month ago, and during the whole of that time has hardly experienced a fine day,' the *West Australian* reported on 4 July. 'Almost three weeks ago he telegraphed from Murgoo – the terminus of the telegraph line northwards from Mullewa – and since that time nothing had been heard of him. It was known that the interlying country towards Roebourne for a distance of over five hundred miles was extremely rough, and that the rivers abounding there were in a flooded state as a consequence of the recent continual rains. All anxiety is now removed, however, for he has arrived in Roebourne.'

Apart from the constant rain, Arthur found the conditions much as he had expected for most of the ride to Roebourne, but he admitted the weather would have been better if his departure had been delayed a month.

'In the main my anticipations were realised,' Arthur recalled. 'Had I waited another month before setting out I would undoubtedly have fared much better, for from the day subsequent to my departure from Perth, right up as far as Roebourne, I experienced terribly severe wintry weather. The rivers and creeks in the Murchison, Gascoyne, Ashburton and West Pilbara districts were all in high flood, and the country for miles upon miles was a perfect quagmire, rendering riding at times an impossibility. Night after night I was compelled to camp out in the drenching rain and at times without shelter.'

If Arthur had waited another month, however, he would have given the White brothers and Mackay a wonderful opportunity to beat him around Australia. As it was, the three rival overlanders were hot on his heels.

Stage Two

Two Chippies and a Squatter

White Brothers and Donald
Melbourne to Rockhampton
5 July to 7 August 1899

WHEN Frank publicly announced in May 1899 that he planned to ride around Australia, the press suggested he should have company on the dangerous journey. 'Frank White, holder of the Perth to Rockhampton and return record, 8480 miles in 152 days, is now preparing for an even greater task,' the *Melbourne Punch* reported on 11 May 1899. 'This will be no less than the feat of riding a cycle right round the continent ... This trip was suggested in these columns some time ago as being a worthy task for any Australian wheelmen desirous of going one better than the old world cyclists. Though adventurous, the journey is not impracticable – but White should certainly take a mate with him.'

Out of the blue, Frank, who was in Perth at the time, received a telegram from Donald Mackay, asking if he could accompany him. Frank must have been ecstatic. He regretted not continuing northwards from Rockhampton the previous

At the last minute Frank White, right, arranged for his younger brother Alex to accompany him on the ride around Australia after Donald Mackay temporarily abandoned the project.

year and becoming the first to ride around Australia, allowing Arthur to get the jump on him, but he had baulked at riding around the continent alone and did not want to go on his own now if he could help it. Agreeing to let Donald join him, Frank arranged to meet him in Melbourne, where they would start the ride. But the day after Donald arrived in Melbourne, important mining business cropped up and he had to reluctantly abandon the ride, at least for the time being.

'White was very much disappointed, as he, like myself, was determined not to go alone as he realised the risk was too great and the remuneration but small,' Donald recalled.

A few years earlier, Donald had offered to cycle round the continent with William Virgin, who had ridden from Perth to Brisbane in sixty days, at the time the longest single ride undertaken in Australia at 6070 kilometres. It was a big ride for a little man, only 161 centimetres tall. Virgin would have completed the ride sooner, but he spent two days in Goulburn, New South Wales, recovering from a dog bite, the 'cyclist's terror'. Donald thought riding round the continent would be a trip of 'risk and excitement'. He also offered to pay Virgin's expenses, but at the last minute Virgin abandoned the idea. Donald then approached the Irish rider Jerome Murif, the first to cycle from Adelaide to Port Darwin, but with no better success. 'So as I did not care for a lonely ride, it passed out of my mind,' Donald recalled.

A week after Donald's withdrawal from Frank White's team, Frank wired him to tell him that the Dayton Bicycle Company had arranged for his younger brother Alex to accompany him and suggested Donald join them in Sydney or Brisbane if he could manage it.

Alex, however, was ill prepared for the ride. He had done practically no cycling in the previous months, just some short rides with the Metropolitan Cycling Club in Perth. And his only other exercise was playing rugby for the Perth Pirates, 'one of the leading clubs of the colony'. In one match he sustained an injury which he worried would inhibit his ability to ride. He fell backwards onto the upturned boot of a player lying on the ground and it raised a lump in the small of his back as big as a hen's egg. On the passage from Perth to Melbourne on the steamer *Paroo*, the lump was a great cause of concern for Alex, but once he started the ride it did not trouble him.

Frank had to wait for Alex in Melbourne, delaying the scheduled departure by four days, and no doubt was growing impatient because in a race around Australia every day counted. Alex arrived in Melbourne on Tuesday, 4 July. Not wanting to waste any more precious time, the brothers departed the next day. They had given Arthur a month's head start.

Frank and Alex rode Dayton road-racers fitted with Dunlop-Welch steel rims, multiplex Dunlop tyres and 6-and-a-half-inch cranks. The bicycles, like Arthur's, had only one gear and the cyclist had to select a ratio for the conditions he was traversing. The White brothers carried three rear cogs (63, 73 and 84 gear inches) so they could alter the gearing to suit the terrain. The weight of their luggage was about 15 kilograms each, including water tanks of Frank's own design, repair outfits, medicine chests and condensed food. They were also armed with revolvers and Winchester rifles, which at times would be their most important items.

Like Arthur, Frank organised the ride so that the journey across northern Australia would be completed in the dry season, avoiding the monsoonal rains that would make cycling an impossibility. The White brothers planned to 'live from hand to mouth' until they reached Port Darwin, after which they would carry sufficient supplies to last from station to station. They would always carry water – at least, that was their intention. Frank anticipated the Fitzroy River region in Western Australia would be the roughest part of the journey. 'We shall go over a tract of country which has been very little explored, although a number of swagmen have crossed it safely,' Frank told the *Australian Cyclist* magazine before departing. 'The alligators in the streams and the mosquitoes in battalions will be our worst enemies, as the blacks are not very aggressive unless you interfere with their lubras, and we are not out on a love-making expedition.'

As optimistic as Arthur, Frank also calculated the ride would take just over six months.

The road out of Melbourne was bad and the White brothers spent the first night at their parents' home in Barkly Street, Brunswick, just a few kilometres north of the city. Out of form, Alex felt 'done up' on the very first day and feared he would not be able to continue. The poor condition of the road and the foul weather did not make it any easier for him. But he joined Frank the next day, riding against a headwind over a rough road to Seymour, at the crossing of the Goulburn River, and pushing on to Avenel, which was the home of Australia's most famous bushranger, Ned Kelly, in his younger years. Kelly went to school there and once saved a boy from drowning in Hughes Creek, which flows through the town. Kelly was awarded a green sash for his bravery in rescuing the boy and was wearing it under his armour when shot down at Glenrowan.

Leaving Avenel at seven-thirty the next morning, the White brothers 'crossed creeks innumerable' and between Winton in north-east Victoria and Glenrowan, where the Kelly Gang made its last stand in 1880, they laboured over muddy roads that were as sticky as a 'glue-pot', carrying their bikes for three kilometres. Then to Wangaratta and Chiltern, where author Henry Handel Richardson lived as a child, doing the last fifteen kilometres in the dark.

At about ten o'clock the next morning the Whites crossed the border at the twin settlements of Albury and Wodonga, separated geographically by the Murray River, Australia's longest river, and politically by a colonial border.

Frank and Alex spent a few hours in Albury where their bicycles were objects of curiosity, attracting groups of interested spectators. They departed after lunch with wishes of good luck ringing in their ears. Alex was now feeling more confident about the ride. The aches and pains of the first day gone, he had ridden himself into fitness and was in 'grand marching order'. A few local cyclists escorted the brothers to the outskirts of town, while one, the pioneering cycle agent and manufacturer Jim Scanlan, went as far as Gerogery, thirty-two kilometres north, near where the bushranger Mad Dan Morgan used to hide in the Yambla Range in the 1860s.

A 'fine fellow', Scanlan gave the White brothers strict instructions to reach Henty, sixty-four kilometres from Albury, that night, so they would not have to camp in the open in wet weather. 'Directly he left us, Frank punctured,' Alex recalled. 'We were riding along the firebreak just close to the railway line. There was plenty of dead stuff across the track, and a twig went into his back tyre. This is the only tyre trouble we have had so far. Well, we were making to Henty when Frank saw the glint of a gear wheel through the bush – and how did the Henty cycling folk turn out! They treated us splendidly and next day we had quite a party as far as Yerong Creek.'

The White brothers continued along the railway line and reached Wagga Wagga, straddling the Murrumbidgee River, fifty-six kilometres further on, in time for lunch, and then pushed on to Junee, another thirty-five kilometres, arriving at sundown. They were now about seventy kilometres from Donald Mackay's home at Wallendbeen.

The brothers had left Melbourne without knowing for sure whether Donald would join them on the ride or not. They visited him at Wallendbeen where they stayed the night. It was the first time Alex had met Donald and he was amazed at his size. Weighing 88 kilograms, he was much bigger and heavier than Frank at 73 kilograms and Alex at 74 kilograms. 'Mackay is a fine fellow — a real giant, and proportionately built. I am a pygmy beside him,' Alex said.

During the brothers' stay at Wallendbeen, Donald told them he was still interested in doing the ride and would aim to meet them in Brisbane. The Whites both hit it off with him and were keen to have his company on the dangerous journey. If they encountered bushrangers or hostile Aboriginal groups, someone of his formidable size and strength would certainly come in handy.

No doubt they were just as impressed by Wallendbeen and may have even been a little envious of Donald's wealth and freedom to do as he chose. The White brothers' background was very different to Donald's privileged life as part of the New South Wales squattocracy. They were descended from a line of skilled tradesmen who eked out a hard-scrabble existence as carpenters and were occasionally broke. Their grandfather John White had migrated to Australia from England in the 1850s. He'd worked in the ship-building industry in London and was involved in the construction of Queen Victoria's royal tender, the *Fairy*, at Blackwall on the Thames. Known as 'Steamer', he'd also had a contract with the Egyptian Transit Company as a master carpenter, joiner and cabinet-maker, servicing steamships between Alexandria, Cairo and Suez. He settled first in Adelaide with his wife and children, including the White brothers' father, Jesse William. The family kept their 'ticket' so they could prove they were free settlers and not convicts. They moved to Stanley on the north-west coast of Tasmania where John White marked out the little township of Blackwall on the Tamar River, selling some allotments and giving to the Church of England and the Wesleyans an allotment each.

Jesse William White, who lived at Black Farm, Circular Head, was a carpenter in the Stanley area. He married a Launceston bookseller's daughter, Mary, and they had twelve children. The first two, Kate and George, were born in Tasmania, but the rest of the family, including Frank and Alex, were born in Wellington, New Zealand. It appears there was a falling-out between John and Jesse, with the father taking legal action against the son for outstanding debts. John did not leave anything to his sons in his will, indicating a split in the family. This was most likely the reason Jesse, who was bankrupt, and Mary moved to New Zealand. Francis Alfred was born on 24 September 1871, while Alexander was born in June 1878.

The White family returned to Australia in 1888 when Frank was seventeen and Alex ten, initially settling in Sydney before moving to Launceston and then to Melbourne. They were involved in speculative building until the Australian bank crash between 1890 and 1893 which ruined them. With the discovery of gold in Western Australia, Frank and Alex moved to Perth and worked on building projects spawned by the gold rush.

There were five White brothers living in Perth at the time. The eldest, George, was a respectable married man, while Arthur, Frank, Alex and Fred lived the life of 'gay bachelors' in the old-fashioned sense. The brothers would row a boat across the Swan River to attend social events, skinny-dipping in the river on hot nights. Another form of White brotherly fun was to rouse mounted police to make them chase them on their bicycles. Fortunately, they could always out-pace the troopers. Whenever a band led a procession through the streets of Perth, the fun-loving brothers would climb up to the second floor of a building and try to drop chop bones into the horns of the brass section.

The White brothers' cheerful exuberance would have been well suited to coping with the demands of long-distance cycling, but Donald was even more irrepressible. Known as 'Don', Mackay was seized with the idea of riding around Australia purely 'for the fun of it'; he loved adventure and wanted to see the country. Of independent means, Donald did not need any emolument from cycle agencies, tyre manufacturers or newspapers. Money was not his motivation. The *Evening News* in Sydney reported that Donald was 'simply doing the trip to kill time, as he puts it. He is very favourably known in Wallendbeen where he is a large property holder'. But it was not just for fun. Donald's aim was to establish a world amateur long-distance record.

Donald was an adventurous, even eccentric, personality. He was born at the Royal Hotel, Yass, in the Southern Tablelands of New South Wales, on 29 June 1870, the son of Scottish immigrants Alexander and Annie Mackay. Alexander had worked for the famous tea and opium trader Sir James Matheson in Hong Kong and held the Chinese in high esteem, telling his children 'it would be as unjust to judge all Australians by the type to be found in Woolloomooloo as it was to judge Chinamen from the average coolie one meets in Australia'. This was quite an enlightened attitude for the times, and had a profound influence on Donald.

Later, Matheson arranged for Alexander to go to Australia to settle land for cattle and sheep grazing. After purchasing Wallendbeen, a rich and fertile 60,000-acre station near Cootamundra, and a number of other large properties, Alexander became a well-known and respected pioneer. The Mackays settled in a slab cottage, which became known as the Rose Cottage after Annie's mother's maiden name. In keeping with his social position and holdings, Alexander built a grand homestead, Granite House, in 1879, bringing out stonemasons from Scotland. 'Wallendbeen' is an Aboriginal word meaning 'stony hill' and it was believed the new house was located on sacred ground. The deeply religious Annie refused to move into the new house, fearing some kind of spiritual retribution.

Annie's respect for Aboriginal culture may have influenced Donald, who had an empathy for the first Australians, which would be demonstrated many years later in a public clash with a prime minister over their treatment. An Aboriginal man named Black Bob, who did occasional work at Wallendbeen, seemed to have a special connection with Donald. Whenever Donald was about to return from one of his many travels, Black Bob would appear out of nowhere like a harbinger of his impending arrival.

Wallendbeen was a wonderful place to grow up. Donald was the youngest of four children. His brother, James Alexander 'Kenneth', eleven years older, was a noted soldier, politician, poet, novelist and horseman who formed the 1st Australian Horse regiment and commanded the Imperial Bushmen's

Contingent in the Boer War. A sister, Annie, was born in 1863, but died of pneumonia at the age of five. A second sister, Jeannie, was born in 1868.

On Christmas Day, 1876, young Donald received a fox terrier as a present. From that day he always owned a fox terrier because 'they always gave a true welcome and were ready to stand up whether things were rough or smooth'. Donald was initially educated by a governess at Wallendbeen Station until he became too much to handle and was enrolled at Wallendbeen Public School in 1881, walking three kilometres a day to attend class before his father bought him a Timor pony to ride. When he was twelve Donald was sent to Oaklands boarding school in Mittagong in the Southern Highlands of New South Wales for 'polishing'.

Alexander Mackay was a strict teetotaller and non-smoker. Like his father, Donald was a non-drinker. When he was sixteen he contracted measles and a gardener at Wallendbeen gave him a bottle of schnapps as a cure. This brought out a rash which covered him from head to toe and he never drank again, except during his thirsty ride around Australia. Donald was a smoker, however. When he was nine he was told that 'smoking stunts the growth'. It was just as well given Donald's great height.

After leaving school at seventeen, Donald took up an engineering apprenticeship with a firm in Sydney, but city life was unappealing and he returned to Wallendbeen where he worked as a jackaroo, hardening his muscles with stock work, fencing, ploughing, wheat harvesting, pressing wool, dam sinking and milking cows. When his father died in 1890, twenty-year-old Donald inherited a part of Wallendbeen, which provided him with a comfortable income and the freedom to indulge his craving for travel and adventure.

A laconic outdoorsman with a dry sense of humour, Donald was the type who would try anything once. One newspaper described him as 'a stalwart specimen of a typical Australian'. He boxed, lifted weights, sculled (becoming a pupil of the former world champion Bill Beach) and cycled, learning to ride on an old bone-shaker. He was also tattooed from neck to toe during a trip to Japan, becoming a 'walking picture gallery'.

He caught the overlanding bug while prospecting for gold in north-west New South Wales in 1895. He bought interests in some gold mines in Wyalong and financed a prospecting expedition to Milparinka and Tibooburra, about 293 kilometres north of Broken Hill. While a buggy carried supplies, Donald and two companions rode bicycles on the journey.

But Donald did not find a speck of gold and returned home. From the inland port of Wilcannia in western New South Wales he rode back to Wallendbeen alone via Broken Hill, Adelaide and Melbourne. By the time he returned home he had been away three months and had ridden more than 3000 kilometres. He had learned a lot about cycling in the bush, which helped to prepare him for the ride around Australia, although nothing could fully prepare anyone for such an epic trek.

In May 1899 Donald made arrangements to sail to England, but the day he was to select his berth he saw a story in the newspaper about Frank's proposed ride and immediately changed his plans. No one who knew Donald was surprised when he announced his intention to do something as crazy as ride a bicycle around Australia. As soon as Donald attended to his business affairs he would meet up with the White brothers, who were already on their way.

After staying at Wallendbeen, the brothers rode to Yass, eighty kilometres away. Having been delayed by headwinds since Albury, they hoped to make better progress when they left Yass the next morning, but the owners of the hotel they stayed at slept in and they had to wait a long time for breakfast. No doubt irritated to be held up, they wanted to hurry across the Breadalbane Plains to Goulburn, ninety kilometres from Yass, but the road was wet and sticky.

Riding on the Great South Road, now known as the Hume Highway, they stopped in Goulburn, Australia's first inland city, 195 kilometres south-west of Sydney, for lunch, and then pushed on to Marulan, arriving at night, having covered 120 kilometres that day. The next morning, crossing Paddys River, which was flowing up to the top of its banks, they experienced the worst part of the journey so far. 'The bridge has long since, I am told, been carried away, and the river was running a banker with the heavy rains,' Alex recalled. 'Anyhow, we plunged in up to our knees, shouldering the machines. It was early in the morning and the water was icy cold.'

After riding through Picton, a small town ninety kilometres south-west of Sydney, the White brothers stopped at Campbelltown for the night, having covered 135 kilometres that day. They left at eight o'clock the next morning with only fifty-four kilometres to ride to reach Sydney, but the road was a quagmire after the heavy rains. Frank described the twenty kilometres between Campbelltown and Liverpool, perhaps the worst in the colony, as being in a 'disgraceful condition for a road within twenty-five miles of the metropolis'. The mud was so deep and the wheel ruts so numerous the road was impassable. It took three hours for them to travel just seventeen kilometres. 'We could not push our machines through it, let alone ride, and all we could do was to crawl along the paddocks,' Alex recalled.

The Sydney Bicycle Club had intended to send a party of local cyclists to Liverpool to escort the White brothers into the city, but there was a breakdown in communication and they arrived in the rapidly growing metropolis where ornate sandstone buildings glistened in the winter sun at 1.25pm on Friday, 14 July, unannounced.

Frank and Alex must have looked a sorry sight when they were met by Mr W. Bulfin, secretary of the Glebe Bicycle Club and representative of the Dayton Cycling Agency, for the riders and their bikes were covered in mud. 'Rough and damp all the way,' Alex said. 'We seemed to follow the rain. Every place we struck had had the rain the day before, and for days before that, so you can imagine what the roads were like. We came down in the mud so often that we soon got used to it, and took such a calamity as a matter of course.'

After finding comfortable lodgings at the University Hotel in Glebe on the western outskirts of the city, the White brothers had a good rub-down and a nourishing lunch. They then proceeded to McLean Bros and Rigg, the Dayton agents, where Alex's bicycle was put on display in the window of the agency, attracting hundreds of curious observers.

There was a wonderful camaraderie among the Australian cycling fraternity, which the White brothers enjoyed during their stay in Sydney. On Saturday afternoon the committee of the Sydney Bicycle Club escorted them around Centennial Park and afterwards to a rugby match at the Sydney Cricket Ground.

In the evening they were guests of the Sydney Bicycle Club at the club's rooms in Elizabeth Street and their health was drunk by more than forty members, who were entertained by a 'fine array' of musical talent. According to the *Australian Cyclist*, the 'indefatigable' honorary secretary of the Sydney Bicycle Club,

Mr C.A. Grocott, proposed the toast, saying that no matter whether an overlander was professional or amateur, they could be sure of a welcome by the Sydney club.

Responding, Frank thanked the club for its kindness to himself and Alex and promised he would 'endeavour to send for the adornment of the club rooms a few trophies from the far north in the shape of alligator skins and Aboriginal weapons, as a memento of the occasion'.

The rest of the evening was spent in 'yarn-spinning, harmony and billiards'. The *Australian Cyclist* observed that:

> Frank White, who is the more experienced rider of the two brothers, is not a bad hand at a narrative, and his previous transcontinental rides have given him some excellent material to work on, and so he found many willing listeners to his story how in his last ride across the Bight he wheedled a store of provisions out of a notoriously close-fisted station holder, known to fame as Charley the Nark, by an innocent trick. Nor does he handle the cue with much less dexterity than he does a story. A couple of games of snooker on the club table gave him an opportunity of showing his pet fancy shots, acquired on West Australian tables; but luck, as it had been all the way from Melbourne, was still against him.

Refreshed after their stay in Sydney, the White brothers set out for Brisbane from the General Post Office at 1.30pm on Monday, 17 July. A large crowd gathered to witness the departure, among it Mr William Rufus George, known as the 'Father of Australian Cycling', who built a 'velocipede' in Bathurst in New South Wales in 1867 from French plans and had the honour of riding the first machine on Australian soil. Many members of the Sydney Bicycle Club were also in attendance. As the chime of the clock died away, the brothers mounted their bikes amid ringing cheers and rode down George Street. The Sydney Harbour Bridge had not yet been built so the brothers did not have the opportunity to cross the most beautiful harbour in the world. Instead, they rode to Windsor, sitting on the Hawkesbury River north-west of Sydney, where they stayed the night.

There were deep concerns about whether the White brothers would complete their journey around Australia. 'On Tuesday last Frank White, the champion overland cyclist, accompanied by his brother, reached Wisemans Ferry about 11am on tour round Australia,' the *Windsor and Richmond Gazette* reported on 22 July. 'If they accomplish the ride, it will be the first time in the cycling history of Australia and it is their intention of putting up a record for the distance ... Considering that there are hundreds of miles of country in those various colonies to be traversed by white men that have never been ridden over, there are big doubts as to the ride being accomplished.'

While the White brothers rode northwards, Donald finished up his business affairs and caught a train from Sydney to Brisbane.

Initially, the Whites made splendid progress, the roads generally being in good order, but they struck a 'muddy run' between Muswellbrook and Aberdeen in the Upper Hunter region. It was 'a hard day's work, having to get off very often to scrape the mud off the wheels,' Frank recalled.

The brothers rode from Scone through 'splendid country' to Murrurundi, where they stopped for lunch. They needed the sustenance because afterwards they had to walk five kilometres uphill. Coming down the other side Frank's chain snapped when a stone lodged in the gear wheel. 'I did a fast bolt to the bottom and pulled up safely,' Frank recalled.

From Murrurundi they headed to the village of Wallabadah, thirty-five kilometres further on, in the New England tablelands, arriving on Saturday, 22 July. The first European squatters arrived in the Wallabadah area in 1830, and during the 1850s a settlement began to develop at the intersection of the two mail-coach runs which came from the north and north-west. The 'Gentleman Bushranger', Captain Thunderbolt, robbed the northern mail coach at Wallabadah in 1867 and also worked on a property west of the settlement.

Captain Thunderbolt, whose actual name was Frederick Ward, was one of Australia's longest-roaming bushrangers until he was shot dead by Constable Alexander Binney Walker at Kentucky Creek in 1870. Bushrangers flourished in New South Wales in the gold-rush years of the 1850s and 1860s, but by the 1890s it was becoming difficult for them to evade capture following improvements in policing and communications. While bushrangers were not as big a threat as they had once been, the Aboriginal bushranger Jimmy Governor (whose life was the basis for Thomas Keneally's 1972 novel *The Chant of Jimmie Blacksmith*) and his brother Joe terrorised northern New South Wales at the turn of the century, mere months after the overlanders rode through those parts.

Hit by a snowstorm at Ben Lomond, the brothers managed just thirty-eight kilometres in four hours. After passing through Glen Innes they experienced more 'hard luck' with headwinds, wet roads and sticky black soil. Eventually, they reached Brisbane's stately stone General Post Office a little before six o'clock on Thursday, 27 July, having completed 2138 kilometres of their ride.

'We arrived at Brisbane last night,' Frank wrote in a telegram that was published in the *West Australian* on 29 July 1899. 'The roads were very rough over the border, and on Monday we had to carry the machines over twenty miles through black soil owing to the rain.'

The White brothers would have been happy to see Donald, who had arrived three days before them. No doubt Frank would have regaled Donald with tales of their ride north and passed on best wishes from members of the Sydney Bicycle Club, but they quickly needed to get down to business. After spelling a day, the trio had intended to depart Brisbane the next day, but it was raining so they decided to make a start the day after. Brisbane was 'looking quiet', but they spent a very enjoyable Saturday night 'doing the theatres'.

In the morning the weather was fine so at 9.45am on Sunday, 30 July, after getting their books signed by officials of the Brisbane Cycling Club, the three overlanders received a big send-off as they pushed off from the General Post Office, escorted by 200 cyclists.

Donald rode a different bicycle to the White brothers, choosing a Dux because it was Australian made. The bicycle was transported from the company's factory in Little Collins Street in Melbourne to Brisbane by steamer. There is a photograph of Donald standing behind his Dux, towering over the machine, which was made especially for him. With a 24-inch frame weighing 27 pounds (13.1 kilos), it was specifically strengthened to carry him as well as his gear, a combined weight of 108 kilograms. The Dux was fitted with Dunlop multiflex tyres, 77-gear and 7-inch cranks. Donald carried two water cans weighing about 7 kilograms, a revolver, ammunition, a set of tools and parts, a camera, a waterproof cloak, a diary, a time-book and a food bag.

'It is the best little wheel I ever rode and although I bumped it over rocks, through great swamps, and crashed into stumps and logs on a thousand occasions it stood up every time, and never needed the slightest repair,' Donald recalled.

The bumpy road was heavy after the rain, but the White brothers and their escort set a brisk pace, while Donald lagged behind. Deskbound while attending to business affairs, he was in poor shape, having been on a bike only twice in the previous month. In Brisbane he'd stepped on the scales and been shocked when he brought up 88.9 kilograms, a full 6.35 kilograms overweight – not exactly the ideal fitness for an around Australia ride.

At Bald Hills, in bushland north of Brisbane, the trio stopped for a round of drinks and had their photograph taken before setting off again. Accompanied now by just six members of the escort, they left amid great cheering and well wishes, many expressing regret at not being able to go with them. It was a common lament.

With the road improving, the party soon passed through North Pine, reaching Caboolture, fifty-one kilometres north of Brisbane, for a late lunch, having been delayed by a member of their escort breaking the fork of his bike while trying to jump a log. On arrival in Caboolture, one of the escort who had expressed a keenness to ride around Australia lay on the verandah of a pub, exhausted, and made discreet enquiries about returning to Brisbane by train.

'Throughout much of the trip we met many misguided individuals like this, who, if they had the time, means, or will, would have come with us,' Donald recalled. 'If they had all come, there would now be a good bike pad around Australia, dotted here and there with the graves of those who had gone contrary to the parable "Boast not in thy strength etc".'

After lunch they started down a muddy track and about a kilometre out of Caboolture Donald had muscle cramps in both legs that were so intense he had to stop riding. Frank gave him a rub-down with whisky and eucalyptus oil to get him going again. Soon they struck the railway line and annoyed the wife of a fettler by riding along the railway cess, the area either side of a track which is kept at a lower level than the sleeper to provide drainage. It was a big improvement on the road, but the sticky soil occasionally clogged their wheels.

The overlanders rode over boggy roads through the Glasshouse Mountains on the Near North Coast and at dusk they reached Landsborough, named for the explorer William Landsborough, the first to complete a north to south crossing of Australia in 1862. Donald 'thanked Heaven that one day of Purgatory was at a close'.

The next morning Donald was stiff and sore again and Frank had to give him another rub-down. The White brothers must have wondered whether this overweight amateur would slow them down and ruin their chances of beating Arthur. But after half an hour's riding Donald felt much better and gradually worked himself into form.

While Donald was now keeping up with his companions, incessant rainfall slowed the progress of all three cyclists. The road was slippery so the overlanders defied regulations and continued to ride along the guttering by the side of the railway track, although sticky mud, which clogged the wheels, resulted in them walking many kilometres on the sleepers of the lines.

At one point, a ganger had 'harsh words' with them, took their names and threatened to report them. They did not take any notice of him and reached the small town of Cooran, thirty-eight kilometres west of Noosa, in time for tea. They arrived just ten minutes before torrential rain fell, promising heavy roads again in the morning.

The weather was just as inclement the next day as the overlanders left Cooran in a 'blinding shower of rain', which continued all day. After stopping in the mining town of Gympie for lunch they had to push their bikes about two kilometres through scrubby paddocks. In the afternoon two of the spokes of Donald's front wheel were torn out by a sleeper that was hidden in long grass overshadowing the cess. Their progress was slowed further by the many railway bridges they had to use to cross over streams, forcing them to walk more often than ride. Some of the bridges were over half a kilometre long and they lost a lot of time. They would walk on the sleepers and run the bikes on two 6-inch centre planks. With characteristic derring-do Frank rode over several of the planks, ignoring the drop from the bridge, but Alex and Donald did not risk it.

Soaking wet, the overlanders pushed on, determined to reach Kilkivan Junction, fifty-four kilometres west of Gympie and the scene of Queensland's first gold discovery in 1852, that night. Arriving at dusk they stayed in a house opposite the railway station, owned by an old man who operated a refreshment room for travellers. They were disappointed to learn that the old man did not have a liquor licence so they had to be satisfied with cups of tea, which were not exactly their ideal thirst-quenching drinks after a long day's ride.

After their meal they adjourned to the parlour where the old man and his daughter entertained them on the piano. Donald joined in, while one of the White brothers hit a tin dish with a stick and the other rang a bell. As the ensemble played on the old man squatted on the floor and thumped it with his knuckles. The cyclists were worried he would break his hand, but eventually he grew tired and, the amusement over, showed them to their rooms.

The overlanders departed at five the next morning, Wednesday, 2 August, and reached Maryborough, a major port town on the Mary River, for lunch, after riding through a deluge for the final twelve kilometres, the water fifteen centimetres deep on the road in places, which forced them to walk much of it. Wet through, they decided to stay the night to dry out their clothes and clean mud off their bikes. In the evening they attended the FitzGerald Brothers Circus, the premier circus in Australia at the time, but they were unimpressed. 'It was a bit flat and we were glad when the show ended,' Donald recalled.

Later, the trio regretted taking so much trouble to clean their bikes because it rained all the next day and the track was muddy again. Crossing the Mary River, they followed the railway track. After leaving Isis Junction, where they made themselves 'top heavy' with a shandy each, the cyclists arrived in the port town of Bundaberg on the Burnett River for a late lunch, but if they washed the meal down with a glass of Bundaberg rum, they did not say. Crossing the Burnett River by ferry, they reached Avondale, a small railway siding, by dark, toiling a considerable amount of the way through mud, rain and headwinds.

The next day, after riding 112 kilometres through more rain and mud, the overlanders reached Bororen, a tiny town fifty-eight kilometres south of Gladstone, at dusk, following a confrontation with fettlers who ordered them off the railway line. The cyclists tried to explain it was impossible to ride on the track because of the undergrowth, but they were still told to go back, to which they replied 'Go to Hades!' When one of the fettlers threatened to throw them off, the overlanders, clenching their fists and pushing out their chests, invited him to try. Deciding discretion was the better part of valour, the fettler, glowering at the overlanders, took down their names instead and they continued on their way, laughing out loud as they rode.

The overlanders ran into numerous stumps as they rode the last few kilometres to a hotel along a bush track in the dark. As it had been raining again during the day they accepted the landlady's kind offer to dry their clothes and they had a good night's sleep. In the morning they rode along the railway line again, but it was not an easy track. Donald and Frank had a nasty fall, going over the edge of an embankment and rolling down a few metres. Luckily, neither of them was badly injured, although Frank bruised his knee.

Soon after, the overlanders left the railway line where it branched into Gladstone and took the road due north to Rockhampton. The country was ridgy and steep and they did a lot of walking. Crossing the Boyne River, a tributary of the Burnett River, they noticed abundant fish, and were tempted to stop to catch some after riding on a diet of salt junk (dried salted beef) and sweet potatoes that was 'becoming too much of a good thing', but they decided to push on to the gold-mining town of Calliope, 113 kilometres south-east of Rockhampton. They reached Calliope around lunch-time and had a 'good, square meal' at a hotel before going on their way. They soon arrived at the Calliope River crossing, which was one of the most dangerous in Queensland. There was a sign on the bank warning those on foot not to attempt to cross it if the water was running more than 'twelve inches deep'.

Descending the sloping bank, the trio shouldered their bikes and started to wade across, the rocks at the bottom very slippery. As the water ran with great speed it was difficult to get across, but they made it. Sitting on a rock, they emptied their boots of water before ascending the steep bank and pushing off across level country again.

It was 'nice running' to Murphy's accommodation house, the overlanders noticing a lot of game birds – quails, pheasants, black ducks and pigeons – perhaps imagining what they might have looked like roasted on a plate. After stopping for a cup of tea at Murphy's they pushed on through 'pretty country', crossing creeks on whose banks luxuriant vegetation grew, to Raglan, fifty-nine kilometres from Rockhampton, where a 'monster' 14-kilogram gold nugget was found in 1867. They spent a quiet evening at the Raglan pub where they were interested to see sixty 'alligator eggs' that had been brought in by an Aboriginal man who had found a nest several kilometres up the creek.

The next morning the country was flat, but passing the post office, which was about a kilometre further on, they struck black soil, which was sticky after the rain. Riding was impossible and pushing the bikes was not much easier as the wheels picked up black soil and dead grass. The Australian artist George Washington Lambert painted his masterpiece *Across the Black Soil Plains* in 1899, the same year as the around Australia rides. The painting depicts a team of draught horses pulling a wagon heavily laden with wool bales across miry, flat lands. The horses tug at the heavy load, just as the cyclists must have strained to push their bikes through the sticky soil. The overlanders may not have known much about art, but they would have appreciated Lambert's painting.

With the sun now shining on firmer ground they made good time. Passing through scrubland, they struck some heavy patches of sand and quartz before reaching the Ten Mile Pub, so named because it was ten miles from Rockhampton, at noon. Just as they finished lunch, a couple of Rockhampton cyclists arrived and guided them to the nearby Three Mile Lagoon where they had arranged to meet the rest of the members of the Rockhampton Cycling Club at 2.30pm. The local cyclists, now numbering about one hundred, escorted the trio into town, arriving at 3.15pm, but they made an inauspicious entry. Turning round a corner to go to the General Post Office, one of the escort fell, causing a mass pile-up.

It had taken the overlanders seven days to travel 640 kilometres from Brisbane, which was an encouraging effort given it had rained most of the way. They rested in Rockhampton, the major port for Central Queensland, just north of the Tropic of Capricorn on the Fitzroy River, for a couple of days. A significant gold deposit at the world famous Mount Morgan, thirty-eight kilometres south-west of Rockhampton, was discovered in the 1880s and the trio took a train to visit the mine. The *Launceston Examiner* predicted that while Arthur had a head start, the White brothers and Mackay would almost certainly catch up to him because they had the advantage of riding as a team.

The White brothers and Mackay would discover soon enough that travelling in company not only enhanced their cycling, but would be the difference between life and death.

In typical cycling attire of the time, Arthur looks like he is about to take a ride through a park rather than an epic journey around Australia.

Stage Three

The Trail Angel

Arthur
Roebourne to Halls Creek
3 July to 5 August 1899

O N a lonely road on the remote north-west coast of Western Australia, Arthur was startled to hear someone crying in a 'heart-breaking fashion' – surprised not just by the sorrowful sound, but by another human voice filling the emptiness. He soon discovered the anguished weeping came from an old man who had lost his horses, packs, tucker and clothes on his way to Halls Creek in the East Kimberley. Even though it slowed him down, Arthur, like a Good Samaritan, or in cycling parlance a trail angel, stayed with the old man and comforted him, probably saving his life.

'He was quite hysterical and lightheaded; but I stayed the night with him and left him in a better frame of mind next morning, when he expressed his intention of following my wheel tracks till met by assistance, which I had subsequently sent out to him from the nearest telegraph station,' Arthur recalled. 'I never heard how he got on, but, as the road is lonely and little frequented, I have no doubt that had I not found him, the poor old fellow would have wandered aimlessly about in the scrub and would have ultimately met with a terrible death.'

It would be hard-hearted to abandon someone in that desperate sort of situation, but Arthur's kindness to the old man when he was endeavouring to become the first to cycle around Australia went beyond the call of duty and was indicative of his willingness to help people, a character trait that would be displayed throughout his life.

It had stopped raining soon after Arthur left Roebourne on the afternoon of Monday, 3 July 1899, and the weather changed completely as he plugged along a red sand plain on the north-west coast. Crossing long and lonely stretches of loose sand, Arthur made slow progress through the ancient landscape until he reached Condon, situated on Condon Creek, between Port Hedland and Broome. While Condon, now an abandoned port, was as remote an outpost as could be found, it had a store and three hotels and must have seemed a veritable metropolis to Arthur in this isolated country.

Beyond Condon, and after a heavy day's trudging through sand, Arthur reached a solitary spot known as Hardys Well, which was where he encountered the pitiful old man. Hardys Well lies on the Kimberley–De Grey stock route, which runs 1850 kilometres through the Great Sandy Desert. 'The experiences and difficulties which are met by a cyclist journeying along the north-west coast are many and varied,' Arthur mused.

He noticed that the little stretches of desert country that were not sandy were all broken up by rat holes, although he did not seem surprised. 'Possibly they are the same as de Rougement writes of, for there are millions of them, and they are a great nuisance,' Arthur recalled. 'If the road is unrideable, and you are forced to walk, your shoes get full of sand from breaking through into these holes. The rats are numerous all over the plains. The rodents are somewhat similar to the common house rat, but have longer fur and hair on the tail. They are said to be migratory and overrun different parts of the country. They live in a similar manner to rabbits.'

The de Rougement Arthur referred to was Louis de Rougement, one of the most colourful characters in Australian colonial history. De Rougement was born Henri Louis Grin in Switzerland in 1847. After moving to Australia he worked in various occupations, including doctor, photographer, and butler to the governor of Western Australia, Sir William Robinson. He also travelled to the north-west coast of Australia on a boat working as a pearler.

In London in 1898 de Rougement passed himself off as a French nobleman and wrote about his adventures in Australia in a British periodical, the *Wide World Magazine*, and in 1899 published a book, *The Adventures of Louis de Rougement, as Told by Himself*. He sensationally claimed to have been shipwrecked at Cambridge Gulf on the north coast of Western Australia and to have spent thirty years living among Aboriginal people. According to de Rougement, he was embraced by cannibals, worshipped as a god and took a native wife.

The general public took de Rougement at his word and he was extremely popular. Henry Lawson claimed de Rougement made 'a bigger splash' in three months than any other Australian writer in one hundred years. But sceptics began to question de Rougement's stories and he was eventually exposed as a fraud, labelled 'the greatest liar on earth'. Whether Arthur regarded de Rougement as a hoaxer, a victim of sceptics or just a good storyteller is impossible to know, but while he saw evidence of rats, he did not mention the 'flying wombats' which de Rougement claimed to have seen.

Arthur rode by day and by night. Night-riding was a common practice among overlanders to avoid the hotter temperatures and stronger winds of the day. Bicycle lights were widely available, and mandatory in most cities, but there is no evidence that the overlanders used them. Heavy contraptions, they were more of a hindrance than a help. Dark-adapted eyes could use moonlight to much better effect.

It was fortunate for Arthur that the moon was full when he was travelling through the North West, which made riding at night less difficult and dangerous; even so, the tall tussock grass sometimes made the track hard to follow. It was easy to get lost in this labyrinth of tall grass. 'The only tracks which one can follow are horse pads — made by a saddle horse with a pack horse alongside,' Arthur recalled. 'Travelling along these in the moonlight is rather ticklish work as all the track you can see is a dark line in the high grass, sometimes as high as the handlebars of the machine. Sailing along a dark lane thus formed, seemingly riding on and through nothing, and not knowing when or where you will strike a stump or stone or drop into a hole — for the country is cut up with big cracks and holes in the limestone — is not the most pleasurable means of travelling.'

The road between Wallal and Lagrange Bay, near the Eighty Mile Beach between Port Hedland and Broome, was very sandy. Arthur reached Lagrange Bay at midnight on Saturday, 15 July, after riding nearly all the previous night through heavy dew and fog. He had entered the Kimberley, Australia's last frontier. Larger than 75 per cent of the world's countries, the Kimberley is a wilderness of spectacular scenery, featuring mountain ranges, limestone gorges and steep ridges. It has an extreme monsoonal climate and sparse population. The Kimberley is also home to the unusual bottle-like boab tree; some are estimated to be 1500 years old. The place is the very definition of remoteness, and Arthur was entering territory previously untraversed by an overlander. It was only in 1879 that the explorer, politician and investor Alexander Forrest, the great-great-uncle of the mining magnate Andrew 'Twiggy' Forrest, named the Kimberley region on an expedition from the De Grey River in the Pilbara to Port Darwin. Arthur would later thank Forrest for blazing the trail across the North West, which made his ride possible just twenty years later.

The road out of Lagrange Bay was also very bad as Arthur rode through pindan country: red soil and low woodland dominated by wattles, eucalypts and tall shrubs. During the long dry season from April to November the plants and grasses die off, so the country Arthur rode through would have looked parched and lifeless, almost alien.

He rode sixty-four kilometres through the pindan via Marshall's Station and Lora Well rock holes to Yardica Well where he camped for the night. From there he travelled another 104 kilometres through Goldwires Well to Roe Station, arriving at eight o'clock in the evening. Then he journeyed across an unrideable 'bumpy and cut-up' plain to Streeter's cattle station where he hoped to have a good meal, but the stockmen were away mustering and he was forced to wait all day for something to eat.

The next day Arthur rode through another sixty-four kilometres of red sand via Taylors Lagoon to Nillababica Tank, arriving at midnight and camping in the scrub. He then crossed the Fitzroy River to Yeeda Station, forty-

one kilometres south of Derby and encompassing much of the
northern end of the Fitzroy and Yeeda rivers, arriving at three
o'clock and staying the night, 'doing all my writing etc'. The
main homestead at Yeeda, constructed of wood and iron with a
bark roof in 1881, was the first house built in the Kimberley. By
the time Arthur rode up it was a fine stone house surrounded
by a garden and a hedge of boab trees, and would have seemed
like a luxury hotel to Arthur after he'd camped so many nights
in the scrub.

He reached Derby at five o'clock in the afternoon of the next
day, Sunday, 23 July, 'having travelled 1673 miles with scarcely
a day's favourable riding'. Derby, sitting on the edge of King
Sound, had been established in 1880 to service pastoralists after
sheep were introduced to Yeeda Station. King Sound's massive
11.8-metre tides, the highest in Australia, made the building
of a wharf necessary in 1885 and the jetty quickly became the
place to be to view the spectacular sunset. If Arthur sat on the
wharf and admired the western sky, he did not say.

It was in this region that the English buccaneer William
Dampier formed such an unfavourable impression of the land,
which was then known as New Holland, when he was the first
Englishman to describe the area in 1688:

New Holland is a very large tract of land ... I am uncertain that it
joins neither Asia, Africa, nor America ...

The land is ... dry sandy soil destitute of water ... the woods
are not thick nor the trees very big ... We saw no sort of animal,
nor any track of beast, but once, and that seemed to be the tread
of beast as big as a great mastiff dog ...

The inhabitants of this country are the miserablest people in
the world ...

With a description like that, no wonder Europeans did not show any interest in colonising North West Australia for another two centuries. Arthur, however, seemed to enjoy Derby, the most northerly point on the Western Australian coast that he touched. He overhauled his bicycle there, putting on new tyres and generally refitting it for the road to Port Darwin. He also bought a new pair of shoes, after wearing out his old ones.

Arthur's original intention had been to keep as close to the coastline as possible, but he now decided to strike across country on the telegraph track once he reached the Fitzroy Crossing police station. He would head for Halls Creek in the East Kimberley, avoiding the desert where he would be unable to obtain food or water.

On Monday, 24 July, Arthur left Derby, following the Fitzroy River on a hard bullock track covered in sandy dust. For the time being he was not isolated. 'There are stations all along the river, mostly utilised for sheep breeding, while others run cattle,' he noted. He arrived at Fitzroy Crossing on Sunday, 30 July, camping there for two days while he sought out a local identity, Fred Ashton, to ask about the track from Halls Creek to Katherine River, which was where he anticipated his real difficulties would begin. 'I have been saving myself for the rough bit across to Queensland,' Arthur noted.

After following the Margaret River from Fitzroy Crossing for eighty kilometres in a south-easterly direction along a horse pad, Arthur headed east towards Halls Creek, traversing mountainous and rocky country. There were plenty of kangaroos and wild turkeys about, but he lived on johnnycakes, a kind of bush bread, and fish, which were abundant in the rivers and creeks. 'You can catch sufficient fish in half an hour to provide for twenty people,' Arthur recalled. 'It is quite possible that de

Rougement caught some of the sawfish of which he writes, for there are plenty of them to be caught, and the blades of some of the fish are over two feet long. The fish didn't seem to grow to any great size.'

At least de Rougement was not exaggerating this time as the predatory sawfish, which are related to sharks, have been sighted 400 kilometres from the Western Australian coast up the Fitzroy River, which also harbours aggressive bull sharks.

From Fitzroy Crossing it took Arthur three and a half days to reach Halls Creek, the centre of the Kimberley goldfields, where a prospector, Charlie Hall, found a huge 28-ounce (nearly 1 kilogram) gold nugget on Christmas Day, 1885. The country Arthur crossed was hilly, but well watered. There was good fishing and hunting along the track, which led through some 'good patches of pastoral country' and also 'several belts of auriferous looking country'. The climate reminded Arthur of Coolgardie, perhaps piquing a bout of homesickness. 'Some two weeks ago there was ice a quarter of an inch thick at Flora Valley, thirty miles from here,' Arthur observed.

He rode into Halls Creek on Saturday, 5 August, just before lunch-time. He was warmly welcomed by the 'kind and courteous' Mr Green, who was the 'warden, postmaster, telegraph master and registrar of everything' in the district. Arthur had heard much about Halls Creek from men who had been there in the gold rush, but when Mr Green showed him around the town he was disappointed. Picturesquely situated among hills, Halls Creek had a post office, police station, government office and stores, but Arthur found the town extremely dull. 'The place is virtually dead,' he recalled. 'A goldfield without diggers or miners, and a diminishing population. The country is very different in appearance to that of the eastern goldfields, being mostly slate, with very little diorite or ironstone.'

Without any distractions in Halls Creek, Arthur put his time to good use, overhauling his bicycle again 'in anticipation of the heavy belt of lonely country I was about to enter'. Also the soles of his shoes had come off, and he managed to find enough leather to repair them.

Arthur was entering what he had described as the 'worst part' of his ride round Australia. There were serious doubts about whether he would make it from Halls Creek to Powell Creek, particularly as he was riding alone. 'According to a prospector named J.D. Phillips of Croydon, North Queensland (who on a bicycle, accompanied by two mates in a buggy, has just come across from Croydon to Perth, via Roebourne, the route lying in the same direction as that which Richardson intends taking), the overlanders will have great trouble in getting through, owing to a bluebush lagoon, twenty-seven miles in width, having to be crossed between Powell Creek and Halls Creek,' the *Bradford Courier and Reedy Creek Times* reported.

It was the intention of Richardson and the White bros. (who are riding round in the opposite direction) to miss this stretch of country; but according to Phillips it is impossible to take any other route than the one which he followed. If this be true and there are no other tracks available, the overlanders will have something to look forward to, as Phillips and his party took three days to cross the lagoon, with the water knee deep. A lively job for a lone cyclist to tackle! As Richardson is now making his way alone across this section of Northern Australia, his progress and movements will be watched with increased interest, and it will be good news to hear that the plucky Dunlop rider has succeeded in making civilisation again, either at Powell Creek – on the overland cable route – or Port Darwin.

The *Australasian*'s cycling correspondent, 'Phillibuster', anticipated Arthur and the White party would meet up shortly. 'Arthur Richardson is making good progress in the north, riding from west to east, and the White bros, with Donald Mackay, are moving along in a rough way from east to west, so that the quartet should meet in the course of a few weeks and exchange experiences.'

If 'Phillibuster' had known what lay ahead, he would not have been confident the overlanders would meet anywhere in this godforsaken country.

Stage Four

Crocodiles and Cockfights

White brothers and Donald
Rockhampton to Charters Towers
9 August to 18 August 1899

A LARGE crowd gathered at the Rockhampton post office to give three cheers for the White brothers and Mackay as they departed at two o'clock on Wednesday, 9 August. Donald chatted to several friends from New South Wales in the crowd before a couple of dozen local cyclists escorted the overlanders for a few kilometres out of town. The country was hilly and they had to cross some creeks, but the track was reasonably good, although Frank's chain was giving him trouble. They met some Aboriginal people who directed them to a branch road to Yaamba, thirty-six kilometres north of Rockhampton, where travellers crossed the Fitzroy River before moving west or north.

Situated on a baking plain, Yaamba was not very attractive, but it was hot so the overlanders stopped at a pub for a drink of homemade portergaff: stout with a dash of lemonade. 'It almost poisoned us!' Donald recalled. Pushing on, they rode

Donald Mackay towers over his Dux bicycle, which was especially designed to carry a weight of around 82.5 kilograms.

on a good road of red ironstone gravel over a swamp timbered with stunted stringybark trees, arriving at a better hotel, the Seven Mile Pub, at sunset, vindicating their decision to keep going.

The overlanders made an early start the next day and at noon they reached Marlborough, a small township 106 kilometres north-west of Rockhampton, close to a significant deposit of high-grade chrysoprase, a semi-precious gem once coveted by Alexander the Great and Cleopatra. After lunch they struggled across bumpy, chocolate-coloured soil, passing cone-shaped hills dotted with kangaroos.

Around four o'clock it started to rain. Riding over flat country, the overlanders saw dingoes near the Styx River, which rises in the Connors and Broadsound Range and enters Broad Sound south of the port of St Lawrence. At dusk they arrived at Willangie Station, which had an old-fashioned bush house, designed to provide shelter for plants and turn rain into mist, on the bank of the river. A Miss Chisolm was 'very hospitable' and a stock inspector gave them valuable information about the roads ahead.

It rained all night and until late the next morning, delaying their departure until 12.30pm. Hundreds of curious Aboriginal people appeared on the plain to watch the overlanders ride across swampy country – and frequently dismount to carry their bikes on their backs, waist deep in water. The cyclists noticed that the Aboriginal people were frightened of the bicycles. As long as they kept riding, the Aboriginal people stayed away from them. If they dismounted, they would advance towards them, but be ready to bolt as soon as they started riding again.

After the cyclists passed Waverley Station the road was drier, but the last four kilometres to the port of St Lawrence, where they arrived at dusk, was 'cut up and sloppy'. As the trio approached the township, they could hear singing and music. On closer inspection they discovered a big crowd of bushwhackers at a pub holding a 'buck dance'. At this time men greatly outnumbered women in outback Australia. While there were no women at this dance, there was plenty of alcohol, dancing and singing of sentimental songs, 'one gentleman leading off with "Then You'll Remember Me"! It would be hard to forget him,' Donald recalled. The tired riders joined in the fun for a while before going to bed at midnight, but they were kept awake by the revellers until three o'clock in the morning. Sometimes they got more rest camping in the scrub.

During the course of the evening a local school teacher 'haunted' the trio, telling Frank his ride from Perth to Rockhampton and back was more meritorious than the expedition of Burke and Wills, which no doubt would have flattered him. The teacher claimed he was also a cyclist and offered to escort the overlanders out of town in the morning, but when the time came he did not turn up. Like most of those hard-living men, he would have been sleeping off the previous night's overindulgence.

Sleeping-in was not a luxury the overlanders could afford and they made an early start. The road was wet as they crossed creeks every few kilometres, carrying their bikes, although the water was not deep. Then they rode over hills of loose gravel and patches of sand before stopping for lunch at an accommodation house. Alex, who was feeling 'seedy' from the night before, fell over a log in the long grass, but did not injure himself.

The road improved as it ran along the coast by Broad Sound in the direction of Cape Palmerston, an area of sandy dunes, beaches and rocky headlands. The overlanders began to see tropical foliage. In the evening they reached Kelvin Grove cattle station, about fifty kilometres south of Mackay. The manager was away so they had tea with an Aboriginal stockman and slept on bare boards in the stockmen's hut with no blankets and bags of chaff for pillows. A swagman was dying of fever in the next room and, as it was too cold to sleep, they listened to his agonising groans all night.

The overlanders rose at daylight and had a breakfast of salt beef, damper and oranges, which grew wild around the homestead. It was still morning when they reached the isolated timber town of Pine Creek, thirty-two kilometres away, where a cricket match was being played against a team from Mackay. The players interrupted their game to give the cyclists a boisterous welcome, but 'there was trouble keeping them from experimenting with our machines,' Donald recalled.

The road from Pine Creek to Mackay, 'the sugaropolis of Australia', as Frank described the town that still produces more than one-third of Australia's cane sugar, was little more than a bush track, sandy and rough. Riding past cane fields, the trio saw hundreds of bare-chested 'Kanakas', who had been recruited from various Pacific islands, mainly the Solomon Islands and the New Hebrides (now Vanuatu), to work as indentured labour on Queensland's sugar plantations.

A rough translation of the word *kanak*, which derives from the Hawaiian language, is 'wild man', 'animal man' or just 'boy', which gives some idea of what Europeans thought of the workers. Ironically, another Polynesian definition of *kanak* is 'free man', something they certainly were not. Some of the workers had been kidnapped, or 'black-birded', which led to accusations of slavery. Britain had abolished slavery in 1833, and the American Civil War, which led to the freeing of African slaves there, had ended in 1865, thirty-four years before the overlanders rode towards Mackay, but 'Kanakas' continued to work on Queensland's cane fields until the early twentieth century.

In the evening the trio attended church in Mackay and then gave interviews to newspaper reporters, who were curious about the amazing ride. They resumed their journey at eight the next morning and had a 'substantial feed' of wild tomatoes which thrived in the scrub. Passing several big sugar mills, they picked up sugar cane that had fallen off trains onto the railway line and sucked it as they rode along, giving themselves toothaches.

The overlanders reached The Leap, a regional landmark, in time for lunch. The place took its name from a brooding mountain, Mount Mandurana, which was dominated by a rocky precipice several hundred metres high. According to local lore, an Aboriginal woman pursued by white pioneers had chosen to jump off the cliff, holding her baby, rather than be captured and face a fate worse than death. The baby survived, caught on a bush in a shawl, and was brought up by white settlers. The Australian novelist Thea Astley used the story as the basis of her novel *A Kindness Cup*, which deals with racist brutality in the 1860s. It is unlikely attitudes had changed much when the overlanders passed through.

At the foot of the mountain was the Leap Hotel. A local sugar grower, who was also named Mackay and claimed to be a Scot, spoke to Donald in Gaelic and became 'very excited' (a euphemism for abusive) when the overlander could not understand him. The sugar grower's insults did not offend Donald. His parents may have been Scottish, but he was a true-blue Australian.

Pushing on after lunch, the trio hit upon a track which was overgrown with long tussock grass, in places almost a metre high and so thick they could not see each other twenty metres away. The riding was very rough across ground strewn with fallen timber and logs, hidden by the undergrowth. Alex ran into a dead tree stump hidden in the overhanging grass and buckled his front wheel and they were delayed until darkness fell while 'trueing it up'.

It was hot the next morning as they crossed the O'Connell River, whose headwaters rise in a valley under Mount Millar in the Clarke Range, part of the Great Dividing Range. On the other side the track was good at first, but they soon encountered swampy country and had to carry their bikes, sloshing through big pools of water extending over the road. The water was a real nuisance, but they would soon be thirsting for just a single drop.

At noon the overlanders arrived at Proserpine, which had only been founded in 1890 after the construction of a sugar mill on the banks of the Proserpine River. The settlement was surrounded by vast flat areas of land used for sugar-cane farming. After lunch they had a good run through picturesque country, passing an orchard where they bought oranges, the fruit a vital source of vitamins on such a long, laborious journey.

Descending the steep, sandy bank of a river, the trio had to wade through thirty-odd metres of fast-running water. On the other side they were stopped in their tracks by a large snake, about a metre long, lying on the rough and sandy road in front of them. They considered their options. They did not dare to try to ride around the reptile, which could be dangerous if aroused. Then Alex, who had a loathsome fear of snakes, got off his bike to kill it. He hit it with a sapling as hard as he could, but it did not move. It was already dead.

The dead snake underlined one of the dangers of riding a bicycle around Australia. While the snake was not identified, some of Australia's deadliest snakes are found in outback Queensland, including the inland taipan, the king brown and the eastern brown, which is the second most venomous land snake in the world. While most snakes flee from humans, aggressive snakes will defend themselves if threatened: if they are accidentally run over by a bicycle while unsighted in long grass, for example.

The overlanders then had some minor mechanical issues to deal with. Frank's wheel was a bit out of line and his pedal was loose, while the heat of Donald's hands had caused his handle grips to come off. They pulled up at a roadside hotel south of Bowen, a port town between Mackay and Townsville, at 5.00pm to fix their bikes and ended up staying the night. The next morning they got an early start. They did not go into Bowen but instead took a turn-off three kilometres out of town where they left the coast and started to cross the peninsula. The road was good, but they had to cross a 'nasty' creek by walking over a railway bridge before stopping for lunch at a hotel near the meatworks, nine kilometres from Bowen. 'The smell from the meatworks being very strong, we felt nearly satisfied before dinner came on!' Donald recalled.

Taking a shortcut through a range of hills, the trio found the main road in about a kilometre, coming out onto a big, rough plain with clumps of trees in the distance. After crossing the plain they had a run of hard riding through tall spear grass, the grass seeds sticking in their stockings, knickers and guernseys, making them look like echidnas on wheels.

It was difficult following the pad in the long spear grass. By dusk each of the riders had had a fall, but no one was hurt, at least not badly. Then darkness fell and they lost the track completely. It was pitch black and they did not know where they were. Frank and Donald fanned out in opposite directions, while Alex remained on the spot. Donald had gone about three hundred metres when he heard Frank shout 'Cooee' and returned to find that he had seen a light in the distance. The overlanders trudged a considerable way through the long grass and at last arrived at a house by the railway terminus at Wangaratta, now known as Bobawaba. There was no hotel, but the ganger allowed them to camp on the verandah with some stockmen, giving them a rug each for the cold night.

Leaving Wangaratta, the overlanders saw 500 head of cattle heading to the meatworks, looking 'clean and fat', which may have prompted daydreams of big, juicy steaks as they set off across some rough plains. At last they entered timbered country and followed a winding road for about a kilometre until, at noon, they reached the Lower Burdekin River, the fourth largest in Australia by volume of flow. A broad stretch of water about 180 metres wide, it was running fast. It was also full of saltwater crocodiles, huge ones, and there was no bridge to cross on.

The overlanders looked at each other, wondering how they were going to make it across, but there was only one way. They took off their clothes and put them on their bikes, which they carried on their heads. Saltwater crocodiles are stalkers: they attack when their prey cannot see them. The trepidation of the cyclists must have been intense as they waded carefully through swirling water, waist deep, revolvers in hand. Every sign, real or imagined, of something swimming in the water would have had the hairs standing up on the back of their necks. In the centre of the broad river they had trouble getting a footing, which only increased their anxiety. It is highly unlikely any of the cyclists would have survived an attack by a saltwater crocodile. It would be a terrible death. Just being bitten would have been bad enough because, at the very least, it probably would have meant the end of the ride for the victim. Fortunately, saltwater crocodiles are mainly active at night and the trio made it safely to the other side of the river, no doubt relieved to be in one piece. 'At last we were on the sand on the other side, feeling satisfied that a little of this wading went a long way,' Donald recalled.

Putting their clothes back on, the overlanders pushed off, stopping at a hotel in Ayr, eighty-eight kilometres south of Townsville, near the delta of the Burdekin River, for lunch. They ate all the hotel had to offer, but still left hungry. The next nineteen kilometres of road were level, but they were delayed when Frank's pedal pin broke. The road then became sandy with many creeks and hills to cross. At five o'clock they arrived at the Reid River railway station, on the Townsville to Charters Towers line, built in 1882 following the discovery of gold ten years earlier.

It was the strangest accommodation they experienced on the whole journey. The dining room was at the railway station, but the bedrooms were half a kilometre away in the bush. After the proprietor showed them the track they mounted their bikes and rode off to their quarters, which were compact and clean. There were no other occupants. After a wash they rode back to the railway station for tea at about 6.30pm, but were told there would be nothing to eat until the 'up train' passed by at 8.00pm, 'so we had to put in the time abusing things in general,' Donald recalled.

Departing at seven o'clock the next morning, the overlanders followed the railway line towards Charters Towers, seventy-six kilometres away, as the road was 'a thing of the past'. Leading at a fairly brisk pace, Frank crashed into a box drain, hidden by grass, and buckled his back wheel into a V-shape. This was a serious accident. The wheel had to be taken off and the spokes removed. Luckily, a ganger came along in his trolley and kindly lent Frank the tools to repair the wheel with solder and wire.

When the trio came to the Upper Burdekin River they did not have to worry about being attacked by saltwater crocodiles because they were able to cross an iron railway bridge. A few kilometres further along they were met at a pub by fifty cyclists who had ridden out from Charters Towers on a sandy road to greet them. They got a good reception and plenty of drinks before resuming their ride. There was a huge crowd at the Charters Towers post office when they arrived that night, Friday, 18 August. After their time-books were signed at the post office the overlanders checked into Ryley's Hotel where they freshened up.

Despite continuous rain and bad roads, they had travelled from Rockhampton in ten days, which would have encouraged them to hope they could beat Arthur around the continent. But the further north the trio rode the more they felt the debilitating effects of a hot climate. 'We are all getting very light weights, the weather being very hot now and it fairly knocks us out,' Frank said.

Charters Towers had been founded on a stroke of pure luck. On Christmas Eve, 1871, a twelve-year-old Aboriginal boy named Jupiter Mosman was accompanying a group of prospectors when their horses bolted after a flash of lightning. While searching for the horses, Jupiter found a gold nugget in a creek at the base of Towers Hill, sparking a gold rush. During the boom years that followed, Charters Towers was known as 'The World', because there was no reason to travel anywhere else.

Realising that almost everyone in town was a 'sport', the overlanders anticipated a fun stay and they were not disappointed. On the Saturday night they received an invitation from the local rugby union to a smoke social (a male-only event where men gathered to smoke tobacco and socialise) at the Masonic Hall in honour of the Mount Morgan rugby players, who had come to play the local team.

At the smoke social, which included singing 'that would have been a credit to any metropolitan talent', the trio was invited to a cockfight the next morning, an enormously popular pastime in outback Australia in colonial times, even though it was illegal. Not having seen a cockfight, Donald and Frank decided to go. Donald went to bed at midnight, but felt he had barely got to sleep when he heard someone kicking his door fiercely and telling him to hurry up or he would miss the bus to the cockfight. Staggering out of his room, Donald ran into Frank in the corridor, almost knocking him over. It was four o'clock in the morning.

Donald and Frank made their way out to the four-horse drag in which the hotel proprietor and several men were seated. A bottle of whisky was passed around and off they went, meeting several other drags along the way. On the outskirts of town they pulled up at a fire near the side of the road. Men sat around the fire smoking, some of them near baskets from which crowing could be heard. Then they made their way across several paddocks to a secluded spot in the bush.

At dawn the cocks were taken out of their baskets and placed in a fighting ring, or cock-pit, a circle about 3.5 metres in diameter and fenced with calico about forty-five centimetres high, supported by small sticks driven into the ground. Metal spurs were attached to the cocks' natural spurs, which ensured a bloody contest. Wagers of up to fifty pounds were taken on the fights. A local told Donald and Frank the story of how he won a big pot by dyeing a champion cock a different colour and beating a good bird at long odds.

The main event was a fight between the champions of Townsville and Charters Towers. Donald and Frank were horrified by what they saw, but they could not look away. 'The excitement was intense,' Donald recalled. 'Though it made me disgusted with myself for coming to such a brutal exhibition, there was a kind of fascination.

'At last the local bird made a lucky stroke, putting the steel through his opponent's neck and puncturing the windpipe. The end was near. Taking full time, the visitor once more stood up, but breathed with difficulty, the blood coming from the wound in his neck and dropping from the end of his beak. Another moment, and with a lurch he fell forward.

'The other bird, looking a little better, staggered over to him, pecking him on the head several times; then, flapping his wings, gave a mild crow. The fight seemed to have given him much satisfaction, and experts admitted it was the best they had seen for many years.'

Donald and Frank had had quite enough of bloodied beaks and ruffled feathers and returned to the hotel at around 8.30am. An hour and a half later a ten-mile road race was held in the overlanders' honour, attracting a big crowd. After riding more than 3000 kilometres from Melbourne, the overlanders may not have wanted to race, but with prize money of a hundred pounds on offer the White brothers decided to enter. The Whites were professional cyclists, after all, but Donald, an amateur, could not compete. Despite his leg weariness and a big handicap, Frank managed to finish third.

The main event of the day, the rugby game between Charters Towers and Mount Morgan, kicked off after lunch. The overlanders went to the ground in a coach with some of the players, which would have made Alex feel at home given his rugby background. The ground was circled by a fence and packed with spectators, but the cyclists, treated like VIPs, were taken inside the ring where they had a good view of the game, which resulted in the local team winning narrowly. The Charters Towers sports celebrated merrily, singing and drinking into the small hours.

The following day, Monday, 21 August, the hotel proprietor, Mr Ryley, took the overlanders on a tour of the mines and cyanide works, including the famous Brilliant Reef, where they enjoyed being 600 metres underground for a few hours before preparing for their departure.

The *North Queensland Register* reported that 'the plucky riders have placed no time limit on their journey, being satisfied with the honour of being the first to succeed in placing a cycling girdle around Australia. They speak in eulogistic terms of the courtesy and hospitality extended to them by the Charters Towers cyclists and footballers. The three look thorough athletes and as hard as nails. Those who have met the frank and gentlemanly trippers will heartily wish them a successful journey, for pleasant it can hardly be expected to be.'

Even with the headstart they had given Arthur, the White brothers and Mackay were growing more and more confident they would win the race around Australia, but they had underestimated the resilience and determination of the lone rider.

Stage Five

Bad Black Country

Arthur
Halls Creek to Wave Hill
6 August to circa 17 August 1899

O n Sunday, 6 August, Arthur made a start on the ride to
Port Darwin, a journey like no other, which would test
his courage, endurance and bush craft to the limit. As far as
Halls Creek he had been travelling through country where he
could communicate with civilisation at regular intervals; as long
as he could reach the outside world he had a lifeline if anything
went badly wrong. But the telegraph line terminated at Halls
Creek and now he was entering a practically uninhabitable and
isolated landscape, with not a road or even a trail, an expedition
fraught with peril. And he was all alone in what was commonly
referred to in those days as 'bad black country'.

Wild and unpredictable, this was a ridiculously easy place
to get lost in. Two billion years in the making, the ancient
wilderness of the East Kimberley consists of gnarled mountain
ranges intersected by sandstone and limestone gorges. The
mountains are not high (less than 1000 metres), but their steep

ridges make this empty and forbidding region very difficult to traverse, particularly on a bicycle, while the deathly silence and pure darkness at night would be unnerving, even for the bravest of overlanders.

From Halls Creek Arthur rode across this rough, mountainous country to Flora Valley Station where he found one of the 'oldest hands' in the Kimberley, who could provide him with information about tracks all the way to Queensland: the legendary pastoralist and explorer, Nat Buchanan. The Irish-born Buchanan had been the first European to cross the desolate Barkly Tableland east to west in 1877 and the first to take cattle from Queensland to the Northern Territory and the Kimberley, crossing the Victoria River country with 4000 head to stock the Ord River Station in 1883. There is little doubt that Arthur followed cattle pads in northern Australia that had been pioneered by Buchanan, who perhaps helped to settle more new country than any other man in Australia, but who died in 1901 with almost no land of his own.

Buchanan tried to dissuade Arthur from continuing his journey, telling him he had no hope of crossing the wild country without pack horses. Arthur respected Buchanan, who knew as much, if not more, about northern Australia than anyone, but it said something about the overlander's independent-mindedness that he ignored the warning of such an experienced and knowledgeable bushman.

The next station Arthur struck was Bootie's Station, otherwise known as 'Koogabring', which got its nickname from the way the manager, Mr Bootie, never let a passerby go without asking if he 'could bring' something back if he ever returned that way.

Arthur rode on through more rough country, scattered with loose rocks and tall grass, with few tracks, to the Ord

River Station, the first to be established in the East Kimberley in 1884. The stone homestead was shaded by wide verandahs supported by rough bush poles and insulated by a corrugated iron roof.

'I got through all right, and, spelling for two days, I got a look at some maps of the country, for there are no roads or tracks from Ord River to the Katherine,' Arthur recalled. 'I also got a good supply of flour, beef, etc.'

When Arthur left Ord River he made a seven-day stage 'per boot' to Wave Hill, about 320 kilometres further on, travelling through the same sort of frightening and lonely landscape. 'Cattle pads provided guiding paths, but they follow down the creeks, and a man can soon get a long way out if he is not careful,' Arthur recalled.

You have to be continually leaving one and crossing a divide till you strike another. All stores for the stations come from Port Darwin and up the Victoria River twice a year, so that there are no wagon tracks. The old Kimberley road has been washed out by the rain for years, and what was a good pad eight or ten years ago is now just the same as the rest of the country – loose, stony ground, with high grass in places, sometimes 6 feet or 8 feet high. Throughout I camped well away from the pads at night, and always continued for a while after dusk for fear of the blacks, who are noted in the district. Some of the gorges through which one passes when getting through the mountains are very solitary and dismal. One of them is known as Swan Creek. It is a long defile, with cliffs on either side covered with brush and scrubby timber. There are always blacks here, for the country is so wild that they can spear cattle and get away into the fastnesses of the mountains, and all the police in Western Australia could not catch them. Day followed day in this manner, and the loneliness at times oppressed me, though I had no misgivings as to my getting along all right and was never discouraged.

Arthur had good reason to be concerned about an Aboriginal attack, as Aboriginal groups had waged a war of resistance against European settlers in the Kimberley throughout the 1890s. The Kimberley was one of the earliest parts of Australia settled by Aboriginal people with the first arrivals landing more than 40,000 years ago, probably from Indonesia. Their descendants had lived in splendid isolation until suddenly the greatest empire in the world intruded into their lives. Invasion or colonisation, call it what you will, the result would be the same for Australia's first people.

The influx of European settlers created tensions with the Bunuba people, who lived in the southern part of the Kimberley, stretching from Fitzroy Crossing to the King Leopold Ranges. With its tropical savannah grassland, the region was prime pastoral country. The Bunuba were driven from their lands and some were forced to work on the newly established cattle stations. If they were caught spearing cattle or sheep, they were chained around the neck, marched to Derby and forced to work in chains, or worse.

A Bunuba warrior named Jandamarra led an armed insurrection against the Europeans. From the age of eleven, Jandamarra worked for white settlers as a station hand and became an excellent horseman and marksman. He was friends with a police constable named Bill Richardson who employed him as a tracker and ordered him to track down Bunuba people who had speared cattle. Among the captives was his uncle Ellemarra, who forced Jandamarra to decide where

Roads were poor and in many places non-existent in the 1890s. The overlanders followed dirt tracks, railway lines, stock routes and camel pads to find their way around the continent.

his loyalties lay. He was given an awful ultimatum. Kill his friend Richardson or be outcast from his people. Reluctantly, Jandamarra shot Richardson, stole some weapons and became an outlaw, beginning one of the most fierce Aboriginal resistance campaigns in Australian colonial history.

Jandamarra waged a guerilla war against European settlers for three years, from 1894 to 1897, using the ranges and caves of Windjana Gorge and Tunnel Creek as hideouts. His ability to seemingly appear out of nowhere and disappear without a trace became legend. He was held in awe by the Bunuba, who believed he possessed magical powers and could 'fly like a bird and disappear like a ghost'.

Western Australia's first premier, Sir John Forrest, ordered colonial troopers to hunt down Jandamarra and crush the insurrection, but this was easier said than done. It was believed only an Aboriginal person with similar mystical powers to Jandamarra was capable of killing him. The police recruited an

Aboriginal tracker named Micki from the Pilbara who tracked down Jandamarra and shot him dead at Tunnel Creek on April Fools' Day, 1897. The death of Jandamarra marked the end of the revolt, but Aboriginal hostility towards European settlers remained, and a lone traveller such as Arthur needed to be on his guard at all times.

Arthur also had to rely on his bush craft to survive in the unforgiving wilderness. He had to live on limited rations and what he could catch in the wild. He made damper with flour, but he had to be resourceful. To save weight, he did not carry a dish to mix the flour in but scooped a hole in the ground and lined it with a gunny bag. He also used the damper for bait when fishing. There were plenty of barramundi, mangrove jack and fingermark bream in the rivers and creeks of the Kimberley. And there were wild figs for dessert. There was no reason to starve in the bush if you knew where to look for food and Arthur's diet was probably better than that endured by the slum-dwellers of Sydney and Melbourne.

Half a day's riding from Ord River, Arthur saw a traveller on horseback coming over a range towards him. It turned out to be a young Aboriginal woman, one of a party of musterers. A musterer had had an accident and she was on her way to the station for assistance. A day later Arthur struck the musterers' camp, in the charge of one man who had left his pack horses and provisions at a river with the injured man and an Aboriginal boy. Later in the day he found the fellow who had been hurt in a terrible plight. Five days before, he had been thrown from his horse against a tree and he was afraid that he had sustained internal injuries. He was helpless in the middle of nowhere.

Arthur shot some birds and made a broth, which was the first food the invalid had eaten for days. For a day and a half

Arthur tended to him and shot some quail on a waterhole to make another good meal. When Arthur left the man he was confident assistance would come from Ord River, but he never heard whether he was rescued or became another victim of an untamed land, a whitened skeleton in the red desert sand.

Once again, it could be argued that Arthur only did what anyone else would have done in the same situation. But he lost a day and a half looking after the injured man – precious time when three wheelmen were pursuing him around the continent.

It took Arthur another two days to reach Wave Hill, a cattle station on high, open grasslands across the border in the Northern Territory, 600 kilometres south of Port Darwin. It was here that he learned first-hand that Aboriginal resistance to European intrusion was far from over.

Not long before Arthur arrived at Wave Hill, the station manager, Mr T. Cahill, and some stockmen were attacked by an Aboriginal group while out mustering in an area where a man known as Paddy the Lasher had been murdered two years earlier. After making camp they sat down for a meal and several spears were thrown at them, hitting one of the men. The stockmen defended themselves and the Aboriginal attackers retreated, but they were lucky there were no fatalities.

Arthur, crossing what was then known as Black Gin Creek and still some hours ride from Wave Hill, noticed a thin haze of smoke about two kilometres down the valley. His loud cooee resounding through the hills soon brought a party of Aboriginal men up the river to within shouting distance. They kept well up on the rise with their spears shipped and gazed at the bike, but would not venture near, seemingly afraid of the machine. Arthur managed to coax one of them to approach, the man moving slowly and hesitantly. Offering the man a piece of tobacco, Arthur learned from him that 'white fella sit down alonga creek'. As Arthur mounted the bike and made off along the bed of the creek the Aboriginal party started yelling and screeching, and while the sound was fearful, he did not feel threatened.

About thirty kilometres down the creek, Arthur came upon a recently deserted cattle camp and that evening he arrived at Wave Hill homestead – or the smoking ruins of the homestead, at least. It had been burned to the ground by Aboriginal attackers who put a fire-stick to the building while the men were away mustering.

The destruction of the Wave Hill homestead would have shaken most travellers, but Arthur steeled himself for the most dangerous part of his journey. He came across the mustering party as he rode away from the station and gave them the bad news about the burned-out homestead. He could do nothing but offer his sympathies to the stockmen and keep riding doggedly, doing his best to maintain courage and hope.

The spirit of Aboriginal resistance at Wave Hill continued sixty-seven years later when a Gurindji tribal elder, Vincent Lingiari, inspired 200 Aboriginal workers to leave their station jobs in protest against low wages and poor conditions that they claimed saw them treated 'like dogs'. The strike against the British pastoral company Vestey lasted seven years and developed from a plea for workers' rights into a battle for land rights, culminating in Prime Minister Gough Whitlam symbolically handing back ownership of the land to Lingiari in 1975 by pouring soil into his hands – long years after Arthur rode through the burned-out station on the way to making history of his own.

Stage Six

Devil-Devil Country

White brothers and Donald
Charters Towers to Normanton
23 August to 1 September 1899

CHARTERS Towers was so hospitable the White brothers and Mackay could hardly be blamed for wanting to stay longer, but they had no choice. They had intended to leave on Monday, but it rained so hard their departure was delayed two days. At 10.00am on Wednesday, 23 August, they reluctantly left this most inviting of towns. The forty-eight hours they had lost would be difficult to make up, but the extra rest helped to prepare them for the perils of what was known up north as 'devil-devil country'.

Frank calculated the overlanders would reach Perth in November if they continued to travel at their current rate, which would put them in a strong position to win the race, but what he did not take into account was that they had completed the easiest part of their journey in riding up the east coast. The challenge for the White brothers and Mackay was to make the same kind of progress in the untamed wilderness of northern Australia.

A dozen members of the Charters Towers Bicycle Club escorted the overlanders for a few kilometres until the road became rough and they turned around. It was a good decision because the track soon became impassable, covered in long grass on a sticky black soil plain, which forced the trio to dismount and trudge through heavy mud, carrying their bikes. 'This was no small job, more especially after the good time we had been having in town,' Donald recalled. 'Every few yards we found ourselves six inches above our usual height, the mud building up on the soles of our boots. This meant pulling up and hacking off the mud and grass.'

Eventually the ground became firmer and they reached the Anabranch Hotel at one-thirty in the afternoon. After lunch they rode on a wet and soft road, crossed the Big Fletcher and Little Fletcher rivers, which were running strong, and arrived at Gainsborough Station at six o'clock, staying the night. 'The cattle are all dead with ticks with which the country is infested,' Frank observed.

The next day the muddy road was 'horribly rough' and the cyclists covered only forty-eight kilometres, doing a lot of walking. Emerging from some low hills they came upon a pretty moon-shaped plain. 'It was a regular basin; its diameter would have been over a mile,' Donald recalled. 'The telegraph line ran across its centre, the road following the same course. It was regular "devil devil" country, and so bumpy that, after a couple of hundred yards, we decided to walk the rest.'

Reaching the far side, they found themselves among small hills covered with loose basalt rocks, which made riding dangerous. Then they were back on black soil, but fortunately it was unusually dry and firm, and they reached Hillgrove Station by evening, where they stayed the night.

The following day, after an early start, the overlanders came across a herd of horses on their way to the Chillagoe tin and copper fields, 205 kilometres west of Cairns. They found an excellent road and covered seventy-four kilometres through good country before lunch, although the grass, cottonwood, ironbark and boxwood were all dead because of a severe frost.

The trio crossed the Basalt River, which was running, having to wade through with their bikes over their heads. On the other side the road was hilly and stony, but they made Clarke River, sixty-nine kilometres away, for lunch on Friday, 25 August.

Leaving Clarke River in the morning, they started out for Christmas Creek Station, another nineteen kilometres further on. Taking wrong turns and losing the track in long grass, they managed to arrive at Christmas Creek at sunset. 'Just as darkness was setting in we sighted the station,' Donald recalled. 'The manager was away, but a manager of an adjoining station — I think the Valley of Lagoons — was on a visit so we had a very enjoyable evening. He had been in these localities many years, and told us of exciting experiences. On one occasion — at the crossing we had seen at the Burdekin — he was swimming across, when an alligator took his horse from under him!'

While at Christmas Creek they had a 'great tussle' with a snake, which escaped into long grass 'minus a foot of its tail'. The big lagoon in front of the homestead was alive with waterfowl as the overlanders departed early the next morning.

At first the road was sandy, but then they went through some pretty limestone hills and clapped on the pace on the harder ground. Donald was riding along the side of a deep guttering when it caved in and he had a nasty fall, which sent him ploughing along the ground. 'When I picked myself up my bike was some yards behind,' Donald recalled. 'On trying to rise I was very giddy, so lay down. In about ten minutes I felt equal to sitting up, and started to examine how much of myself was intact. Fortunately, no bones were broken, but a good deal of skin was missing off both hands, also from the knees and elbows.'

The overlanders stopped at a nearby creek for lunch and a strong cup of tea brought Donald back to his 'normal condition'.

From there the country was level, but there was still a lot of black soil, which made for rough riding to Lynd Station where they stayed the night. Even though the next day was a Sunday, they were up well before daybreak as the station manager was an early riser with breakfast ready at 5.00am.

Departing, the road was good, but a strong headwind slowed them down. Late in the morning they stopped on the bank of the Lynd River and washed their clothes, lying in the shade for an hour until they dried in the searing heat.

The overlanders made another start at three o'clock and after a kilometre they met several men driving a herd of cattle. One of the drovers was a Mr Blakeney, the station manager of Carpentaria Downs, which was a few kilometres away. Blakeney told the cyclists to go to the station and mention to the ladies he had told them to call, an invitation they could hardly refuse.

The ladies of Carpentaria Downs made the overlanders feel right at home in a pleasant two-storeyed house, and by the time Mr Blakeney returned they had already enjoyed refreshments. Later in the evening they went down to the lagoon, which Mr Blakeney said was full of crocodiles, but he promised they would not bite. It was probably because they were freshwater crocodiles rather than 'salties', as the length of one, about 2.7 metres, which had been near the garden the day before, indicated. Mr Blakeney swam far out into deep water, and when no crocodiles appeared the cyclists cautiously followed him in and had an invigorating swim, washing the dust and the dirt from their weary bodies.

From Carpentaria Downs the overlanders rode west on a cattle pad over flat country watered by small creeks, which harboured crocodiles. About eleven o'clock, after travelling thirty kilometres, they crossed the Einasleigh River, a tributary of the Gilbert. The Gilbert–Einasleigh River, which flows northwards to the Gulf of Carpentaria, is one of the largest river systems in northern Australia. Although it is a seasonal river, the Gilbert–Einasleigh has the sixth-highest discharge of any river in Australia, but in the dry season it was just a trickle of water in a wide bed of sand.

If the overlanders had read the adventurer Arthur C. Bicknell's book *Travel and Adventure in Northern Queensland*, published in 1895, they might have been on the look-out for a 'wood devil' on the banks of the Einasleigh River. An old bushman told Bicknell that the 'wood devil' was as tall as a man, walked about on its hind legs, had long arms and huge hands and made a strange moaning noise. Bicknell asked the old man to direct him to where the 'wood devil' might be seen. Climbing a tree, Bicknell waited for the creature and when it appeared he shot it.

'There sure enough he lay, as dead as any stone, shot through the heart,' Bicknell wrote. 'He was no more a wood devil than I am, but you can call him one if you like. He was nothing but a big monkey, one of the largest I have ever seen, with long arms and big hands, as the old man had described. These big monkeys, or apes, are common in Nicaragua, but this one was certainly the largest I have ever come across.'

As if the overlanders did not face enough danger already from snakes, crocodiles and hostile Aboriginal people, they had to deal with wood devils too, although what a Nicaraguan ape (perhaps a spider or capuchin monkey) was doing wandering around northern Queensland was anyone's guess.

The town of Einasleigh, 330 kilometres south-west of Innisfail, is on the Copperfield River, just before the junction with the Einasleigh River. The name Copperfield was a reference to the ore discovered there in 1866 by the pioneering geologist and photographer Richard Daintree, whom the Daintree Rainforest is named after. A few kilometres from their crossing, the overlanders noticed hundreds of miners pegging claims in a copper rush. The thought of joining the rush and making a small fortune might have tempted them, but they did not have any time to spare if they were to beat Arthur.

Riding across hilly, timbered country, the overlanders passed thousands of two-metre-high termite mounds, with some of the cathedral mounds reaching as high as five metres. The mounds represented an amazing feat of co-operation by the termites and that was the trio's main advantage over Arthur: the benefit of teamwork.

The overlanders headed towards the mountainous country of the Newcastle Range, which at 779 metres is one of the highest localities in Queensland. On a blazing hot afternoon they struggled across the Stockmans Range, a limestone and basalt spur of the Gregory Range, lying south-east of Croydon. The primordial landscape dates back 1.6 billion years, long before dinosaurs, or bicycles, roamed the earth. 'Anyone riding horseback there is compelled to carry a lot of horseshoeing implements because the horses shed or loosen their shoes at every mile almost,' Frank recalled.

As the overlanders started to ascend the range, which was steep in places, they marvelled at how bullock drivers ever managed to get their teams over the rugged track. No sooner did they top one rise than another would appear in front of them, but the view behind of rivers winding through open, level country was spectacular. At the very top of the range riding was exceedingly difficult because of loose boulders lying everywhere.

Even though kangaroos and dingoes were plentiful, the overlanders could find no sign of water. The ephemeral nature of the watercourses on the range meant there was usually no surface water in the dry season because there was virtually no rainfall. Their throats were on fire when, at sunset, they reached Charleston, a mining town established in the 1880s, but which was then practically deserted.

Originally known as Finnigans Camp and renamed Forsayth in 1910, Charleston township consisted of a pub, a store and a post office under one roof and some rudimentary huts. The old landlord warned the cyclists against drinking the beer because it was 'injurious' to anyone who was not accustomed to it. Whether they accepted his advice is unclear, but they were thirsty so they probably risked it. After tea the whole population of thirty bushwhackers sat on the verandah, listening to an accordion, the townsfolk taking it in turns to play it. 'Our host said all the townspeople were musical,' Donald recalled. 'This was a matter of opinion and might have been disputed by some.'

After a huge plate of porridge for breakfast, the overlanders departed at eight o'clock in the morning, not sorry to see the last of the small mining camp. The road was hilly, but exceptionally good, and with the wind behind them and the porridge providing fuel, they travelled sixty-four kilometres in two and a half hours to Georgetown, a gold-mining town on the Etheridge River.

Georgetown was one of the real locations mentioned several times in the 1950 novel *A Town Like Alice* by Nevil Shute, about a young Englishwoman who uses an inheritance to redevelop a small, derelict outback town.

The overlanders entered what appeared to be the best hotel in town. Before they had time to settle in they were interrogated by a newspaper reporter, who would not leave them alone. The annoying journalist's enquiries took even more time because he stuttered. Eventually, the reporter had his story, and the cyclists headed off to lunch, but the scribe reappeared with several friends and joined the overlanders, so they had to repeat themselves.

The town crier notified the townsfolk of the overlanders' intended departure at one-thirty and gave the trio a memorable send-off. 'By the time we finished lunch it was our advertised time to start, and, on going out, saw the bell man — a short, fat, dirty fellow doing eighty per cent of his walking on one leg, which was much longer than the other, and did most of the work,' Donald recalled.

> As he stepped onto the verandah he gave a fast, furious ring of the bell, and announced to the assembled multitude in a voice that might have been taken for a cart axle in want of grease: 'Roll up! Roll up! Roll up! And see these marvellous freaks of nature, as they move from our town at half past one this day, on their perilous and meritorious trip on wheels from the Poles to the Equator, from the scorching plains of Central Australia to the ice-clad peaks of the Snowy Mountains. Roll up! Roll up!'
>
> His eloquence paralysed. Truly, it is a pity that such a man should waste his talents in such desert air. I asked him to have a drink, which he accepted, saying that the dryness of the climate had materially affected his voice. In a confidential manner, he told me if we intended going through any cold climates to put a thick coat of grease over the nose. He said he had suffered much from frostbites when in the far north. If being minus half his nose goes for anything, he may have been telling the truth.

Several hundred miners cheered the overlanders as they mounted their bicycles. 'Had great trouble getting away, the people being very hospitable,' Frank recalled. But they managed to push on, riding towards Croydon, a gold-rush town at the heart of a vast region of dry savannah grassland. The original track had been pioneered by Ludwig Leichhardt in 1844—45 on an overland journey of 4800 kilometres from the Darling Downs in Queensland to Port Essington in the Northern Territory. After crossing the sandy bed of the Etheridge River, the overlanders rode in inescapable heat along a good track for thirty kilometres to Cumberland, a gold-mining town on the Gilbert River. On arriving, they found the entire population in a drunken state after burying a popular resident. The townsfolk invited the trio to join them in 'drowning their sorrows', but they politely declined and pushed on.

In a few kilometres the overlanders stopped at another hotel, which was more like a bush shanty. As they approached the hotel they were intrigued to see three bicycles leaning against a verandah post and decided to have a look. The trio need not have feared they had any extra competition on their ride around Australia. Inside were three Salvation Army men drinking beer. Bicycles were a common form of transport for clergymen in the outback.

The temperature on the road was '100 degrees in the water bag', but the overlanders reached Forest Home Station on the Fanning River in good time and got a warm reception from the manager, Mr Henry Wilson. Before tea they had a swim in a large lagoon in front of the house and spent the evening playing cards and hearing stories of cattle stealers, who had caused a lot of trouble for the station over many years. 'Two days before we arrived one had been caught red-handed,' Donald recalled. 'But local juries seldom convicted this class of criminal, and it was thought improbable that this duffing expert would receive his just deserts.'

The trio discovered there was, in fact, some sympathy for cattle duffers in those parts. Riding over a reasonable road on the 107-kilometre stage to Croydon (also mentioned in *A Town Like Alice*), they stopped at a halfway hotel for lunch. The proprietor was defensive of the thieves, arguing it was harsh to arrest 'innocent' men for stealing cattle and that juries should not convict them because it was 'needless expense'.

It was terribly hot and the overlanders, feeling drained, had a rest after lunch. Starting once more, they found the track sandy, but rideable. They were amused to see the snakelike tracks in the sand made by the Salvation Army men, who in the previous days must have wobbled all over the road, having imbibed a little too much good cheer. Now and then the trio would laugh to see the prints of parts of their anatomy where they had fallen.

On Wednesday, 30 August, just outside of Croydon, the overlanders were met by thirty riders from the Croydon Bicycle Club, including Mr Vince Creagh, the League of Wheelmen secretary. After a round of drinks at a pub they started for the town, stopping at a Chinese market garden where they enjoyed oranges and bananas, before reaching the post office and getting their books signed. The trio then checked into the Queen's Hotel and had a bath, shave, tea and a good night's sleep, which was a rare luxury on this hardest of journeys.

The White brothers and Mackay were anxious to meet up with Arthur somewhere in northern Australia to glean information about the route across the North West, but they did not know his whereabouts. 'Should strike Richardson soon,' Frank wrote in a telegram to the *West Australian*. 'Cannot hear of him here. Wire me Normanton where he is. Want to see him particularly.'

Under a big blue sky, the overlanders were farewelled by a crowd of miners at first light the next morning and were escorted by two local cyclists out of town, passing mines and mullock heaps. The track was sandy so they followed the newly built railway line from Croydon to Normanton. In 1886 the Queensland government had decided to build a railway line from Cloncurry to Normanton. Then, with the discovery of gold at Croydon, the line was deviated twenty-one kilometres, reaching the town in 1891 and ending there after the gold ran out. (Today, the unique line survives as the Gulflander tourist railway, while Croydon and Normanton are part of the Savannah Way, which runs from Cairns to Broome.)

In 1899 the railway line was little better from a cyclist's point of view than the track, so the trio ended up following a pad running parallel with the line. Riding in the low scrub they each lost a spoke, which cost them an hour for repairs. By the time the overlanders had covered just sixteen kilometres the heat was so intense and the sand so loose that riding was almost impossible.

The trio arrived at the Blackbull Hotel, about halfway between Croydon and Normanton, at two o'clock in the afternoon. As their water had run out a couple of hours earlier, the thirsty cyclists 'opened the ball on hop beer and during our stay of one and a half hours put twelve bottles in safe keeping!' When the mail train to Normanton stopped in Blackbull, the trio felt a strong temptation to get on board and take a comfortable seat. The track ahead through the scrub for the next thirty kilometres was said to be sandy, and as the train departed they consoled themselves with another beer, dreading the upcoming stage.

Pushing on at three o'clock, the overlanders broke away from the scrub and came upon some small plains, the harder ground enabling them to make up some time. They reached a linesmen's camp at Haydon on Clarina Creek where they got an enthusiastic reception from men who were amazed at what they were attempting. Over tea they joined in a debate with the linesmen on the big political question of the day, federation, before turning in, appreciating a good camp after a hard day's riding.

While defence and trade were seen as the main benefits of federation, cycling also had much to gain from nationhood. Alfred Deakin, a leader of the federation movement who would become Australia's second prime minister, told the *Australian Cyclist* on 20 July 1899 that:

> The cyclist from New South Wales paying a visit to Victoria will no longer be required to pay duty on his bicycle before he can cross the old border, or require to have his luggage searched for suspected hidden articles liable to be assessed for customs duty. Federation will sweep away this obnoxious system, so that the tourist or man of business may pass from one colony to the other whenever and wherever he pleases [and] induce the shire councils and similar bodies to improve existing roads which have hitherto been neglected and construct new ones leading to districts in another colony. The benefits which will thus accrue to cyclists, tourists, and those who travel by road can scarcely be over-estimated.

The overlanders would have endorsed Deakin's observations on the state of the colonies' roads. How they must have wished federation had already come!

The overlanders enjoyed a nourishing breakfast and some 'priming of square' (gin) before farewelling the linesmen early in the morning. The dry, dusty road was rough, and they saw spinifex grass for the first time on the ride. They came to a depression in the level country, which turned out to be the Norman River, 'a long stagnant pool with a few lilies resting on the surface'. Crossing a railway bridge, they reached a wooden pub where they had a snack, mended a punctured tyre and exercised with some dumb-bells, perhaps to strengthen their upper bodies after so much pedalling.

'The bulbs were of unequal weight and in time were calculated to break up a Hercules, though the landlady told us the proprietor, a German of considerable magnitude, played with them as a cat does with a mouse!' Donald recalled. 'This remarkable man could also stay under water for five minutes at a stretch! The landlady seemed a bit disconcerted when I suggested she must mean a beer tap.'

After continuing across black soil plains and red gravelly ridges the overlanders arrived at Normanton, a river port on the Norman River, just south of the Gulf of Carpentaria, on Friday, 1 September. The town was 'a place of medium size and altogether notable for ugliness', according to Donald. Riding up the main street, they stopped at a hotel opposite the post office, running into an escort of local cyclists just starting out to meet them. In no time at all the locals were entertaining them with 'long beers' at the hotel.

In the evening the townsfolk of Normanton gave the overlanders a smoke social. After listening to some of the locals singing in the 'weird and dismal strains' of the Australian bushman, the weary overlanders were in bed by midnight. Just as he was getting to sleep, Donald heard a commotion in the drawing room and rushed in to see an all-in brawl, which quickly broke up and was followed by more singing. 'I sneaked back to my room only to hear some wretch with a shrill voice, intermixed with hiccups, sing "The Last Rose of Summer". And I slept.'

The overlanders did not know it yet, but the party was over.

Stage Seven

Alone in the Wilderness

Arthur
Wave Hill to Victoria Downs
Circa 17 August to circa 19 August 1899

T HE most difficult stage Arthur experienced during the whole ride was from Wave Hill to Victoria River Downs, across one of northern Australia's most remote regions, rarely seen by white men. If Arthur had any pioneering spirit, this was where he would need it most. The ancient untamed wilderness was 'exceedingly rangy, rough and absolutely trackless'. The run of the Victoria River, the longest singularly named permanent river in the Northern Territory, provided some sort of direction, but it was impractical to ride a bicycle over this course. Arthur would need to find some way to navigate the wildest stage of the ride or risk becoming hopelessly lost or worse.

Fortunately for Arthur, there were certain people who knew this 'unknown' land like the backs of their hands: the Aboriginal inhabitants. Even though Wave Hill homestead had been burned to the ground by local Aboriginal people, the station manager, Mr T. Cahill, advised Arthur to visit an

Aboriginal camp on the banks of the Victoria River to ask them to show him a shortcut across the ranges and also carry his provisions.

If Arthur had any reservations about approaching potentially hostile Aboriginal people for assistance, he did not show it. He took Mr Cahill's advice and arranged with two Aboriginal men to help him, but only one turned up at the time of departure and he did not meet with the overlander's unqualified approval. 'He was anything but a beauty,' Arthur recalled. He was 'evil-looking' with a 'peculiar squint in his eye'. Arthur was distrustful of his guide from the start. But he was not in a position to be choosy.

An overlander had to be well stocked during this stage of the ride. Arthur packed flour, meat, tea and sugar into two 22-kilogram bags, into one of which he also put his camera. Strapping these bags together by the top, the Aboriginal man carried them across his shoulders. They started off with 160 kilometres walking in front of them and no track. The Aboriginal man said he knew a shortcut across the hills, which he called 'short fella', and Arthur agreed to try it. It was terribly heavy work tramping along a stony creek, then over a range and down along another creek. By sunset they had tramped thirty kilometres, but at least they were making some kind of progress. In a race around Australia, if a rider was standing still he was going backwards.

Arthur and his guide camped on a creek in long grass, but from the moment they stopped he could see that the man was uneasy and eventually he asked to be allowed to go back, explaining that there were 'too many black fella all about'. Arthur had noticed plenty of tracks around the waterhole so he guessed he was telling the truth, but he could not let him go.

He warned him any attempt to desert would result in 'severe punishment'.

The tension between the overlander and his guide increased after that confrontation. After tea they started cutting grass to make a camp. The Aboriginal man worked at the spot where they had crossed the creek, while Arthur went lower down and lost sight of his guide. This was the man's chance to escape and he took it. With a 'good armful' of grass cuttings, Arthur started back and as he rounded the bend he saw the guide absconding with his tucker bags, running up the opposite bank.

Arthur had no chance of catching him, as he was already about seventy metres away, but he was within firing range. Taking out his pistol, Arthur fired a shot and the ball split against the bank just in front of the guide's nose. With a yell of terror he dropped the tucker bags and his spears and 'scrambled into the long grass like a dingo'. Arthur never saw the man again, but suspected he would join other Aboriginal people in the area. 'As they are in that locality as wild and treacherous as any in Australia, I packed up my traps and cleared,' he recalled.

Arthur now had to find his own way through the wilderness. For hours he tramped over the ranges, scrambling through canyons and gorges and sloshing across creeks, up one gully and down another, travelling at the snail's pace of about three kilometres an hour.

At two o'clock in the morning, Arthur rested at a small spring, exhausted. He could go no further and fell into a deep sleep. When he woke up the next day he had no idea where he was. 'All the blacks in Australia could not have kept me awake and the sun was fairly high when I awoke next morning in a wild and desolate spot and in possession of little knowledge as to my whereabouts,' he recalled.

The overlanders noticed that Aboriginal people were generally curious, but afraid of bicycles, although these two warriors do not seem concerned about the machines.

Arthur was lost and alone in the wilds. It would be hard to imagine anything worse, even for someone as intrepid as Arthur. To be sure, the travelling was difficult, but the intense loneliness was even harder to endure. And there was the constant fear of being attacked by a hostile Aboriginal party. It was not so bad during the day, but in the blackness of night Arthur's nerves were on edge. How much more could he take?

'While daylight lasted I was all right for I followed the lay of the country and knew that I must strike the river in time,' Arthur recalled.

Even without actually getting bushed I had a most perplexing and uncomfortable time of it. At times I fancied that I was making great headway, but just as I would begin to congratulate myself upon getting out of a nasty predicament I would come slap up against a blank wall in the shape of an impossible line of ranges or sheer cliffs, and oft I would be forced to go up a gorge or down a creek to look for a gap to get through, humping the machine over stones and through an expanse of thick, high grass – sometimes far higher than myself – with the continual dread of receiving a shower of spears; scrambling up the sides of ranges as steep as the walls of a house, and down the other side the same thing occurs again. Sometimes the blacks would follow along the tops of the cliffs for miles, occasionally showing themselves, and probably waiting for me to camp, but at sundown I would boil my billy and then push on again into the dark, and slinking through the grass like a dingo, camp away from the bike, with no fire and myriads of mosquitoes to worry me till dawn.

In order to survive, Arthur adopted the traveller's motto: 'When in Rome do as the Romans do.' In 'blackfellow country' he 'lived like a blackfellow'. After his tucker ran out he lived on what he could catch. His diet included lily roots, the size and shape of an onion, which he found by groping in shallow pools under waterlilies. He also dined on wild figs, berries and fish, although kangaroo and other game were scarce.

If things were not bad enough, they suddenly got a whole lot worse when Arthur caught a fever. One of the greatest fears of a lone traveller is becoming ill and not being able to look after oneself, as there is no one else around to act as nurse or carer. And the remote reaches of the Northern Territory was one of the last places on earth anyone would want to be sick, all alone. Arthur's fever was an ailment his father could have easily remedied at home. But a debilitating illness was potentially a greater danger in the wilderness than crocodiles and hostile

Aboriginal people combined. After a while, his body aching, Arthur could not go on much longer. Was this the end? Not even halfway around? Would he simply disappear like Ludwig Leichhardt, never to be seen or heard of again?

The situation was grim. These few days were about as awful as it got for him on the whole ride. Then, one fine, clear morning, Arthur somehow managed to clamber to the top of a red sandstone cliff. Looking down he saw winding away through the hills the Victoria River, the 'Big Vic', a river of life. The moment was as dramatic as the setting. Following the course of the river along a very rough pad, and feeling sick and exhausted, he struggled to Victoria River Downs Station a day or two later; he could not remember how long it took. How he did it, who could know? It was sheer indomitable will. But he got there just in time before he collapsed altogether.

The Victoria Downs manager, Mr Watson, nursed Arthur back to health, insisting he stay until he was well again. Whatever feeble protests Arthur made about needing to continue his journey to become the first to ride around Australia, Mr Watson dismissed them. Arthur's wellbeing was the manager's only concern. He had to recuperate, however long it took – race or no race.

Arthur greatly appreciated Mr Watson's warm hospitality, the kindness of a stranger. It was the sort of thing Arthur would have done for someone in the same predicament.

'I must have looked a pretty object with my beard half grown, my shoes tied together with pieces of hide, and the soles made of greenhide laced onto the uppers,' Arthur recalled. 'You can imagine how welcome under the circumstances was the hospitality extended towards me by Mr Watson, the manager. For ten days, while I suffered terribly from a sort of low fever, he tended and nursed me, and had me fit and well for the journey to Katherine which was an eight or ten days stage.'

Victoria River Downs, known as the 'Big Run', had been stocked in the early 1880s and would become the largest cattle station in the world. No doubt Arthur knew he was lucky to strike it when he did or his ride around Australia, perhaps even his life, may have come to an abrupt end. As it was he lost ten precious days, which gave the White brothers and Mackay a great chance to catch up — but he had come to the stark realisation that surviving was more important than winning.

Like all of the overlanders, the White brothers were commercially exploited, but
without the support of sponsors such as Dunlop the race around Australia would
never have taken place.

Stage Eight

Plains of Hell

White brothers and Donald
Normanton to Camooweal
3 September to 12 September 1899

O N Sunday morning, 3 September, the White brothers and Mackay set off from Normanton for Burketown, an isolated river port 241 kilometres further west on the Gulf of Carpentaria. After receiving 'mixed directions' from a mailman, the overlanders were escorted out of town by a dozen cyclists for about sixteen kilometres. At first the track was sandy and undulating, but soon became level and thickly timbered. Coming out onto a large grassy plain they rode into a strong headwind for about half an hour before reaching an oblong-shaped lagoon where cattle grazed on the banks. After a farewell nip with their escort they followed a cattle pad running across the dry grass plains and reached Armstrong Creek for lunch, camping on its bank near a large pool overshadowed by trees, which provided welcome shade from the malignant sun.

While eating sandwiches, they heard a horse bell ringing from the other side of the creek. It was a group of miners in a buggy who were heading north to inspect mines that were being opened on the McArthur River in the Northern Territory. They crossed over to meet the miners, who insisted on giving them food, beer and whisky, and entertained them with stories of their adventures on the goldfields of Western Australia and north-west New South Wales.

Farewelling the genial miners, the overlanders crossed a rough plain before reaching Magowra Station on the Bynoe River in the late afternoon, where they were heartily welcomed by the station manager. After a nip they joined the station hands in a swim in a bathing hole, washing off the dirt and sweat that 'coated' them. Refreshed from the swim, they watched Aboriginal workers perform acrobatic feats before being summoned to tea by the cook, who vigorously kicked an iron tank because he did not have a bell to ring. Tall tales were told over tea before the overlanders went early to bed for a much-needed rest.

This unforgiving land was haunted by the memory of the explorers Burke and Wills who had perished on their ill-fated expedition just thirty-eight years previously. In 1860–61, Robert O'Hara Burke and William John Wills led an expedition of nineteen men from Melbourne to the Gulf of Carpentaria, a distance of 3250 kilometres, to make the first successful, documented south–north crossing of the continent. Doomed to failure by poor leadership, bad luck and errors of judgement, the expedition left Melbourne on 20 August 1860 and reached Cooper Creek in South Australia – as far as European explorers had ventured – on 11 November where they formed a depot. On 16 December, Burke, Wills, John King and Charlie Gray set off for the Gulf, leaving William Brahe in charge. The party reached the Little Bynoe River on 9 February 1861, just forty kilometres from the coast, setting up their most northerly camp, Camp 119. Burke and Wills attempted to reach the sea, but mangroves were impenetrable and they turned back just a few kilometres from the coast. With supplies running out, the party left Camp 119 on 13 February for Cooper Creek, arriving just nine hours after the depot had been abandoned, exhausted and malnourished. Tragically, Burke, Wills and Gray died on the return journey, while King was rescued.

Like the overlanders, Burke and Wills had been engaged in a race with explorer John McDouall Stuart, the pursuit of glory making them do impulsive and foolish things, which ultimately cost them their lives.

The overlanders were now just a few kilometres from where Burke and Wills made their final, poignant camp, but for them there was no turning back. The next morning the trio reached the Flinders River, the longest river in Queensland, flowing for 1004 kilometres, and named in honour of the explorer Matthew Flinders, who was the first to circumnavigate Australia and identify it as a continent. While the overlanders were not on an expedition of exploration, their 'circumcycling' of the continent shared the same spirit of discovery as Flinders' voyage.

Cautiously dipping their pint mugs in the muddy river, Alex and Donald were startled by a sudden splash in the water, and fearing an attack by a crocodile attempted an immediate retreat, but Donald got stuck in the mud. 'Unluckily, in my hurry, my feet sank in the soft mud,' Donald recalled. 'By the time I staggered out, my mate, who had reached a safe position, saw that our supposed enemy was a large fish. Near the opposite bank he had seen the head of one, as it came to the surface, similar to the one that had frightened us. I afterwards learned that they were a large species of catfish.'

The overlanders then rode across undulating country of low gravelly ridges dotted with stunted trees and darkened by flocks of black cockatoos. They reached Ironstone Creek at about four o'clock in the afternoon and boiled their quarts with water remaining in pools in deep depressions. Then they pushed on over rough plains which changed from red to chocolate to black soil, walking much of the way until they entered woodlands again.

After staying overnight at Inverleigh Station, they crossed empty rough country, known as the Devil's Punchbowl, on their way towards the Leichhardt River, named after the ill-fated Prussian explorer. The disappearance of Leichhardt on his last expedition remains a mystery. In 1848 he set out from the Condamine River on the Darling Downs in Queensland to reach the Swan River in Perth. He was last seen on 3 April 1848 at Macpherson's Station near Coogoon on the Darling Downs. It is believed he died somewhere in the Great Sandy Desert in Western Australia.

The fate of Burke, Wills and Leichhardt should have been a dire warning to the cyclists, who were traversing the same treacherous country as the explorers, that errors of judgement or even sheer bad luck would be punished severely.

The Leichhardt River was wide, but dry at the teamsters' crossing with big pools of water at either side. The overlanders tried to get a drink, but the water was brackish so they pushed on, thirsty. Riding for about an hour and a half through woodlands they were met fifteen kilometres from Floraville Station, near Leichhardt Falls, by a welcoming party bringing whisky and water, which was 'very acceptable' after an eighty-kilometre dry stage. They reached Floraville, sixty-four kilometres south-east of Burketown, as darkness fell and rested on the wide verandah. 'We had great delays owing to sticks getting in the wheels and breaking the spokes and we had to put twelve in in three days,' Frank recalled.

A staging post, telegraph station and watering hole, Floraville was close to the place where the police superintendent and renowned bushman Frederick Walker was buried. In 1861, Walker led a party in search of Burke and Wills. While he did not find the explorers, he did locate Camp 119, the most northerly camp of their expedition. Five years later Walker was commissioned to find a route for a telegraph line from Cardwell, a coastal town between Townsville and Cairns, to the Gulf of Carpentaria. He arrived at Burketown at the height of an outbreak of 'gulf fever', thought to be typhoid, fell ill on the return journey and died at Floraville on 19 November 1866, aged forty-six, yet another courageous, but doomed, victim of this fatal country.

The next morning the overlanders followed the telegraph line across seemingly endless rough grassy plains. The region had been originally named the Plains of Promise by Captain John Lort Stokes of the *Beagle* in 1841. Stokes discovered the mouth of a river which he named the Albert, after Queen Victoria's consort, Prince Albert, and travelled in a longboat for 128 kilometres seeking fresh water. The surrounding countryside, having recently experienced favourable seasons, was in good condition, influencing Stokes's choice of a positive name. If Stokes had ridden a bicycle across the plains in the dry season, he might have given them a different name. Plains of Hell perhaps? 'If the road to Hades was as rough, the traveller would be too weary to care what happened to him by the time he arrived,' Donald recalled.

In the afternoon the track changed from hard black soil to loose dust, the wheels sinking several inches. After a few kilometres the cyclists came upon a chain of lagoons and another rough track which they followed until they reached the banks of the Albert River at sunset. Hailing a boat, they were ferried across the river, which was deep and about ninety metres wide, to Burketown, roughly thirty kilometres inland from the Gulf of Carpentaria.

Burketown was the kind of frontier town where, according to the press of the day, 'everyone carried a pistol and where a successful shopkeeper could ride well, shoot well and be an able pugilist'. The overlanders' stay coincided with a visit by a famous, or perhaps infamous, squatter, Harry Readford, who had travelled from his station on the McArthur River, 320 kilometres further west on the Gulf.

Thirty years earlier, Readford had performed the greatest feat of cattle-duffing in Australian history. Working as a stockman on Bowen Downs Station near Longreach in Queensland, Readford realised that remote parts of the property were rarely visited by station workers. With two accomplices he mustered a herd of 1000 cattle and drove it through the searing heat and dust of the Channel Country, an eerily empty region of red sandhills, and across the Strzelecki Desert to Marree in South Australia, where he sold the cattle for £5000.

Readford was arrested in 1872 and tried at Roma in western Queensland in February 1873 on a charge of cattle-stealing, but the jury members were so impressed by the magnitude of his achievement that they found him not guilty, prompting the judge, Charles Blakeney, to remark: 'Thank God, gentlemen, that verdict is yours and not mine!'

The novelist Rolf Boldrewood based the character of Captain Starlight, an honourable bushranger, in the Australian classic *Robbery Under Arms* in part on Readford. When the cyclists met

Readford in Burketown they were impressed by his larger-than-life personality.

'He was a man who, one could see at first sight, would be equal to anything from wooing a lady to winning a kingdom, standing 6 feet, 4 inches, and proportioned as Hercules,' Donald recalled. 'In his younger days he had done exploring work of no small extent, and marked many of the tracks that now exist in these parts. On hearing of our project, he was much interested, and gave good information, and, if we had been going via the McArthur, offered to pack any dunnage we might have as far north as his station. Now that he was in town, he was having a good time, practically taking possession of the pub, serving behind the bar, and flirting with the ladies; in fact, the lion of the day!'

The next day the overlanders inspected the local boiling-down works on the bank of the river a kilometre out of town. Donald was impressed with a gigantic sausage machine, which he described as a flytrap. 'They flew around it in thousands, heeding not the fate of many of their number who at every turn of its iron jaws went to that bourne whence none return,' Donald recalled. 'Still, their extract is distributed all over the world and, though they die, it may be only to assist in restoring health and strength to suffering humanity.'

The overlanders left Burketown on Thursday, 7 September, with Camooweal as their next major destination, about 700 kilometres distant in a south-westerly direction. The heat was unbearable so they decided to pull up early and spend the night at the Brook Hotel, a rough teamsters' hostelry on the Nicholson River.

'The hotel was anything but inviting, and seemed to be an accommodation house for pigs, poultry and some pet goats, one of which was anxious to have the tea off the same plate as Alex,' Donald recalled.

> The company was few, and anything but select. One man seemed nearly dead, suffering a recovery, with a bit of fever chucked in; but he pinned his faith on rum and Holloway's pills, taking a dose of each at frequent intervals. The other two just arrived as we did, and were soon merry.
>
> Here it is the quantity, and not the quality, of the grog that tells. Soon they were shouting for us in a reckless manner. It was a case of drink or fight, and sooner than be unsociable, we chose the former, generally only taking water, as the landlady had kindly warned us to stand off hard tack.
>
> At length we slipped away and got to bed, only shortly afterwards to be aroused by the landlady cursing someone in a masterly fashion. It turned out afterwards that one of our friends, being refused a drink, had started to set fire to the house, but on being detected he got a nip that soon put him to sleep.

It turned out the landlady had given him a drink with knock-out drops in it.

The next day the overlanders crossed the Barkly River and followed a monotonous teamsters' track, sandy and then black soil, until five in the afternoon when they reached Barrett's Hotel on the banks of the perennially flowing Gregory River, near Gregory Downs Station, one of the first cattle runs in the Gulf Savannah. It was a big improvement on the previous night's accommodation.

Before tea the trio had a swim in the river and came across a group of Chinese men camped in the scrub. They suspected the Chinese had slipped across the border from the Northern Territory to avoid paying the poll tax imposed by the Queensland government, which was designed to keep them out of the colony. From the beginning of the gold rush in the 1850s to federation in 1901, an estimated 66,000 to 88,000 Chinese arrived on the goldfields, including 20,000 in north Queensland, which created tensions with anti-Chinese Europeans who wanted to rid the colonies of the 'yellow agony'. The cyclists questioned the Chinese about the country they had traversed, but they did not understand, or perhaps pretended not to, saying only 'No savvy'.

Pushing on the next morning, the trio was heartened by a road that was good for the first fifteen kilometres, but then they struck loose rocks, which made riding difficult. By midday it was terribly hot so they decided to have a rest by the Gregory River, which was deep and clear with plenty of fish. Sitting over the water in a paperbark tree they threw in their lines. After an hour Alex had caught just one fish, which they cooked for lunch, but the overlanders were very nearly lunch themselves.

Just as they were about to leave, the cyclists noticed the head of a crocodile under a large pandanus palm that drooped over the water. Alex and Donald both shot at the creature with their revolvers, but there was a big splash and it vanished beneath the surface.

Back on the track by two o'clock, they rode over loose, gravelly hills until night began to fall. They had to reach Police Wells outpost before dark or camp without water, which would not be very pleasant. The road followed a dry creek, but coming round the bend they soon arrived at the station. They had done this run 'on the cadge', or hoping to obtain a free meal, and were disappointed to learn that rations at the station were just about out. There was some rotten beef, however, and they were so hungry that they ate it. 'The meat had been on hand for heaven knows how long; but there was some, and if they could eat it, we could!' Donald recalled.

During the night they all suffered from abdominal pain, diarrhoea and vomiting. Frank and Donald were only mildly ill and had recovered by the morning, but Alex's case was more severe. It was with less vigour than usual that the overlanders set off, and by mid-morning Alex was unable to ride any further. He was feeling so weak that Frank and Donald had to support him on foot while wheeling their bicycles. He would suffer bouts of gastroenteritis for the rest of the journey, which raises the question: why did he continue? An unproven rider, Alex almost certainly had to complete the course to fulfil his contractual obligations to his sponsors. Stoically, he pushed on. But his illness slowed down the trio and put their chances of beating Arthur in real jeopardy. Riding as a team, the cyclists were learning, had its advantages and disadvantages.

One of the ways to manage gastroenteritis is to maintain fluids, so Alex's malaise was not helped by a scarcity of water on the dry plains. Craving a drink, the exhausted overlanders' mouths were dry and their tongues swollen. They began to see mirages shimmering in the distance, which tormented them even more. They sluggishly followed a track across ridgy country to where a Mrs Webber had kept a hotel. It was now closed, but Mrs Webber still lived in the building with her two daughters. The hungry trio asked her for something to eat and drink, but she refused, saying it would be improper to encourage them when there were no men in the house. They eventually managed to persuade her to sell them some chops and a tin of peas. They also bought a melon from an old man who had a garden by the side of the creek.

The meal seemed to revive Alex and the overlanders headed for Morstone Downs Station, sixty-four kilometres away, one of the westernmost homesteads in Queensland. Riding across rough limestone country, they found a small pool of water near the dry Douglas River, but it had been fouled by a dead kangaroo and was undrinkable. Alex was by now feeling very weak and thirsty. After another hour's walk he had to lie down. Donald found a few drops of water in his water can, which restored Alex a little. It said a lot about Donald's character that he would give his last water to his sick mate.

With grim determination, the overlanders decided they had to reach Morstone Downs Station that night, no matter what, so that Alex could recuperate properly. At ten o'clock they came to a shearers' camp on the banks of the O'Shannassy River and, after a cup of tea, one of the shearers escorted them across the river to the Morstone Downs homestead where Alex received much-needed nursing from the station manager's wife, Mrs Murray, who also gave him some medicine.

In the morning Alex was feeling a little bit better and they pushed on. With limestone boulders covering the area, they followed a rough, stony track. 'Truly the station was well named,' Donald recalled. 'Morstone; it was far more stone than grass.' By mid-afternoon Alex was exhausted again and they stopped at the O'Shannassy Hotel so he could rest for the night, but it was closed. The proprietress sold them a bottle of whisky, which helped them through a miserable night.

The following morning, Tuesday, 12 September, the overlanders pushed themselves to ride the last thirty kilometres across the plains, against a strong headwind, towards Camooweal, the last Queensland town before the Northern Territory border.

'We started from Burketown on Thursday last,' Frank wrote in a telegram which was published in the *West Australian* on 16 September. 'We have taken six days in travelling 240 miles, camping and crossing the sand plains. We went short of water, and with mirage shimmering all round we suffered intensely from thirst. Alex and I have also been ill. The lot of an overlander in Queensland is not an enviable one.'

The overlanders could see the galvanised tin roofs of Camooweal, situated on a plain, half an hour before they rode up the main street of the small town. 'The town itself is the most desolate I had seen,' Donald recalled.

> On entering it, one was inclined to abandon hope. But we found it to the contrary. On the inhabitants learning who we were, we received an invitation to a social that was to be given that night to Mr Thorpe, who was retiring from the police force. Being a trifle off, we decided to go to bed. An old man was left in charge of the hotel; also in charge of many babies. These soon started to perform. How I prayed that a modern Herod would appear! At last I thought my prayers had been answered, as the old boy, who had been nursing one of the infants on the verandah, lost his temper and began to criticise it and its parents back to the third and fourth generation. Then there was a thud, followed by most hellish yells. My heart failed me. He had not put it down hard enough, though. He now whistled like a steam engine. This was the signal arranged if things got to extremes, and soon the happy mother arrived. Eventually, we got to sleep, the infant's sobs having a soothing effect, the mother's method seemingly being hammering and shaking alternately.
>
> Next morning the town slept till about ten. It was not till dinner that some of our friends came out, and then only in their pyjamas.

Camooweal, with both South Australian and Queensland police stations (South Australia had annexed the Northern Territory in 1863), a customs house, stores and pubs, was the last town the overlanders would strike before Port Darwin, 1400 kilometres away. They heard bad accounts of the track to Powell Creek telegraph station, 643 kilometres away, with 'long dry stages and not a tree for days with the ground very heavy', and decided to spend an extra day in this outback metropolis.

'We hope to reach Powell Creek in about eight days,' Frank wrote in a telegram. 'The route we will take is from here through Powell Creek up the telegraph line to Port Darwin, back again to Katherine Station towards Halls Creek, and thence along the same route as Richardson to Perth. We hope to strike better tracks after the next four hundred miles. If not, we will have to go very slowly. The weather is very hot and it is raising blisters on our hands.'

It was almost enough to make them want to turn around and go back, forgetting all about the folly of riding a bicycle around Australia.

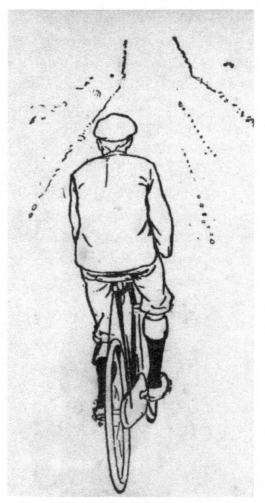

The loneliness of the long-distance cyclist was often harder to endure than thirst, hunger and weariness.

Stage Nine

Worst Country in Australia

Arthur
Victoria Downs to Katherine
Circa 30 August to 9 September 1899

A S he ventured into the 'worst patch of country in Australia', Arthur was glad to have company. While the overlander had been recuperating at Victoria Downs, Mr Watson, the manager, was asked to travel to Port Darwin on business, so he and an Aboriginal boy, Dolo, driving nine horses between them, set off alongside Arthur on his bicycle.

The travelling companions rode through spectacular wilderness country for over a week. It was not always possible for Arthur to ride across the rugged sandstone and limestone terrain and he spent part of the journey tramping on foot. He had become used to that, but for the first time on his ride water began to be scarce. Nothing if not resourceful, Arthur used the old bushman's trick of sucking on a small stone, which kept his mouth moist and reduced the sensation of thirst.

They were on constant watch against attacks from hostile Aboriginal groups in a region where 'more men have been murdered by the blacks than on any other part of the track,' Arthur recalled. 'No one in these regions goes out mustering or even to the creek for a bucket of water without firearms, and even our black boy carried a big revolver. It was amusing to see him each morning tracking off after the horses, revolver in one hand and bridle and stock-whip in the other, in regular Deadwood Dick fashion.' Deadwood Dick was a fictional highwayman character who appeared in a series of dime novels published between 1877 and 1897 by the American writer Edward Lytton Wheeler, a self-styled 'sensational novelist'. First de Rougement and then Wheeler: Arthur's taste in literature tended to the melodramatic and bloodthirsty.

One midnight the travellers had a scare while camping in high grass near the Little Gregory River Gorge, an area of dramatic escarpments. Arthur had been tramping all day and was terribly tired. The night was dark and still, but the quiet was interrupted by the blast of two shots from a revolver close to the heads of Arthur and Mr Watson. Roused into action, they leaped to their feet, ready for a fight with Aboriginal marauders. They were relieved to discover that the Aboriginal boy, Dolo, had shot only a dingo, which had smelled their meat rations and was trying to help itself.

The semi-arid landscape gave way to dry savannah woodlands and rocky hills as they passed three deserted cattle stations: Willeroo, Delamere and Price's Creek. The homesteaders had been forced off the stations by hostile Aboriginal people. 'Willeroo was the nearest to Victoria Downs, and carried 12,000 head of cattle, but the blacks had most of them, only 3000 head having come off the station,' Arthur recalled. 'The last manager, Mr Scott, was speared there about two years ago. Mr Watson told me that the place was often the scene of battle between the natives and whites ... so aggressive as to occasionally spear horses and cattle alongside the stockyard, and on one occasion they had the cook — a Celestial [a Chinese national] — besieged for days while the others were away.'

Arthur was still out of contact with the civilised world and there was a lot of concern for his welfare, particularly after reports that Aboriginal warriors had attempted to kill a constable in the Katherine region and a local couple had disappeared, as the *Evening News* in Sydney reported on 30 August:

Many people laughed at the idea of the overland riders, the White brothers and A. Richardson, meeting with trouble from the North Australian blacks; but a telegram from Katherine (on the overland cable route) states that the blacks round the Katherine district have attempted the life of a mounted constable, spearing his horse, and following him for two days. Further disquieting information is to hand stating that a Mr and Mrs Kingston went out for a ride in the same district, and have disappeared. It is supposed that the blacks have killed them. Large search parties are now out searching for them; but no further tidings are to hand. As Arthur Richardson is now engaged in traversing this very stretch of country on a cycle, and is unattended, considerable anxiety will be felt until word is again heard of the hardy cyclist. The Dunlop trio, F. and A. White and D. Mackay, will also have to pass through this part of Australia; but as the party are properly armed with repeating rifles they will not be the cause of the same anxiety as Arthur Richardson.

The Dunlop Tyre Company wired Perth to ask if anything had been heard of Arthur and received a reply that there had been no intelligence of him since he left Halls Creek. Some of Arthur's friends wired Katherine, asking officials at the telegraph station to be on the '*qui vive*' for the lone traveller and to contact Perth immediately when they knew of his whereabouts.

It was Saturday, 9 September, before Arthur's whereabouts were established. The first to ride a bicycle through the region, Arthur justifiably felt a sense of achievement as he wheeled into Katherine Station, 354 kilometres south of Port Darwin, at about four o'clock in the afternoon. 'You can imagine what a feeling of satisfaction I experienced when we crossed the river and proceeded to the telegraph station, after traversing the solitary and difficult belt lying between Halls Creek and the line,' Arthur recalled. 'It was the first time that a cycle had been through the country, but it had stood splendidly.'

The Katherine telegraph master, Mr Henderson, and his wife gave Arthur a 'hearty' welcome and Arthur put his friends' and family's minds at ease when he sent a telegram to announce his safe arrival. 'The last 240 miles to the Katherine has not had any wheel traffic on it for four years, so that I could not travel much faster with my bike than Mr Watson with the horses,' Arthur wrote in the telegram which was published in Kalgoorlie's *Western Argus* on 21 September. 'We got in here this afternoon. My bike tyres are all right, and I am going strongly.'

Katherine, situated on relatively flat plains on the banks of the Katherine River, began as an outpost of the Overland Telegraph Line between Port Darwin and Port Augusta in South Australia. One of the greatest engineering feats in Australian history, the construction of the 3200-kilometre line in 1872 was the nineteenth-century equivalent of the introduction of the internet. Prior to the telegraph line, it took weeks and even months to send communications between cities, towns and settlements because of the tyranny of distance of the vast Australian continent. Australia had also been isolated from the rest of the world. News and letters travelled by ship, horse and coach and would take up to five months to reach their destination. But an undersea cable from Port Darwin to Java in Indonesia in 1871 had connected the lonely continent to the world.

The town of Katherine, still a tiny settlement when Arthur reached it, has an important modern connection with Australian cycling. The 2011 Tour de France winner, Cadel Evans, was born in Katherine Hospital on 14 February 1977. Evans spent his early childhood in the small Aboriginal community of Barunga, eighty kilometres east of Katherine. Arthur could not have imagined that the remote hamlet would one day give birth to one of Australia's greatest cyclists. Or maybe it was just the place to breed a champion.

Arthur was back in 'civilisation', but not everyone thought he was out of the woods just yet. The *Quiz and Lantern*'s cycling correspondent, 'Spokes', hoped that Arthur would have protection with him when he visited Port Darwin, Australia's wild northern frontier town. 'It is to be hoped that Arthur has a persuader with him. It saves a deal of argument,' 'Spokes' wrote on 31 August.

Arthur certainly had no time or inclination to argue.

The White brothers, Frank and Alex, spent an enjoyable time in Sydney during their ride around Australia.

Stage Ten

A Life and Death Struggle

White brothers and Donald
Camooweal to Monmoona Creek
14 September to 28 September 1899

O N Thursday, 14 September, on a stinking hot afternoon, the White brothers and Mackay departed from Camooweal on the most hazardous stage of their journey so far, which would see them involved in a life-and-death struggle in the desert. They were crossing the Barkly Tableland, a rolling black soil plain of treeless grassland which runs from western Queensland, where the views stretch on forever, into the eastern part of the Northern Territory.

William Landsborough had discovered the tableland in 1861 and named it after the governor of Victoria, Sir Henry Barkly. But it was not until Nat Buchanan and Sam Croker crossed the tableland in 1877 that the land was opened up for settlement. The Barkly region covers 21 per cent of the Northern Territory, but with a population today of just over 6000 people, the tableland still has the lowest number of inhabitants of any region in the Top End. The overlanders were about to find out why so few people lived in this harsh country.

Giving their heavy coats and vests away to locals in Camooweal, the overlanders rode in the lighter attire of shoes, stockings, shorts, sweaters and hats. Wearing shorts was considered quite risqué in the Victorian era, but the heat was so unbearable the overlanders had no regard for social etiquette. Striking out over the plain, they had trouble picking up the track, which was in terrible condition, but an Aboriginal man came to their assistance and showed them the way. While some Aboriginal people were hostile, others were helpful to the overlanders to the point that it is uncertain whether they could have managed the ride without them.

The overlanders trudged along loamy country, making slow progress until they reached the Northern Territory border which was marked by a pole surrounded by rocks. A board nailed on the pole displayed the rules and regulations of admission to Queensland, something federation would soon get rid of. Sitting on the heap of stones, the overlanders made a toast to the success of the ride with a sip of their precious water.

The sun was setting, but they pushed onwards across the plain in search of water, as their supplies were running low. There is little permanent surface water on the Barkly Tableland, particularly in the dry season, and they could see the concern in each other's eyes.

At eight o'clock they reached the ironically named Happy Creek, which, sadly, was dry. In moonlight they followed the track along the bank of the creek and finally found a fine pool of water and had a drink before making camp. The night was extremely cold and with practically no covering they were almost frozen. They thawed out in front of a fire and, leaving at daylight, headed for the 'interminable' plains, the sun beating down on them mercilessly.

The overlanders reached Avon Downs homestead, fifty-seven kilometres west of Camooweal, at midday after a bumpy ride over stony ground. The trio inspected the homestead, the woolshed and the mia-mias (shelters) of the Aboriginal workers. In the evening they had a game of cards with the station manager before sleeping in comfortable beds, although the 'infernal screeching' of a pet brolga woke them in the middle of the night.

Alex was feeling sick again so they stayed at the station for an extra day and a half. He was still weak when they set off on the morning of Sunday, 17 September, and they made slow progress, covering only twenty-eight kilometres before lunch. Afterwards, they entered what was known as the Little Desert, red spinifex country with low scrub. After a few kilometres they reached the Big Desert, a stretch of red sand and stunted timber.

By mid-afternoon their water cans were empty and they began to be tormented by thirst. They tramped for several kilometres through spinifex country, keeping a watchful eye out for death adders. These most venomous of snakes were not sighted by the overlanders, but had left hundreds of tracks in the red sand.

At dusk the trio reached Lorne Creek, ringed by a few stunted coolibah trees, and gulped down 'gallons of water' before camping for the night in a tin hut, part of a deserted outpost of Lorne Creek Station.

In the morning they broke camp just as the first rays of sunlight touched the tableland. They met a mailman who gave them information about the track, warning it would be 'hard going'. The riding was difficult, but the overlanders soon got out of the pindan country, reaching Ranken Downs at about eleven o'clock. The water in the Borrodo (Ranken) waterhole was thick, or hard, because of minerals in the bedrock, and the area was dotted with the whitened skeletons of cattle. They had a 'good feed of rice' and rested for a couple of hours before setting off again across the big sandy plain for Buchanan Creek, forty-eight kilometres away.

Riding into a hot headwind almost strong enough to knock them off their bikes, they had to dismount and walk when the track became loose. Running out of water, they suffered terribly from thirst, a mirage cruelly teasing them. Just when they were ready to despair, the screeching of a flock of galahs helped them to locate the creek. They quenched their thirst, but soon endured irritating pangs of hunger after eating all of their remaining food.

The overlanders had a couple of hours rest and then decided to push on to Alexandria Station, travelling by moonlight. With large, loose rocks on the track they walked most of the time until they came to a chain of waterholes where the track ended. They camped the night, hoping to find the track in the morning. At daylight they climbed a tall coolibah tree and saw plains stretching to the horizon. Behind them was flat mulga country. The awful realisation that they had gone the wrong way dawned on them and they had to retrace their steps to Buchanan Creek.

After leading their bikes over sandy country for a few kilometres the overlanders had a rest under some gidgee (stinking wattle) trees. As they recuperated, an emu strode past them and they took a shot at it, but missed. The emu sprinted away, followed by some chicks, which the cyclists chased, managing to catch one, taking it with them in case they could not find food.

Back on the plain with a harder track and the wind behind them they picked up the pace, sighting the tin roofs of Alexandria Station at midday, having been twenty-one hours without food. According to Donald, they 'felt more like kangaroo-dogs than human beings!'

Alexandria Station is now the second-largest pastoral property in Australia, after Anna Creek Station in South Australia. For the overlanders it was an oasis in a vast grassy plain and they certainly appreciated the warm hospitality extended to them by the manager.

Alex was feeling sick again so their departure was delayed until five o'clock the following afternoon. The extra rest would not do them any harm for it was going to be a long, dry stage across the fearful tableland, but they could not afford to lose too much time. After crossing a creek near the station, they had a bad run and camped after just thirty-two kilometres, but the ground was full of ants and they had a restless night. In the small hours of the morning they set off by moonlight, which guided them along a narrow pad between tall tussock grasses in which their pedals caught frequently.

Even though he was still crook, Alex was setting the pace with Donald riding second. All of a sudden Donald ran into Alex's back wheel, and the next thing he saw was his mate lying on top of a figure in a heap on the ground. 'The shrieks emitted were enough to make one's hair curl,' Donald recalled.

At last we got righted, and I found that Alex had run over a Chinaman, who had been lying across the track. He told us he had so camped for fear of losing the track. On rising to his feet he staggered. I feared the collision had done him some serious harm, but we soon learned that he was nearly dead for a drink. We gave all we could spare, for in his state he could never have got to the next water, twenty miles ahead. (As it was, I often thought of him afterwards as bleaching on the plain, where many of his countrymen had perished in attempting to walk across.) We waited to see him have a drink and then said adieu.

At midday the overlanders struck a muddy creek and made tea out of the thick water, which refreshed them. About twelve kilometres from the creek, pushing their bikes over water-worn pebbles, they reached Brunette Downs, now the second-largest cattle station in the Northern Territory after Alexandria.

The overlanders spent the afternoon watching stockmen brand cattle, doing as many as sixty an hour, which impressed them enormously. After playing crib with the manager, Mr James Hutton, in the evening, the weary cyclists went to bed. They were having a good night's sleep until they were woken by the noise of the homestead's cook preparing breakfast at four o'clock in the morning.

The early wake-up call got the cyclists on their way by six o'clock and they headed for Anthony Lagoon, thirty kilometres away. The track crossed black soil plains with patches of gidgee trees, and a headwind made riding unpleasant. They struck a creek which was 'literally brown with whistling ducks', according to Donald, but as they had provisions they did not try to shoot any of them. About a kilometre from the creek a big flock of pigeons flew over them in their thousands, darkening the sky. There were numerous snake tracks in the sandy soil, so once again they kept their eyes wide.

At dusk the overlanders reached Anthony Lagoon, a permanent water source fed by Creswell Creek. Although it was very low, it was a 'fine sheet of muddy water' ringed with coolibah, lignum, bluebush, verbine and tussock grassland. There were pelicans, waterhens and ducks in the water, while the trees were full of galahs, parrots and hawks making a raucous noise.

The trio had travelled about four hundred kilometres since leaving Camooweal and needed a spell. A police station established near the lagoon in 1895 to keep a watch over the cattle passing through the area provided the overlanders with comfortable accommodation, including a relaxing bath, which soothed their tense muscles.

They spent the next day resting and preparing for their run across to the Overland Telegraph Line, which they expected to strike at Renner Springs in the heart of the Barkly Tableland, 240 kilometres away, on their way to Powell Creek. In the evening they watched Aboriginal stockmen herding a flock of 'Territory sheep', or goats, one of which was killed and cooked to provide the cyclists with a good supply of meat. They also obtained a rough map which showed where water could be found and they were elated to hear from the trooper that they would have a good hard track all the way.

In high spirits, the overlanders left Anthony Lagoon in the early morning of Monday, 25 September, but contrary to what they had been told by the trooper, they found the track so rough that it was difficult to ride. Maybe the track was good for a camel or a horse, but not a bike. They had travelled only thirty-two kilometres by the time they stopped at a dry watercourse for lunch, the stunted wattle trees providing little shade on the glaring plain.

Walking across the monotonous terrain, they were shocked to discover that their water canteens were leaking and almost empty. 'I always considered them of service for irrigation purposes only,' Donald recalled. It was a situation they could laugh about later, but it would not have been very funny at the time. It was serious, deadly serious. With a long dry stage ahead, the lack of water was a big problem which could threaten not only the ride, but their very lives. They had only two options. They could return to Anthony Lagoon to fix the canteens and start again or push on to Eva Downs, a deserted sheep station, where they expected to find water.

In a fateful decision, they chose to continue. It was understandable that they did not want to retrace their tracks and lose precious time, but if they reached Eva Downs and did not find water there they could die of thirst. It was a risk they were prepared to take to win the race.

As the sun began to set, Frank lay down exhausted. It was decided that Alex and Donald would press on and return to him with water when they found it. The pair trudged on until dusk when they also lay down and fell asleep, only to be woken by Frank who had caught up to them. All three were now extremely tired and thirsty, but they had to summon whatever energy they had left and keep going because to remain on the dry plain for any length of time without water meant almost certain death. A person can go three weeks without food, but water is a different story. In a harsh environment like the Australian outback a person needs water after three days or they will perish. The overlanders were running out of time.

Donald and Frank had to rouse Alex from a 'kind of stupor' before they departed. They lost the track and had to wait until the moon rose at eleven o'clock 'like a ball of fire' to find it again. Then they saw a flickering light, indicating a camp fire. Again, they lost the track and were guided by a star. Coming to a dry watercourse, Alex rested while Frank went up the creek and Donald down, but they found no water. Donald climbed a corkwood tree and spotted the flickering light again, which seemed quite close. They pushed on across the plain until they reached the camp fire near a hut on Eva Downs Station at about midnight, having taken nineteen hours to travel seventy-seven kilometres across an awful track that they had been told was good.

At the camp site they encountered an Aboriginal group who were most likely Gurindji people, though Europeans at the time would have referred to them as 'Myall blacks'. A 'Myall' was an Aboriginal person who had not come under the influence of European civilisation; weary as they were, the trio would have been on their guard when they were greeted by naked tribesmen with spears in hand. But these 'Myalls' were not hostile. Taking pity on the cyclists, the Aboriginal group directed them to a waterhole about a kilometre away. The waterhole was full of beetles, but that did not stop the overlanders from slaking their thirst. 'We did not even wait to strain it through our teeth!' Donald recalled.

In the morning the overlanders realised their supplies were running out. They had only taken enough rations from Anthony Lagoon to last two days, which was how long they had expected it would take them to reach Powell Creek. They pushed on once more across the black soil plain, following a cattle pad and leading their bikes through the dry tussock grass. At about two o'clock they stopped for a late lunch, 'groggy in the legs'. Tying their sheets between two bushes to provide shelter, they had a snack and drank the last of the water in their canteens. Donald and Frank lay down for a while, but when they got up to make a fresh start they felt light-headed and nauseous. 'We realised that we had just missed a heat stroke by the skin of our teeth,' Donald recalled. 'The great heat from the ground has often this effect on people when they are weakened.'

With Alex leading the way, they walked their bikes along the pad in deathly silence until they came to another dry watercourse. Donald could go no further and he threw himself on the ground. In the red glow of the setting sun they held an emergency meeting. They were about 112 kilometres west of Anthony Lagoon and Powell Creek was about eighty kilometres further west. There was no water in their canteens and they were running out of food. They might find water at Bundora Creek, which lay ahead of them, but they might not — which would be disastrous.

The trio decided that Alex should push on alone towards Powell Creek and bring water back to Donald and Frank when he found it. As Alex disappeared in the distance, Frank tried to dig for water in the dry creek, but soon gave up the fruitless exercise, while Donald's mood turned black.

'For more than a whole day at times we had no water, riding and walking under a tropical sun,' Frank recalled. 'Once, when Alex went on in search of the precious fluid, Don and I lay down utterly exhausted. It seemed hopeless to push on. We could scarcely crawl, and poor Don, in a weak moment, actually proposed a course which would have brought our journey to a sensational close.'

Feeling helpless, Donald and Frank decided to follow Alex. As they staggered to their feet, swaying, they were shocked at how wobbly they were. Struggling along, they soon had to lie down again. The heat was so intense they stripped off all of their clothes except their pants. At daylight there was no sign of Alex. They decided that Frank, being the stronger rider, should take Donald's bike, which 'ran the lightest', while Donald would follow with Frank's bike and the heavy dunnage. It was the first and only time on the journey that all three cyclists were separated from each other. At least they would have got an idea of how Arthur felt throughout his ride.

Donald plodded on doggedly with hawks flying just above his head. He did not want to become a meal for the scavengers so he pushed himself for another kilometre until he came to a dry watercourse where he saw Alex's tracks in the sand, although there was no sign of his companion. To escape the unbearable heat he slunk into a big crack in the plain and fell asleep. When he awoke, several hawks were sitting on the ground above him so he wearily took out his revolver and shot at them.

Pushing off again, at last Donald saw a speck on the horizon. It was Alex, who had just managed to get to water in time. Donald gulped it down. 'If I had had a chance, I would have liked to start on a 400-gallon tank!' Donald recalled. At twelve-thirty, Alex and Donald made their way to Bundora Creek, eight kilometres away, where they found Frank fast asleep.

Meanwhile, anxiety was growing about the welfare of the overlanders, who had not been heard of since they left Camooweal. 'From Camooweal they intended striking west until they reached Powell Creek, a stretch of some 400-odd miles of very rough and dry country,' the *Macleay Chronicle* reported on 12 October. 'But for all that, the Dunlop trio should have covered that distance in two weeks, so that we can only suppose that either the wheelmen are travelling very easy stages or are delayed by illness or accident.'

The *Chronicle*'s concern was fully justified. The overlanders had survived a desperate situation, but their troubles were far from over. Powell Creek was still sixty kilometres away and they barely had enough food for one person. They would not all make it to Powell Creek, yet they could not trek back the way they had come. They had to move forward, but how? They held another emergency meeting and decided that Frank, who was a bit more refreshed than the others, should go ahead with all of the food and try to reach Powell Creek and send out a rescue party. In the meantime, Alex and Donald would head to Monmoona Creek, fourteen kilometres away, and hopefully find water.

Frank had a meal of sago and meat, a bath and a rub-down before riding off at half past three in the afternoon with the fate of his companions resting on his shoulders. He had taken Donald's bike again because it 'ran lighter' and was stronger, something he never mentioned in any of his telegrams in case he upset his sponsors at Dayton.

Alex and Donald set off at dusk, intending to do as much of their travelling as possible in the cool of the night. After a couple of kilometres Alex had to 'cry a go' and they lay down in the dry tussock grass. At daylight they made another start. Donald was feeling refreshed, but Alex was still weak, although he never complained. Donald broke the silence with a 'pious ejaculation' after stepping on a snake. He took off a shoe and 'battered the reptile out of recognition'.

At last they sighted Monmoona Creek and the sweet perfume that wafted on the breeze told them there was water in it. They were greeted by galahs, corellas and parakeets, which 'screeched as if possessed'. After quenching his thirst, Donald built a mia-mia to shelter Alex from the sun. 'The rest of the day passed quietly, neither of us feeling very talkative,' Donald recalled.

In the morning the hungry cyclists tried to shoot a bird, but had no luck. Then they spotted a galah's nest low down in a tree and Alex caught two chicks, which were no bigger than a turkey egg, but sufficient to make a pot of galah soup. Afterwards they had some tobacco and as another night passed they began to wonder despondently whether Frank would reach Powell Creek and send help. If they stayed out here in this godforsaken country much longer, they would surely die, and all for a dream that was fading fast.

A. MACDONALD, who rode 2596 Miles (from Port Darwin to Melbourne) in 33 Days, mounted on a

SWIFT CYCLE

Fitted with DUNLOP TYRES.

Sole Agents: THE AUSTRAL CYCLE AGENCY, LTD.,

391 GEORGE STREET, SYDNEY, and at Melbourne, Brisbane, Adelaide, etc.

Aided by sand which had been set by rain, Albert MacDonald's record-shattering ride from Port Darwin to Melbourne in 1898 was unimaginably fast at the time.

Stage Eleven

A Happy Time

Arthur, White brothers and Donald
Katherine to Powell Creek;
Bundora Creek to Powell Creek
10 September to 3 October 1899

IT took Arthur three days to ride from Katherine to Port Darwin, arriving at dusk on Tuesday, 12 September. He was met at the Ten-Mile Camp by several members of the North Australian Cycling Club, who escorted him into town. Why did Arthur bother to go to Port Darwin instead of just continuing east? The track to Queensland led eastward from Katherine and he would have to double back to resume his journey.

Perhaps Jerome Murif's transcontinental ride from Adelaide to Port Darwin two years earlier had influenced him. Murif, the pioneering Irish rider, departed beachside Glenelg on 10 March and took seventy-four days to cover the 3150 kilometres, which was regarded as a slow time. But Murif deliberately rode at a leisurely pace, spending a week touring Alice Springs. He also had to negotiate endless sandhills, which he described as 'like cycling up and down a stairway, with the stairs of unequal heights and width, blindfolded'.

Typical cycling clothing at the time included shirt, vest, jacket, knickerbockers, stockings, shoes and cap, but Murif eccentrically wore pyjamas for comfort, carrying a spare pair to change into whenever he arrived at a telegraph station or homestead. On reaching Port Darwin on 21 May, Murif dipped his bike in about a metre of water at a place he called Bicycle Point to complete his journey from ocean to ocean. 'I looked fondly upon the bicycle which had served me so well, pressed gently one of its handles and whispered, "Thanks Diamond,"' Murif wrote lovingly of his bike.

Like Murif, Arthur dipped his bike in the sea, demonstrating the bond between the overlanders, who were the only ones who truly understood what it was like to ride across a harsh continent on a bicycle.

But Arthur had a more practical reason for going to Port Darwin. His tyres were completely worn through with burrs, and new covers were waiting for him in the town. It was also a chance to completely overhaul his bicycle before the arduous journey over the Barkly Tableland. He was a bit worn out too, which was understandable given how far he had come since leaving Perth and the kind of difficult terrain he had traversed. The press detected his fatigue: 'Arthur Richardson has reached Port Darwin and although safe and sound, and with Dunlops in first class order, yet there is a distinct strain of tiredness running through his report,' the *Quiz and Lantern* noted on 21 September. 'He will recuperate for a day or two at the capital of the White Elephant. With his attendant luck Arthur should run across the White brothers very shortly. They are almost due at Powell Creek.'

Referring to the Northern Territory as the 'White Elephant' was common at that time. The Territory had been part of New South Wales from 1825 to 1863, except from February to December 1846 when it was part of the short-lived colony of North Australia. Then, in an 'excess of enthusiasm and adventurous imperialism and driven by a compulsion to outdo its neighbouring colonies', South Australia annexed the Territory in 1863, 'in the biggest land grab in Australian history'.

But growth and development in the Northern Territory were disappointing. The isolation, hostile climate and lack of water frustrated plans for settlement and agriculture. By 1901 the Northern Territory's cost to South Australia had reached £2,114,205 and was growing annually. The scepticism of some South Australians about the Northern Territory's economic potential was echoed by the journalist W.J. Sowden, who wrote of it in 1882 as 'that extreme northern country of ours, which we have called by courtesy the Northern Territory, but too often, with bitterness, our white elephant'. In 1910, W.J. Denny, South Australia's attorney-general and minister for the Northern Territory, admitted that the administration of the Territory had been 'a hideous failure' and he negotiated a transfer to Commonwealth control the following year.

The Northern Territory may have been a financial burden, but Arthur found Port Darwin with its 'novelties and peculiarities' an extremely hospitable destination. Port Darwin was certainly different to other Australian cities and towns of the time, and perhaps still is. While the rest of Australia was predominantly Anglo-Celtic in colonial times, Port Darwin was already a multicultural society. The Larrakia Aboriginal people had already lived in the Darwin area for thousands of years when Darwin Harbour was first seen by a European,

Lieutenant John Lort Stokes of the *Beagle*, in 1839. The ship's captain, John Clements Wickham, named the harbour after the famed evolutionist Charles Darwin, a former shipmate. In 1869 a permanent white settlement, originally known as Palmerston, was established. The discovery of gold at Pine Creek in 1871 accelerated the town's growth, bringing an influx of Chinese miners, while other Asians and Pacific Islanders arrived to work in the pearling industry. In the 1890s the Chinese community began to arrange public events in Port Darwin, which Arthur may have witnessed. According to a local historian, Kathy De La Rue, 'The Chinese New Year had always been celebrated in Darwin and ... the general European response was composed of about equal parts fascination at the alien festival, annoyance at the noise of the fireworks and fear that the whole town would erupt into flames.'

Arthur was warmly welcomed at a smoke social given by the North Australian Cycling Club at the Town Hall on Saturday night, 16 September. Mr C.E. Herbert, president of the club, cited Arthur's 'many good qualities' and assured him that the club in particular, and Territorians in general, were very pleased to welcome him after his difficult and long journey and would all be delighted to hear of the successful accomplishment of his ride round Australia on a bicycle.

After being toasted in bumpers of champagne, Arthur briefly replied, thanking the club for the hearty welcome extended to him and proposing a toast in turn to the club. The club members then raised Arthur on their shoulders and triumphantly marched him around the room, which no doubt would have embarrassed him. After an enjoyable evening, which included much singing, the company broke up just before midnight.

Thoroughly enjoying himself in Port Darwin, Arthur was strongly tempted to stay longer, but he was anxious to keep his rendezvous with the White brothers and Mackay at Powell Creek to glean information about their route, particularly the hazardous journey across the Barkly Tableland. If he had been aware of the dire straits the trio had found themselves in, he probably would have left sooner to try to offer assistance.

Reluctantly, Arthur departed Port Darwin on Monday, 18 September, and was given an escort by members of the North Australian Cycling Club, who accompanied him for a few kilometres along the road before wishing him bon voyage as he followed the telegraph line down to Powell Creek, just as his overlander contemporaries Alfred Mather, Tom Coleman and Albert MacDonald had before him.

On 12 August 1897, Coleman and Mather, backed by Dunlop, had left Port Darwin for Adelaide, attempting to beat Jerome Murif's time. Maher broke his fork north of Barrow Creek, a small town about 280 kilometres north of Alice Springs. Coleman pushed on ahead but became ill and had to cut the Overland Telegraph Line — which signalled his need for help — at Ti Tree, well known for its sweet water, 193 kilometres north of Alice Springs. 'In all my experience I have never yet met such terrible going,' Mather recalled. Resuming their ride, Coleman and Mather broke Murif's record, but by only a few days, which was viewed dimly given the support they had received.

In 1898, MacDonald, a telegraph operator from Powell Creek, rode from Port Darwin to Adelaide in only twenty-nine days, an unimaginably fast time, even if he had been aided by tailwinds. MacDonald continued to Melbourne, completing the entire 4178-kilometre journey in thirty-three days and five and a half hours.

Arthur was looking forward to Powell Creek, MacDonald's old stamping ground, which was one of eleven stations built along the Overland Telegraph Line to service faults and to relay morse code signals. There was nothing particularly distinctive about the station. The house was made of stone and tin with wide, latticed verandahs, overgrown with flowering creepers. There was accommodation for stockmen and staff, a workshop and outstation, three water tanks and a well. But it was famous among overlanders, teamsters and linesmen for the warmth and hospitality extended by the telegraph master, Mr Kell, and his wife.

'It was at this oasis in the desert that MacDonald, who sped across Australia from north to south in less than one month, spent five years of his life,' Arthur recalled. 'The other cyclists who have been through – Murif, Mather and Coleman – all speak in glowing terms of the excellent treatment meted out to them at this, one of the most important stations on the line. When day after day a man toils along under the broiling sun, and night after night hides himself away in the solitary bush or dreary scrub, it is some comfort and encouragement to know that ahead a warm welcome is awaiting him.'

The ride from Port Darwin to Powell Creek was uneventful as Arthur followed the telegraph line, day-dreaming about the warm welcome he would receive and his rendezvous with his fellow around Australia racers. Instead, Arthur was shocked when he saw Frank, who had arrived at Powell Creek just a few hours before him on Friday, 29 September: it was not so much the fact he was there, but the poor state he was in – dead tired and worried sick about Alex and Donald. 'Frank White was in a most exhausted condition, and was exceedingly anxious as to the condition of his brother and Mackay, whom he had

Riding from Port Darwin to Adelaide with Alfred Maher, Tom Coleman fell ill and had to cut the Overland Telegraph wire to signal for help.

left without food or water fifty miles out on the baking plains,' Arthur recalled. Arthur must have wondered about the deadly country he was about to traverse if the White brothers and Mackay had been reduced to such terrible straits there.

Downing a couple of fortifying ales, Frank, the noted yarn-spinner, almost hysterically told Arthur all about their misadventure, although he would have had no need to embellish his story. On a scorching hot day he had struggled on for nearly one hundred kilometres until he discovered, to his horror, that he had been riding in the wrong direction. He then walked all night until he struck water at ten o'clock the next morning. Later in the day, after being lost for twenty hours, he reached the Overland Telegraph Line at a deserted station forty-eight kilometres south of Powell Creek. He must have been overcome with joy and relief because all he had to do was climb the pole and cut the line, which would signal his need for help. He tried to climb the pole, but he was too weak! Even though his life, and the lives of his brother and mate, depended on it, he could not get up that damned pole. He had no choice but to push on, and travelling at a slow and agonising pace managed to 'crawl' into Powell Creek at three-thirty in the afternoon, 'more dead than alive'.

Some critics were not too impressed when Frank admitted he would have cut the Overland Telegraph Line if he had not been too weak to climb the pole. When Coleman had severed the telegraph line two years earlier he was hauled over the coals and fined 150 pounds, an average yearly wage, by the South Australian government, but Frank might have found himself in even more trouble. On 28 October the *Sydney Mail and New South Wales Advertiser* suggested there would have been a 'tremendous outcry' if communication with Britain was stopped while the Australian colonies were involved in the Boer War in South Africa:

> From time to time we hear of the adventures of the Brothers White and Mackay, who are proceeding on cycles round Australia one way, and Richardson, who is doing the same thing in the opposite direction. They are tasting of thirst, hunger, dangers from blacks, from swollen rivers, from alligators, and fierce mosquitoes, and rough country and wild vegetation, and what good it is all going to do is not evident. They are not prospectors who can discover for us new mineral country, or competent pastoral engineers, or scientists who could add to our knowledge of the fauna and flora. They are simply out record-making. And suffering all sorts of dangers and discomforts in the process. The overlander was even going to do as a predecessor once did – cut the overland wire so that someone would come out and find his weary and hungry and thirst-stricken person. Thus at the very moment when war trembled in the balance eastern Australia would have been cut off from the world because a cyclist wanted to break a record. We were only saved that because he hadn't strength left to climb the pole. *Cui bono!*

Despite the grumbling of this journalist, most of the press and the public were behind the overlanders.

As soon as Frank arrived at Powell Creek, Mr Kell arranged for two Aboriginal stockmen, supplied with food and water, to rescue Alex and Donald. Frank and Arthur were extremely anxious as they waited for their comrades, keeping each other's hopes up that the rescue party would find the cyclists in time. Frank must have felt sick to his stomach after recruiting his younger brother for the dangerous journey. If through some magical looking glass Frank could have seen Alex and Donald struggling in the desert, he would have felt far worse.

* * *

The galah soup had seemed to soothe Alex, but he was still too sick to go on. Then, during the night, they spotted a fire in the distance and their spirits rose, hoping it was a signal from a rescue party, but in the morning no one came.

For two and a half days, the pair — sunblasted, starving and psychologically rattled — lay by the side of the waterhole with nothing to eat. Donald confided in Alex that he felt so bad that if he had the pluck he would shoot himself, but then pulled himself together. Instead of staying where they were and starving to death, they decided to take as much water as possible and find those who had lit the fire — or die in the attempt.

Somehow they managed to lift themselves up and set off, albeit groggily. The hours dragged on, but at midday Alex sighted a pack horse drinking at a creek. Then two Aboriginal stockmen rode up to give their horses a drink. It was the rescue party. They were saved! If Alex and Donald had had the strength they would have leaped in the air, but broad grins sufficed to express their joy. The stockmen could not speak much English, but they told the cyclists they had been sent by Mr Kell from Powell Creek to bring them in and that Frank had arrived there safely, although exhausted.

The stockmen had come by a shortcut through thick, low scrub, but it would be impossible to go back that way with the bikes. At five o'clock Donald and Alex had a 'splendid meal' of corned beef and damper and felt ready to head south for Renner

Springs, regarded as the border between the tropical north and the red centre of the Territory, and then follow the telegraph line north to Powell Creek.

Their bicycle tyres were flat and Frank had the only pump so Alex and Donald loaded their bikes onto the pack horse, which 'bucked them off in great style'. They took one of the bikes to pieces and loaded it onto the horse without any trouble, agreeing to push the other bike between them. After staggering through low gum scrub and dry swamps they camped for the night, 'but to get to sleep early was out of the question, for our guides were vocalists,' Donald recalled. 'Lying on the dry grass (having just taken off all their clothes), they chanted native songs for hours. The songs embodied themselves in two lines, which they kept repeating. When I awoke in the morning it was still ringing in my ears.'

Crossing the Ashburton Range, they finally came to the Overland Telegraph Line, that symbol of civilisation in the wilderness. Following the line across some rough limestone country they at last reached Powell Creek, oasis and sanctuary, on Tuesday, 3 October.

Donald, who was in the lead on his bicycle, came through a gap in the hills and found himself at the back of the house just 200 metres away. Passing a garden, he walked up a slope and ran straight into Arthur and Frank, whom at one point he must have thought he would never see again. The overlanders greeted each other ecstatically, thanking their lucky stars they were all still alive. 'Indeed, it was a happy meeting,' Donald recalled. After being introduced to Mr and Mrs Kell, Donald sat down and excitedly started to narrate the story of their terrible ordeal just as Alex — sick, weary, but determined as always — arrived on his reassembled bicycle with the Aboriginal stockmen.

Arthur was full of admiration for Alex and Donald when they arrived at Powell Creek. 'For two days we were in a state of unrest, but one evening at sundown the [stockmen] who had been sent out with pack horses and provisions returned with the two wheelmen, who had nearly perished, but who, in their dogged persistency to cycle round the continent, refused to ride the horses, but came in on their wheels by easy stages,' Arthur recalled.

It is interesting to note that Arthur's version of events had Alex and Donald reaching Powell Creek at sundown, while Frank claimed they arrived in the morning. This was a major discrepancy in their accounts, but perhaps explained by the fact that Arthur did not relate his story to 'Pedal' of the *West Australian* until five months later, and his memory may have failed him, while Frank gave an immediate report in a telegram from Powell Creek.

'Shortly after my arrival A. Richardson arrived, looking well, just too late to go with the relief party, which arrived back safely this morning with Alex and Mackay,' Frank wrote in his telegram. 'We are now all resting here, and recovering slowly, under the hospitable treatment of Mr and Mrs Kell. Richardson has come through so far without a water can, but is at work on one now. He will have a very rough time from here to Normanton. We very much doubt whether he will get through at all; but he is determined to go. We will require a solid spell here.'

In another telegram from Powell Creek, Frank revealed that the White brothers were 'quite out of funds' and did not know what to do. He never explained how they solved their financial problems. Perhaps their sponsors wired them money or maybe Donald paid some of their expenses.

The meeting of the overlanders in Powell Creek was a momentous occasion. A headline in the *Australian Cyclist* announced that the 'cycle has girdled Australia'. It was a 'happy time' the overlanders spent together at the telegraph station. The four of them badly needed rest, particularly the White brothers and Mackay, and they spelled for three days, recuperating under the care of Mr and Mrs Kell.

The overlanders occupied their time overhauling their machines, and Arthur made some water cans which carried three quarts. While the cyclists were rivals in the quest to ride around Australia, they were also comrades. They exchanged notes on their experiences — information of 'inestimable value' — discussing the tracks they had just travelled, getting lost in the bush and encounters with hostile Aboriginal people.

'The next three days which we stayed there were about the most pleasant of the whole trip, and by the time we left we were quite satisfied that the glowing accounts given by the transcontinental riders as to Mr and Mrs Kell's hospitality were in no way exaggerated,' Donald recalled.

> We had several walks in the surrounding country during our
> stay ... During one of our walks we saw the graves of several
> blacks. The bodies are laid on a stage, built up a tree, generally
> about 10 feet from the ground. It is then covered over with leaves.
> Sometimes a year or so afterwards the bones are buried. When it
> is a mighty hunter or fighter who is buried, the young men come
> when the body is in a state of decomposition and stand under
> the stage so that the juice from the body may drop on them, in
> the belief that such juice may impart to them the prowess of the
> departed warrior.

The fact that the overlanders had all made it to Powell Creek alive gave them encouragement that they could successfully navigate the rest of their journeys, although each party was doubtful about the chances of the other. The White brothers and Mackay did their best to dissuade Arthur from attempting to cross the unforgiving Barkly Tableland on his own, fearing for his life, but he was determined to go. The trio gave Arthur their maps and wished him good luck, although they knew it would take more than luck to survive the hellish landscape he was about to enter.

Interestingly, the *West Australian* newspaper was confident Arthur would make it around Australia, but was 'extremely doubtful' about the prospects of the White brothers and Mackay. 'Richardson will now have a lonely ride of six hundred miles to Camooweal in Queensland and from there down the eastern coast his ride will be a triumphal one,' the newspaper reported on 30 September. 'The troubles of White's party are only just commencing and I am extremely doubtful as to whether they will be able to get through. The season when they will be crossing to Halls Creek is anything but favourable.'

The night before the overlanders' departure they enjoyed a musical evening. Mrs Kell played the piano and sang, with the cyclists joining in. Afterwards, over a beer, they agreed to meet again in Perth if they all survived the journey. It must have occurred to the White brothers and Mackay that if they made that rendezvous, Arthur probably would have won the race, but it was an appointment they never expected him to keep.

Stage Twelve

A Keen Disappointment

White brothers and Donald
Powell Creek to Katherine
6 October to 28 October 1899

A S soon as the White brothers and Mackay recovered from their ordeal they set off for Port Darwin at 5.00pm on Friday, 6 October, a day before Arthur resumed his journey. If anyone needed an extra day's rest it should have been the trio, following their near-death experience in the desert, but their desperate desire to beat Arthur drove them on. They also had to cross northern Australia before the arrival of the wet season when monsoonal rains might flood rivers and make some areas impassable, which would end their hopes of completing the ride, let alone winning the race.

From Powell Creek to Port Darwin the White brothers and Mackay, like Arthur, followed the Overland Telegraph Line. Compared to what they had just endured, this was a fairly straightforward ride – if there was such a thing in the wilds of northern Australia.

'We will have to battle up to Port Darwin by easy stages to get strong again in order to tackle the Kimberley track,' Frank wrote in a telegram from Powell Creek. 'We have done so much walking so far that I think we have made a great mistake in taking bikes in place of wheelbarrows. Our feet are all blistered with walking. The temperature this month has never been under 100 degrees. In the shade.'

After riding twenty-two kilometres north of Powell Creek, the overlanders reached Ferguson Creek, where a group of linesmen were camping with bullocks and goats on a big waterhole. After a cup of tea the linesmen asked an Aboriginal man to guide the trio to the main camp two kilometres further up the creek. In the darkness the man carried a fire-stick, 'more to frighten away evil spirits than show light,' Donald recalled.

During a good meal the captain of the party, Bill Pibus, asked the overlanders if they knew Arthur, who had recently passed this way, and remarked: 'If he could only stay in the Northern Territory for a time, what a fine curser he would make!' Donald explained to Pibus that cursing was a talent that came naturally to cyclists.

With a tent for a mattress and a few rugs the overlanders had a good night's sleep before setting off in the morning. They had to walk two and a half kilometres to the track, but then they had a good run to South Newcastle Creek. After crossing the creek, they struck a rough open plain, arriving at Newcastle Waters Station at dusk.

'This is a splendid station, the cattle being fat and free from tick,' Frank wrote in a telegram. 'There is plenty of permanent water and over one hundred miles frontage to the river. They stocked 4000 head of cattle in 1892 and since then they have sold 12,000 head and there are 11,000 head still remaining there.'

The overlanders were met near the 'substantial, but not picturesque' house by one of the owners, Mr S. Lewis, who congratulated them on the success of the journey so far and offered them liberal quantities of 'square' or gin. While waiting for tea, they went down to a large pool 200 metres from the house and had a swim in the milky-coloured water.

During tea the trio noticed that the dining-room wall was decorated with a dozen rifles. They had also seen about thirty dogs around the house. When asked why he kept so many dogs, Mr Lewis answered that they were to protect the place against a night attack by Aboriginal marauders.

Alex was suffering from gastroenteritis again so they stayed at Newcastle Waters for another day. Donald spent the time inspecting the stockyards and, with Frank's help, fixing his bicycle saddle. After tea Donald had an engrossing conversation with a Mr Chambers, who had just come down from Daly Waters and who had been in the South Australian Survey Department. Mr Chambers captivated Donald with stories about the explorer Ernest Giles, the leader of five major expeditions in Central Australia between 1872 and 1876, inspiring in him a desire to one day return to Central Australia to map the interior of the continent.

'Finding I was inclined to investigate some of the yet unknown interior, we talked of the many possibilities (most men would say improbabilities!),' Donald recalled. 'The hope I cherished was to sally forth in the dim future and prove the third great drainage system of Australia.'

Mr Lewis would have been happy for the overlanders to stay for a few weeks, but they were anxious to push on. After a two-day spell Alex's health had improved, but none of them were fully fit following their ordeal. Leaving Newcastle Waters on the morning of Monday, 9 October, they rode into a headwind and reached Frew Ponds, a basin with excellent water, at about four o'clock in the afternoon. This was the spot where the two ends of the Overland Telegraph Line were joined together on 22 August 1872, completing the transcontinental link. There was an Aboriginal camp at Frew Ponds and the women were employed cleaning wattle seeds, which were ground between flat stones and made into a cake. As they were leaving, the cyclists noticed three Aboriginal warriors, their bodies smeared with clay, an ominous sign of things to come.

It was starting to get dark when Alex saw a 400-gallon water tank near the track, a wonderful sight for thirsty cyclists. There were in fact three iron tanks which filled with water in the wet season and usually still held water in the dry season. For once the riders thought their luck had changed, but they were mistaken. As they approached the tanks they were bombarded by mosquitoes which attacked their faces, hands and feet. After drinking deeply and replenishing their water cans, they fled from the water, but the mosquitoes followed them and they had no sleep that night as the cursed insects tormented them.

The overlanders were still tired when they pushed off again at daylight and struck several kilometres of sand crisscrossed with numerous snake tracks. Alex killed one snake that was three metres long. Riding through timbered country they arrived at McGorie's Waterhole, where the water was very thick, but they still had a drink. Several kilometres from Daly Waters a stick got caught in Alex's chain and broke it. They walked the rest of the way to the Daly Waters telegraph station, 620 kilometres south of Port Darwin, arriving at two o'clock in the afternoon. The temperature was '108 degrees in the shade' and they were happy to lie down on the station's verandah and cool down.

After a pleasant stay in Daly Waters the overlanders set off around ten o'clock on Monday morning, 9 October, for the Ironstone Tank, fifty-five kilometres away.

On the track they met a man who was driving two pack horses, one of which bolted through the scrub when confronted by the bicycles. 'There was no opportunity for a yarn,' Donald recalled. 'We saw him but for a moment, but methinks I hear his curses still. He had disappeared and we reckoned it was expedient to follow his example.'

At the Ironstone Tank they found two iron tanks on the side of a dry waterhole. There was a little water in one of the tanks and although a bit muddy and red in appearance, it made good tea. After crossing some small, gravelly, ironstone hills they struck a well where they had their meal. They had intended to camp there, but the mosquitoes were so bad they continued to ride until dark when they found a place with fewer mosquitoes, but more ants. 'During the night they did not forget to let us know the fact,' Donald recalled.

Approaching Elsey Creek, ninety kilometres south of Katherine, the trio passed through country timbered with pandanus palms and paperbarks, which was like 'a tropical garden'. On reaching the creek they could see Elsey Station on the opposite side. They were warmly welcomed by the station manager, John McLennan, the 'sanguine Scot of the Never Never' who was later made famous by Jeannie Gunn's iconic novel *We of the Never Never*, and were soon enjoying 'cocoa and every luxury of the season'. They were persuaded to stay the next day, spending their time yarning, swimming, eating and watching Aboriginal stockmen break in horses.

The first white woman to settle in the remote region, Jeannie Gunn (née Taylor) was born in Melbourne in 1870, the daughter of a Scottish Baptist minister. After working as a school teacher, in 1901 she married the pastoralist, explorer and journalist Aeneas Gunn, who was a partner in Elsey Station, 483 kilometres south of Port Darwin. The following year Aeneas became the station's manager. Jeannie was discouraged from accompanying him to the station because she would feel 'out of place' as a woman, but she was determined to go and won over the stockmen with her courage, humour and horseriding skills.

Sadly, Aeneas died thirteen months later from blackwater fever and Jeannie returned to Melbourne where she wrote her novel about her experiences on the station, helping to create the legend of the Australian outback 'where men and a few women still lived heroic lives in rhythm with the gallop of a horse in forbidding faraway places'.

Thanks in part to the overlanders, the outback was not just living in rhythm with the gallop of a horse, but with the whirring of bicycle wheels.

In the evening the overlanders visited an Aboriginal camp and tried to glean information about the country they were about to traverse, but the Aboriginal people were not forthcoming. Donald expressed concern about the negative influence of European civilisation on traditional Aboriginal culture. 'The only good point they seemed to have was generosity among themselves,' Donald recalled. 'They share everything. But I heard that even this custom is dying out since mixing with the whites.'

Returning to the homestead, the overlanders asked Mr McLennan if he had any sandpaper with which they could clean their tyres. He did not, but took the trio into a paddock where he pulled some leaves from a fig tree, the rough under-surface making a splendid substitute. If the overlanders were to succeed in riding bicycles around Australia, they had to be adaptable.

Reluctantly, the trio left Elsey Station in the morning. Riding for about thirty kilometres through thickly timbered country and then black soil plains, they reached Bitter Springs, a series of thermal pools surrounded by palms, as the semi-arid desert landscape gave way to a lush, tropical paradise. The water was 'as clear as gin', and while it had a decidedly sulphurous smell, the taste was passable.

At five o'clock they arrived at Gum Waterhole where they intended to stop for tea and perhaps camp, but a few minutes after they lit a fire a dozen Aboriginal warriors arrived, coloured in red ochre and brandishing spears which were almost three metres long with glass points. Laying the spears on the ground, the warriors advanced to the camp and asked the cyclists for 'bacca'. The trio's response was a 'bit abrupt' and the warriors departed, grumbling in their own language.

After their meal the overlanders decided to push on, anticipating they would receive a 'warm reception' from the warriors if they camped there for the night. It might have been a wise decision, for just as they were leaving they saw a mob of Aboriginal people coming up the creek.

The overlanders headed for Katherine, eighty-six kilometres away, the gathering place for a different type of overlander – stockmen on gruelling cattle drives. As they approached the settlement, the cyclists stopped to 'spruce up a bit' in case there was a white woman at the telegraph station. They were nothing if not gentlemen, these overlanders. In the end they bypassed the telegraph station and went straight to a pub. A group of about thirty drovers and bushwhackers was congregated on the verandah, some lying asleep, others propping up the posts.

Dismounting from their bicycles, the overlanders received an invitation to have a drink with the bushwhackers, who had just buried a man who had been found dead a few kilometres away. 'Being decomposed and smelling badly, a hole was dug on the windward side, and the corpse pushed in with long poles,' Donald recalled.

After many rounds at the bar, they adjourned to the dining room for lunch, followed by some bushwhackers, who sat at the opposite end of a long table on which one of them had fallen asleep. 'They seemed a jolly lot,' Donald recalled.

Their remarks would need to be heard to be appreciated. They were men of all ages – short and grizzly, long and tanned. The one who located next to me seemed to have his face in bad repair, but apologised for same by saying that an alligator had bitten him when getting a drink.

Just as we were leaving the table, one, who said he was a vocalist, asked if any of us could play the piano, which I noticed in one corner of the room. Unfortunately, White accused me of being able to do so. Vainly declining, I was escorted to the piano. There was nothing else for it. So at 3.00pm the concert started. After each song, drinks! By 4.00pm drinks were being brought in at the middle of songs. In fact, it became about a three-minute service between the bar and parlour.

By 4.30 things were very merry. I had not been able to keep up the pace. And now the top of the piano was stacked with drinks, not counting many that had been spilt over same – also, over myself. But I was now entering into the show in earnest. As the firewater splashed over me, I was refreshed. The evening was hot. Under any circumstances, external application would be preferable to internal! The pace had been killing, but with frequent intermissions. For instance, when a performer was thought to be singing out of tune, he had to pay the penalty with a hit under the ear. It would then generally take some minutes for him to prove he was correct. Although much of the furniture got upset, it was a welcome respite.

In the evening it was proposed that the party should have a swim in the river to freshen up for tea. It was a magnificent stretch of deep water, shaded by the overhanging branches of giant trees on the bank. They all dived into the water without any clothes. One bushwhacker, though, did not join in, instead sitting on the bank. Suddenly he sprang to his feet and shouted, 'Alligators!' There was a mad dash to reach the bank, but there was no sign of any 'alligators' or the practical joker. Cursing in the 'startling lingo of the NT', the bushwhackers decided to return to the dining room for tea before adjourning to the bar.

'After a smoke, during which many tall adventures were narrated, mostly bearing on horsey subjects and shooting blacks, it was considered time to again start the concert,' Donald recalled.

Truly this performance would have satisfied the most fastidious Celestial. Again I had to be the musician. The afternoon performance, coupled with the heat and liquids I had consumed, made me reckless, so I sat down and played off accompaniments with the confidence of a professional. Noise – and that in big quantities – was the thing required. They got it. Handfuls of wrong chords were all the same. So long as they could remember the words, they could sing them to anything, from a blackfellow beating a sheet of bark with a yam stick to an orchestra. Recitations, songs, curses, competitions – all followed in quick succession, till at last, about twelve o'clock, I worked up an excuse and slipped out, but had to run the gauntlet, for my friend, whose face looked like a butcher's shop, steadying himself by grasping me firmly by the shoulder, wished to congratulate me.

We must have a drink! I asked to be excused. He remarked it must be drink or fight! As he said it he drew close, glaring into my eyes. I may forget that look, but his breath never! I could stand no more, and giving him a shove, slipped out onto the back verandah as he sat on the floor showering curses on me ... Before long I heard voices demanding that I should return; but as I did not answer, one of their number filled my position.

About 1.00am I got to bed. At last the infernal music stopped ... Never have I met a freer-handed or better lot of fellows – true bushmen. Although rough, how could they be otherwise when living as they did, practically out of touch with civilisation.

After managing to grab a few hours sleep, the overlanders were up at six o'clock in the morning and after a dip in the river sat down to breakfast, not feeling any ill effects from the night before. As soon as they had eaten they headed off towards Port Darwin, 317 kilometres away, amid the good wishes of the bushwhackers, or at least those who were not sleeping it off.

The trio had not originally intended going to Port Darwin because it meant doubling back over hundreds of kilometres to Katherine, but, like Arthur before them, they had arranged with a firm of cycle agents to ship a complete set of new tyres and other accessories to the town so that they could overhaul their bikes for the hazardous journey across the North West.

They reached Edith Creek, a clear-running stream fringed by pandanus palms, for lunch. After crossing the creek over a fallen tree, they found two men camped in a clump of palms.

Alex's gastroenteritis was playing up so they decided to rest for a few hours. The bushmen had some brandy and Alex had a nip and lay down. When he felt better the trio farewelled the campers and made another start over slaty hills, the monotony broken only by a couple of graves. Crossing two more creeks they got into granite country, the track as rough as any they had ridden on.

As evening fell, Alex was very weak and they had to walk. In the dark they took the wrong track and ended up at Spring Vale Station, which was managed by the bushman, drover and explorer Alfred Giles. After fighting off dogs they reached the house and were given refreshments and directions. Around nine o'clock they saw a light in the darkness and followed it to a house where Mr and Mrs Neilsen welcomed them with a bottle of 'square', while their curious children gawked at the around Australia riders.

The next day the trio reached Pine Creek, 226 kilometres south of Darwin. As they were walking down the main street they ran into Mr N. MacDonald, the brother of the overlander, who ran one of the three stores in town. MacDonald invited them to stay with him and showed them around, introducing them to 'many leading citizens' of the town. 'One old veteran, who had fought in India ... claimed to have been perforated by both lead and spears,' Donald recalled. 'On one occasion [in India] he crawled home resembling a porcupine and on examination was found to have seventeen spears in different parts of his anatomy!'

Pine Creek had been named by the Overland Telegraph Line construction worker Sidney Herbert in 1870 for the pines growing there. The discovery of gold in 1871 had led to the construction of a railway line between the settlement and Port

Darwin, which enabled the cyclists to ride along the side of the tracks to Adelaide River, 112 kilometres further on.

The overlanders enjoyed a good meal at the Adelaide River refreshment rooms, and after enquiring about accommodation were directed to a deserted police station. A group of Aboriginal people was occupying most of the building so the cyclists set up camp on the verandah where they were sheltered from the rain that had just started to fall. It was hot and steamy, and just fifty metres from the river, so the trio was soon attacked by a 'myriad of mosquitoes' which bit through everything except the soles of their shoes.

Without any breakfast the overlanders set off at daylight for Stapleton, a small settlement situated on Stapleton Creek, ten kilometres north-west of Adelaide River. After crossing a railway bridge over the river, the line wound through hilly country where the riders had several falls, rolling down among stones and wet grass. At last they reached Stapleton, where the local ganger, on learning they were the around Australia cyclists, invited them to his house and offered them the best of everything, including homemade beer and an invitation to call in again on their way back from Port Darwin.

Passing through Rum Jungle, they crossed the Darwin River, its banks covered with luxuriant tropical trees and ferns. At four o'clock in the afternoon they reached the Ten-Mile cottages and found some local cyclists who had come out to greet them and escort them into town. Nearing Port Darwin, they could see 'unmistakeable signs' of a recent cyclone with huge trees strewn on the ground in all directions. Arriving at the Victoria Hotel at 5.45pm on Wednesday, 18 October, the White brothers, at least, had completed half of their tour of Australia.

The first thing the overlanders did was have a shave, their beards having grown two and a half inches over the previous month, making them look like anything from 'an escaped convict to an orangutang'. After tea they went up to the balcony for a smoke and were approached by some local cyclists to go for a moonlight run, but they 'brutally refused', saying such a ride had no attraction for those who at that moment 'cursed the sight of a bicycle'.

The overlanders received a shock when they went to the shipping agency the next day to find that because of a mistake the shipment of new tyres had not arrived. The tyres would be put on the next boat, but they would not reach Port Darwin for twenty-five days.

This was a huge setback. A three-week delay would ruin any chance they had of beating Arthur if he continued at his current rate of progress. And if they waited for the tyres, the wet season would arrive and crossing flooded rivers would be impossible. But the alternative was not exactly promising either. They would have to ride on threadbare tyres through the most difficult and dangerous part of their journey.

The trio almost abandoned the ride at this point. 'We hoped here to refit; our tyres were done, but, as you know, there were none to be had,' Frank recalled. 'We felt like giving it up, but we made shift with some inner tubes.'

Despite the setback, the overlanders still managed to enjoy themselves in Port Darwin. 'I can't say our stay had not been without its bright spots,' Donald recalled. 'We were taken out for several drives, including an enjoyable picnic to the jungle ten miles out. We also had many strolls about the town and to the gardens; and also spent an evening with Mr Paddy Cahill, the famous buffalo shooter.'

Paddy Cahill was the most popular man in the Northern Territory. A 'stocky, broad-shouldered extrovert, with ruddy complexion and ever cheerful manner', Cahill was known as the 'Buffalo Bill of the Northern Territory'. One of the first buffalo hunters to shoot from horseback, much of Cahill's success was attributed to his horse, St Lawrence, which was sure-footed and manoeuvrable over grassy plains covered with buffalo tracks and potholes. Visiting Port Darwin in 1898, Banjo Paterson listed the main topics of conversation in the town as the 'cyclone (of 1897), G.R. (the government resident) and Paddy Cahill'.

A couple of years earlier, when the craze for cycling was first sweeping the Australian colonies, Paterson, a noted horseman, had gently mocked the bicycling boom in his poem 'Mulga Bill's Bicycle'. The poem recounts a bushman's unsuccessful attempt to learn to ride a bicycle, and though it quickly became one of Paterson's most popular poems, its preference for the horse over the new-fangled technology of the bicycle was already a lost cause at the time of publication.

The day after the overlanders arrived in Port Darwin, Cahill married Maria Pickford at St Mary's Star of the Sea Catholic Church, but within three weeks of the wedding he covered 300 kilometres in three days to help his partner William Johnston, who had been gored by a bull. During his later years, Cahill, a recognised authority on Aboriginal matters, acted as a Protector of Aborigines on a reserve based on his idyllic property, Oenpelli, in Arnhem Land.

The White brothers had a look at a Chinese joss house, or temple, but Donald did not bother as he had seen many on his travels in Asia. There was a new temple idol in the joss house as the Chinese worshippers had taken the old one to the end of a pier and thrown it into the sea after the recent cyclone. Most of China Town had been blown down and they were angry that the 'joss' had not protected them.

The locals' nerves were still on edge after the cyclone. The day before the trio departed there was an earthquake, which shook the town. 'All rushed from the houses, fearing another catastrophe was about to happen,' Donald recalled. 'However, with the exception of the houses and inhabitants' nerves getting a good shaking, no damage was done.'

Against the advice of local cyclists who warned them not to try to cross the North West on patched-up tyres, the overlanders departed Port Darwin at 2.30pm on Wednesday, 25 October. They knew they had to cross the North West before the wet season arrived. 'It practically meant annihilation if, after leaving the Katherine, the wet should set in, as the country was a network of watercourses which became very wide and deep, and abounded in alligators,' Donald recalled. 'To make the position worse, Alex White was a poor swimmer. We tried to purchase [tyre] covers locally, but without success, so decided to try and patch our old ones and trust to luck.'

Frank's luck soon ran out. Approaching Pine Creek on the way back down to Katherine, Frank's main crankshaft was damaged and he had to walk his bike into town. Along with punctured tyres and damaged forks, broken cranks were the most common problem facing cyclists in that era. As his bike 'required a little doing', Frank suggested that Alex and Donald go on ahead to Katherine to make arrangements for pack horses to carry their gear over the hilly and stony country towards the Victoria River, while he remained at Pine Creek to repair his bicycle.

On 28 October, after purchasing supplies for the next stage, Alex and Donald were just about to go out to lunch in Katherine when they received a telegram from Frank, which read: 'Crank broken. If I cannot mend same go on.' Donald admitted he was 'much surprised' at the news, but did not elaborate. At daylight the next morning Alex rode back to Pine Creek to see if he could help Frank. If the bike could not be fixed, Alex would bring back a few 'necessities' that Frank had with him.

The country between Katherine and Pine Creek was so difficult that Jerome Murif had offered a gold watch to anyone who could ride it in ten hours. It is not known whether Alex, who rode from Pine Creek to Katherine in five and a half hours, ever collected his gold watch from the overlander. Donald, meanwhile, filled in his spare day touring the Kintore Caves, twelve kilometres west of Katherine, which contain rare fauna and evidence of a long history of human occupation.

Alex returned to Katherine without Frank, whose disappointment at having to abandon the ride was 'keen'.

Given Frank was the more experienced rider and Alex was constantly sick and holding the party back, it may seem surprising that Alex did not pull out of the journey instead and give his bike to Frank. But Alex needed to complete the ride to fulfil his contract with his sponsors. If he dropped out now, all of his trials would have been for nothing. The same thing may have applied to Frank, although it is possible, as a famous overlander, that he had guaranteed monies from his sponsors. There may also have been a gentlemen's agreement among the overlanders that rides begin and end on the same bike. Certainly, Frank would not have been keen to ride across the wilds of northern Australia on his own while trying to catch up with Alex and Donald.

The *Northern Argus* commiserated with Frank, although the newspaper intimated that an accident on such a difficult journey was almost inevitable. 'Frank White has by this time arrived back at Port Darwin and left there by the S.S. *Chang-Sha* for Melbourne and it is to be regretted that such a plucky rider should be forced to give up his ride through no fault of his own,' the newspaper reported on 8 December. 'But when attempting such a ride as that of touring around the Australian continent such accidents are only to be expected and it is a matter of good luck if they do not occur.'

The *Northern Territory Times and Gazette* reported more accurately that Frank left Port Darwin on the *Guthrie* bound for Sydney. 'Mr F. White, the cyclist whose machine broke down whilst attempting to ride around Australia, left by the *Guthrie*,' the newspaper reported on 8 December. 'He spoke very highly of the hospitality meted out to him by Territorians. We hope he doesn't mention this fact south, else we'll have a few more fame-seeking cyclists dropping in upon us, and the overlanding fad since Murif's and MacDonald's ride is being very much overdone.'

The Dux Cycle Company could not resist a dig at their rival bicycle manufacturer, Dayton Bicycles, after Frank's breakdown. 'The Dux Cycle Company is particularly proud of the manner in which Don Mackay speaks of his mount,' the *Australasian* reported in Melbourne on Saturday, 9 December. 'Writing from Port Darwin, he states that his machine is standing splendidly. As subsequent events have proved, one of his companions, Frank White, would have given something considerable to be able to have said the same of his wheel. Mackay was fortunate in his choice.'

With the worst part of the journey lying ahead, Donald would need his trusty Dux to continue to 'stand splendidly' or the consequences could be catastrophic.

Circumcycling Australia.

After the weary desert country comes Powell's Creek.

AN OASIS IN THE WILDS.

Powell's Creek Telegraph Station, 510 miles from Port Darwin.

A sanctuary in the desert, Powell Creek telegraph station was famous among the overlanders for its hospitality.

Stage Thirteen

Edge of Madness

Arthur
Powell Creek to Townsville
7 October to 10 November 1899

ARTHUR had endured tremendous hardship on his ride so far – hunger, thirst, exhaustion, loneliness and illness – but now the lone cyclist felt he might descend into madness as he crossed the endless plains of the Barkly Tableland. It was enough to drive anyone insane. The temperature was '115 degrees in the shade' when Arthur departed Powell Creek on Saturday, 7 October, setting off on a journey that the White brothers and Mackay had strongly warned him against. Alex and Donald had survived the tableland only because Frank was able to reach Powell Creek and send out a rescue party. But Arthur was on his own. There was no one to save him.

Fortunately, one of the dangers Arthur had feared had all but dissipated as the country was 'too dry and open' for hostile Aboriginal groups to threaten him at that time of year. It would be a relief to be able to camp without fearing a 'shower of spears' raining down.

Nevertheless, after what had happened to the White brothers and Mackay, Arthur still faced a daunting task. Day after day he travelled over open plains as hard as flint, while the ruts that grazing cattle had made in the pads across the plains rendered them all but unrideable. Hot easterly winds blew head-on at gale force against the overlander and the tropical sun beat down upon him. With the plains seemingly cracking in the heat, cycling was extremely trying and wearisome.

Paradoxically, Arthur got lost in a 'labyrinth' on these wide open plains. One night he camped at a waterhole and the next morning he selected what he thought was the correct track from the many which led from the hole, but found that it did not follow in the right direction. He tried many others, but without success, and he had the unusual experience of being 'bushed on an open plain'.

Arthur noted that cattle travelling in mobs in the dry season can smell water when within two or three kilometres of a hole, and once they do they stampede from all directions. This accounted for the labyrinth of tracks in which he found himself and which caused him 'to have lunch there as well as breakfast'. Eventually he found the right path and rode well into the night to make up time, for the sight of his diminishing provisions caused him to become 'feverishly anxious'.

'That week of cycling will never be forgotten by me,' Arthur recalled. 'From morning till night I toiled on over the arid plains and through the low-lying scrub country. Sparing in the use of water which I carried and only drinking when forced to, I was constantly tantalised and tempted by the shimmering mirage which seemed to accompany me.'

One day Arthur rode or tramped with a shimmering lake in front of him that was so calm and clear that it almost became a reality. He camped for lunch in the shade of a tree, 'the leaves of which could have been shot off with a saloon rifle in ten minutes'. He was feverish and hot-headed, and rode like a madman until he reached the deserted Eva Downs Station where he camped for the night. The place was only a log humpy with the iron roof half blown off. The blasting hot winds which swept across the plains 'howled dismally through the cracks of the building, while the swinging sheets of roofing iron creaked incessantly'.

Arthur was so exhausted that the next day he simply lay on the floor. 'I altogether forget leaving that place, but I can remember being quite terrorised during the night, because of my half-demented condition and the dirge-like moaning of the wind,' he recalled. 'Through it all the one thought uppermost in my mind was that of conserving the water in the cans which I had made, but the want of food must have driven me away from Eva Downs and urged me onward.'

He had only ridden for about four hours on an excellent pad, which the Whites and Mackay must have missed during their miserable departure from the lagoon, when he noticed a sudden change in the country. The bare hot plains gave way to scrubby stony land with actual watercourses, not mirages. Lying in a deep hollow was a fine lagoon, oval in shape and containing a fair amount of water. He came upon a settlement and soon learned it was Anthony Lagoon Police Station. Mr Giles, the trooper, made him comfortable and he had a bush shower by standing on a box while Aboriginal workers threw buckets of water over him. He stopped at the station for a couple of days until 'thoroughly well' again, physically and mentally.

The next stage to Brunette Downs, 229 kilometres north-west of Camooweal, was also waterless, but it was not as monotonous and the journey took only two days, although he did see 'signs of a visitation of rats'. The open, grassy downs country alternated with red loamy rises and flats with low timber and scrub. Arthur camped at a small waterhole on the first night and the next afternoon reached the station. Thirty thousand head of cattle were carried on Brunette Downs, managed by James Hutton, whom Arthur described as 'one of the best known and most popular men in northern Australia and western Queensland'.

Arthur spent a couple of days at Brunette Downs, which ran a herd of goats, providing milk and a welcome change from beef. Heavy rains fell while he rested at the station, and by the time he departed the black soil plains were unrideable. The 106-kilometre stage to Alexandria Station, against strong headwinds and over bumpy plains, was extremely rough.

From Powell Creek Arthur had pursued essentially the same track as that followed by the White brothers and Mackay, but now he decided to take a shortcut. Instead of keeping southeast along the track to Camooweal and then heading north to Burketown, he cut across country and struck the Camooweal–Burketown Road about 320 kilometres north of Camooweal.

Arthur entered mountainous country over the Queensland border and reached Herbert Vale Station, one of the westernmost homesteads in the colony, just off Wilfred Creek. At Lily Lagoon he hit the mail road to Burketown, running parallel with the pretty Gregory River 'with its fine wide waters fringed with fig trees and pandanus palms' and followed it for a couple of hundred kilometres.

While Arthur was taking his shortcut, some back in civilisation were beginning to wonder what had happened to him. 'No word has come to hand from Arthur Richardson, who left Powell Creek two or three weeks back. He is due at Camooweal any day,' the *Morning Bulletin* reported.

But Arthur had bypassed Camooweal. He reached Burketown on Monday, 23 October, nearly five months from the time of starting. The shortcut saved him nearly 480 kilometres travelling, but he paid a heavy price, enduring a long, exhausting stage of 173 kilometres across a waterless wasteland.

'Many of the dry stages here, though not very long, have to be walked,' Arthur recalled. 'There is nothing more disheartening than walking against strong headwinds on the endless black soil plains, knocked up and short of water. Still, when the stations or camps are reached, there is always a very hearty welcome. You are asked to stop a week, and feel like accepting, and putting off the trip till after the wet; but the next day you get your head down to it again.'

In Burketown, Arthur received a telegram from Percy Armstrong, who, drawing on his own overlanding experience, gave him directions about which route to take from the Gulf of Carpentaria down the east coast, where his 'troubles' would be all but over.

'Dear Arthur, by the time you receive this you will have all your troubles practically over and will be in civilisation,' Armstrong wrote.

```
The road to Normanton will not be too good,
but it is passable. From there you will go
to Croydon and when you get there be sure to
call on D.P. Viles, commission agent, who was
an old boss of mine, and give him my kind
regards. You will find a lot of my old friends
in Croydon. From there you will go via the
```

Gilbert to Georgetown, across the ranges to
Charters Towers or Townsville. The turn-off to
the Towers is at Continong, a few miles before
you come to the Burdekin. The road turns to
the right. I think that you had better take
the straight-on road, cross the Burdekin, go
through Argentine and on to Townsville. You
will be welcomed there and will be able to get
tyres if necessary. From there you will find
it better to go down the coast roads. I went
inland through Ravenswood, Clermont, Emerald,
Springsure and Taroom, and the going was vile.
The coast roads will save you weeks of toil.

As soon as you are on decent tracks, I want
you to push on for all you are worth so that
White and party will not have a chance with
you. Your progress down the east coast will be
like a triumphal march. You will have the best
weather and the roads will be good.

The ride is becoming more interesting every
day. I had a letter from Humbers and they
say that the *Wide World* people will take up
the ride. They want you to get all the quaint
photos that you can, and the more out of the
way they are, the better for the purpose.
Get in plenty of notes so that a splendid
description may be written up. As long as
you give them the material they will do all
the padding, and you will have some idea of
their ability in this direction after the de
Rougement story.

The photos are a necessity. Also remember
that the matter must not appear in any other
magazine or they will not touch it, so do
not give the eastern writers any particular
information. Of course you can tell them enough
about the trip so that they will not have
a set on you, but do not give them anything
under your own name, and no photos. If you get
in good matter I think you will do well out
of the copy of the ride. Above all, plenty of
photos even if you have to buy them.

When you are in civilisation you must wire
the *West Australian* every day if possible. It
is a better advertisement to them to get the
wires often and it is better for us. You need
not mind about the expense to them as they do
not consider it. They have been complaining
that you do not advise on every occasion.
Wishing you a good time from the time you
receive this.

I remain yours sincerely,

For Armstrong Cycle Agency, P.W. Armstrong.

Armstrong's exhortation to Arthur to 'push on for all you are worth so that White and party will not have a chance with you' dispelled any notion that the solo rider was not in this race to win it. It would be wonderful to see what Arthur saw through the lens of his camera, but unfortunately there are no known photographs of his ride.

Arthur dragged himself away from Burketown and on Saturday, 28 October, he reached Normanton where he was delayed after a money wire was sent to the wrong place. 'Arrived here yesterday. Shall have to stay till Monday, as money wired me went to Burketown by mistake, and was posted from there per boat, which is stuck on a mudbank,' Arthur wrote in a telegram published by the *West Australian* on 31 October.

> The spell will do me good, and I am giving the machine an overhaul. Left Burketown at about five in the afternoon. Going out twenty miles to a camp, but I had to ride back again twelve miles to escape the heavy rain. I got a very heavy wetting next morning for twenty miles. The mailman had to scrape the mud off the buggy wheels, so you can guess how I got on. Making Floraville telegraph station for the night, I rode thence on fair roads to Inverleigh Station. From there I had a very bumpy road to Normanton. The bike is now cleaned and looks as well as when I left Perth, and the tyres are all right. I am also all right.

The White brothers and Mackay were not the only ones who did not think Arthur would make it across the Barkly Tableland. The *Australasian* reported on 11 November that Arthur, against all expectations, had successfully negotiated the dreadful stretch of country. 'Contrary to expectations, Arthur Richardson, the overlander, succeeded in negotiating, apparently with ease, the 400-mile stretch between Powell Creek cable station and Camooweal ... Richardson has now traversed the most trying portion of his ride, being within easy reach of civilisation henceforward.'

When the White brothers and Mackay heard the news that Arthur had crossed the Barkly Tableland safely, they would have had mixed emotions. They would have felt a sense of relief that their fellow overlander had survived, but they also would have realised that they could not win the race unless some accident or disaster prevented Arthur from finishing. The race around Australia was Arthur's to lose.

The worst of the ride now well behind him, Arthur reached Georgetown at noon on Thursday, 2 November, and sent a telegram to the *Western Mail*, which published it on 11 November.

> Arrived here this morning. The road was rather heavy and through mostly sandy and granite country. Leaving Croydon some of the cyclists came out a few miles to see me fairly on the road. There is a good deal of cycling there but only one agency. Mr Creagh, who looked after me, gave me the run of the shop, etc. From here I go along the old Townsville road via Carpentaria Downs. At Townsville I shall refit. My apparel is now a total wreck, and I had to go into long pants at Burketown, having got through the leather round the knickers etc. Whites and self took a full day and a half from Croydon here, and the local cyclists take only ten hours.

In fairness to the overlanders, the locals had not already ridden thousands of kilometres.

The *Evening News* in Sydney calculated that on arrival in Georgetown Arthur had averaged thirty-two miles (fifty-one kilometres) per day, 'which is very good travelling, considering the country passed through'. But while Arthur was making good progress, this was certainly no time to become complacent. He still had more than half the continent to ride around and who knew what lay ahead.

On his way back to civilisation, Arthur crossed the Great Dividing Range in Far North Queensland without incident.

The road from Burketown to Townsville was well travelled and the ride uneventful compared to what he had experienced in the wilds of the Top End and the North West. Certainly, Arthur saw plenty of crocodiles all the way across northern Australia and down to southern Queensland, but he did not have any 'hairbreadth escapes' from the prehistoric predators, at least none that he mentioned. Crossing fine pastoral and mining country, he was met with nothing but kindness from miners, teamsters, homesteaders and townsfolk alike.

One morning, after a steady climb of forty kilometres to the top of a range running parallel with the coast, he got a glimpse of Townsville lying on Cleveland Bay, about fifty kilometres away. 'The first view of the eastern ocean was a fine streak of blue on the horizon,' Arthur recalled rather wistfully.

Australia's first transcontinental cyclist, Percy Armstrong, left, rode from Croydon to Melbourne in 1893. He was accompanied as far as Sydney by R. Craig.

Reaching Townsville at one o'clock on Friday, 10 November, Arthur had left the wilderness behind him. The unofficial capital of north Queensland, Townsville had been founded in 1864 as a port for the fledgling pastoral industry and named after the Sydney investor Robert Towns, who financially backed the settlement. Townsville was originally just a muddy track through a mangrove swamp, but the discovery of gold in the hinterland in the late 1860s accelerated its development from rudimentary huts to gracious brick and masonry buildings. By the 1890s Townsville had become a rip-roaring town of more than 13,000 people, some of whom might even have remembered Arthur from the time his family briefly lived there.

'Arrived here this morning, so can consider I am now in civilisation,' Arthur wrote in a telegram which was published in the *West Australian* on 18 November. 'From Georgetown to here the road is very rough and hilly. I also had a lot of trouble about the road, and cannot get reliable information regarding the turn-off roads, and have had several times to cut across ranges onto the road as far as twenty miles. Here there is plenty of water and tucker, and I strike camps every night. From here I will travel through the towns, and then south. The machine, tyres, etc, are still in splendid condition, and I am quite well, though rather lightweight.'

Arthur still had a long way to go to reach his final destination, but he would now have a comparatively easy ride from Townsville to Adelaide and would have been feeling supremely confident about finishing first — though he knew it would take just one mishap to shatter his dream.

Bicycle manufacturers and tyre companies sponsored the overlanders' rides to gain publicity and credibility for their products.

Stage Fourteen

Ambush!

Alex and Donald
Katherine to Derby
30 October to 16 December 1899

FRANK'S withdrawal left Alex and Donald to traverse 'the worst part of Australia' without their leader and most experienced rider. Frank had saved their lives once, but now they were on their own in the most dangerous place on the continent. Not only would they face harsh terrain, but the stage from Katherine to Derby would take them through the 'bad black country' where Aboriginal warriors were resisting European intrusion.

Alex and Donald would be out of communication with civilisation for much of this portion of the journey. After nearly dying on the way to Powell Creek they must have approached this leg of the trip with some trepidation. If they became too ill or exhausted to continue, their chances of reaching their destination alive would be very slender. The pair faced the challenge with characteristic courage and determination, but they realised that the ride ahead was very dangerous. 'For the first time on the trip things looked serious from the start,' Donald recalled.

At four o'clock on Monday, 30 October, Alex and Donald got their books signed at the Katherine telegraph station and an hour later, after a round of drinks, they pushed off amid good wishes and cheers. The road from Katherine to Victoria Downs was a 'network of creeks'. They followed the trail of their hired pack horses, which had gone ahead, down to the King River, a tributary of the Daly River.

Passing Springvale Station, the overlanders came to a creek where they found the leader of the pack-horse party, a man named Anderson, fast asleep on the bank under the shade of a paperbark tree, with three empty gin bottles nearby. Donald told Anderson's female Aboriginal companion, Albunga, that he and Alex were continuing and gave her 'strict orders' to bring Anderson along as soon as he was awake.

The overlanders and the pack-horse party camped in the fork of the King and Katherine rivers. The stockmen did not seem to be in a good mood and the cyclists worried they might not accompany them further. Alex, Donald and an Aboriginal stockman went fishing at a point where quite a lot of small crocodiles cruised slowly at the surface of the river. Alex took a shot at a seven-footer, but missed. While many fish could be seen swimming in the clear water, they only managed to catch a few, which they cooked in damper back at the camp.

Making an early start the next morning, they reached Sardine Lagoon where they noticed a tree marked 'Richardson, A.R, V.R.D., 200m', so they knew they were on the right track. Leaving the Katherine River, they cut across savannah woodland to the Flora River, fringed with dense riverine vegetation and dotted with deep pools, where they heard the rumble of the beautiful Kathleen Falls. The track did not pass in sight of the falls so the overlanders left the pad and carried their bikes through the scrub to the edge of the water, but they had trouble getting a clear view because of the tropical foliage. 'It was a fine sheet,' Donald recalled. 'The falls were some hundred yards up from where we stood. The drop was about fifteen feet, breadth thirty yards.'

The country between the Flora and Ord rivers was considered the most dangerous in the whole of Australia for Aboriginal attacks. The overlanders had seen a lot of Aboriginal footprints in the area and now on the other side of the water they could hear Aboriginal people talking in loud voices. They then saw about twenty painted warriors carrying spears heading upstream, but they did not seem to notice the cyclists.

The overlanders soon came upon evidence of Aboriginal resistance to European intrusion, arriving at the 'burned ruins' of Price's Creek Station, where they camped for the night, the fish in the creek providing a good meal.

Black clouds darkened the sky and the party got hit by a violent storm, accompanied by high winds and a spectacular outback sound and light show of thunder and lightning. 'At last it was over,' Donald recalled. 'Wet through, we at last got the fire going and spent the remainder of the night cursing our luck.' Even worse than the drenching they received, the storm was a warning that the wet season could arrive in earnest any day to wash away their dreams.

After the tempest, riding on the sticky black soil was impossible. They could not even wheel the bicycles so they had to tramp, carrying their machines on their backs. Entering hilly country, Alex and Donald were able to ride again. They arrived at Shipton Creek, where water was supposed to be obtainable, ahead of the pack-horse party. The creek was dry, but not empty. There were fresh Aboriginal tracks in the sandy bed. Looking around, the overlanders saw twenty Aboriginal warriors about one hundred metres down the creek. Without warning the warriors shipped their spears and ran towards Alex and Donald at full pace, fanning out in a semicircle. The country was too rough for the cyclists to ride faster than the warriors could run, so they had no choice but to stand and fight.

'I reckoned it best to get in the first shot, so taking as quick a sight as I could, fired at two big, fierce, painted devils who were steadying their spears,' Donald recalled. 'I let go two chambers. But I only saw where one bullet landed – just in front of one of my friends. He made a wild bound into the air. I thought [bullet] no 1 had him.

'They all seemed nonplussed, and dropping their spears, held up their hands. I demanded an explanation. A small thick-set individual (the only linguist) asked for bacca in a very subdued voice.'

Hearing gunfire, Anderson galloped up, but the situation had been defused by the time he got there. Speaking the local Aboriginal language, Anderson discovered there was a *gilgai*, or small lake, about a kilometre away. The warriors led the overlanders to the water. 'Seeing us on the bikes seemed to interest them very much,' Donald recalled. 'They stared at us and gesticulated in a manner that looked quite French.'

On Saturday, 4 November, the party passed the ruins of Delamere Station. Their supply of dried meat had nearly run out and Anderson rode towards Mount Needham to hunt for a stray bull or cow, while the rest continued to Willeroo outstation, which they reached at about eleven o'clock. Setting up camp, they waited for Anderson, who returned at dusk, but without a cow. Anderson managed to round up some cattle the next day and one of the pack-horse party shot a cow with a rifle, while the rest of the herd bolted. The beast was butchered and the meat was salted down in a log hut.

The next day the party reached another deserted house, just a hut and an outhouse, at Aroona Creek, which had been the site of several attacks by Aboriginal warriors and was believed to be haunted. 'As the night was hot we camped outside, but were fortunate in not seeing any of the ghosts that were supposed to haunt the place,' Donald recalled.

Earlier in the day Anderson shot a 'fat steer' with a rifle and it provided the party with a 'sumptuous' meal that night. In the morning the overlanders parted company with the pack-horse party and continued their journey across this inhospitable country on their own.

Nothing had been heard of the duo since they left Katherine and friends and family from Western Australia to Wallendbeen were starting to worry about them. 'No particulars are at hand this week from the White brothers and Mackay, who left Katherine Creek nearly a fortnight back for Halls Creek in the Kimberley district,' the *Queenslander* reported. 'As the country to be traversed consists of some 450 miles of heavy and mountainous bush tracks, the Whites are likely to have a hard time in negotiating what Arthur Richardson described as the most dangerous part of Australia. Besides the water being scarce in this section, the blacks on Victoria River are very hostile, and likely to cause trouble if met with.' Clearly, news of Frank's withdrawal from the ride had not yet reached some of the press on the east coast.

The pack-horse party had given Alex and Donald a rough sketch of the track to Victoria River, a pad running through slightly undulating country of black soil and long grass. Soon it took them up between two rocky hills and a view 'unequalled in Australia' lay before them. 'The country dropped suddenly some hundred feet,' Donald recalled. 'It was known as the Jump Up. Forming a perfect half circle, it gradually opened out, with the sides regular corridors of round, stony hills, making a splendid background against a tropical blue sky.'

At 3.30pm on Friday, 10 November, Alex and Donald arrived at Victoria Downs Station where they received a friendly reception from Mr Watson, who had accompanied Arthur to Port Darwin and was just as hospitable to them. After refreshments they had a swim in the deep, wide river. The evening passed with cards and yarns before a comfortable sleep in greenhide hammocks.

In the morning Alex was feeling sick so they decided to rest at the station for another day before pushing on. Instead of taking Arthur's route by Wave Hill, which was south-west from Victoria Downs, Alex and Donald decided to take the northern track to Wyndham, on the coast of Western Australia, because of concerns about the state of their tyres. There was just one problem. This way would take them through the notorious Jasper Gorge where two white teamsters, Mulligan and Ligar, had been brutally, though not fatally, speared by Aboriginal warriors a year earlier.

The night before Alex and Donald arrived at the station, Mr Watson and his stockmen had fired on some would-be Aboriginal attackers creeping towards the homestead. In their haste to escape the bullets, the warriors had dropped their spears. Alex and Donald had a close look at the weapons. They were 3.5 metres long, with stone points, fifteen centimetres in length, shaped like leaves. The points were fixed onto the shafts by gum made from spinifex, resembling cobbler's wax. Alex and Donald imagined the damage the spears could do and hoped they would not see their like at such close quarters again.

As they rode to Jasper Gorge, Alex and Donald had the uneasy feeling they were being watched. They did not see anyone in the bush, but they sensed someone was there. If they were being followed, their pursuers were keeping their distance, staying out of rifle shot, perhaps having learned from bitter experience. At night the overlanders took turns to keep watch, sleeping away from their camp fire, which would be a target for spears.

On Monday, 13 November, as the duo approached the entrance to Jasper Gorge, they heard the 'shrill yaki' yell of an Aboriginal warrior. Looking up they saw a man on top of a rocky peak waving his spear threateningly, then disappearing. Even more disturbingly, they noticed a signal fire near the spot where they had seen the warrior. The overlanders did not need to guess the message and entered the gorge cautiously.

The narrow passage was a deep gully twelve kilometres long. It was impossible to ride over the loose sand and rocks so they had to walk the bicycles. Before long, on a ledge about sixty metres in front of them, they spied a band of Aboriginal warriors shouting and waving their spears. It was an ambush. The overlanders did not have time to think. Diving for cover, they crouched behind a large boulder, took out their revolvers and fired. Like apparitions, the warriors disappeared.

Alex and Donald pushed on as fast as possible, but the warriors soon reappeared on another ledge, this time out of firing range. The cyclists nevertheless let off another volley of shots and the warriors vanished again, only to appear and disappear at intervals over the next hour. 'We were always pleased to be able to see them, as passing under the cliffs we expected either to get a spear or shower of rocks down on us,' Donald recalled.

The besieged overlanders still had about five kilometres to go before they could exit the gorge when the rocky bottom of the defile gave way to heavy sand, which made wheeling the bicycles even more difficult. In the intense heat, the narrow passage felt like a cauldron. 'Between it and the thought of being skewered at any minute made the yards seem miles,' Donald recalled.

At last the gorge opened out to a dry, well-timbered ravine running parallel with Jaspers Creek. The warriors were nowhere to be seen. Realising they could cycle on the firm ground, the overlanders mounted their bicycles, aiming to ride away as fast as they could, but Donald's back tyre was flat and he had to stop to pump it up. The timing could not have been worse.

Donald was hurriedly disconnecting the pump from the valve when Alex looked around and saw the warriors charging through the long grass on the bank of the creek. Dropping the pump as Alex yelled a warning, Donald drew his revolver and fired as the warriors let out a terrible cry and threw their spears, which whizzed past the heads of the overlanders. With Alex and Donald both shooting, the gunfire soon had the warriors retreating to the creek. The duo quickly reloaded their revolvers, jumped on their bikes and took off.

But they were still not out of danger. On the other side of the creek several Aboriginal men had gathered. Alex and Donald let off some long-range shots at them and they disappeared. They then passed the area known as TK Camp, where Mulligan and Ligar had been speared, but they felt relatively safe the further they progressed in the more open, rideable country.

Alex and Donald continued to pedal well into the night until they were satisfied their attackers had been left far behind. They camped at Bobs Grave Spring where they tried to keep their eyes open in case they were pursued. Eventually they fell asleep, exhausted. After they had nearly perished in the desert, the attack by hostile warriors marked the second time on the journey that Alex and Donald had narrowly escaped death. How many lives did they have?

In the morning Alex and Donald looked back at the dangerous and desolate country they had crossed and were glad to be finished with it. Pushing on, in thirty-five kilometres they reached the safety of a police station at Timber Creek, a small town on the banks of the Victoria River, where they relaxed by having a swim. Enjoying the cool water, they might have laughed about their hair-raising escape at Jasper Gorge, comfortable in the belief that their troubles with Aboriginal attackers were behind them. But when they looked up from the water they saw two warriors coming towards them with spears. They yelled for help and Trooper O'Keefe rushed out of the police station, sending the warriors on their way with a few shots of his rifle.

Alex and Donald rested for a day at the police station and enjoyed a delicious meal of barramundi, which Trooper O'Keefe caught in the river, before riding to Auvergne Station, fifty kilometres west of Timber Creek on the Baines River, where they stayed at the homestead. Donald went for a swim in the lagoon and shocked the Aboriginal workers who had never seen a man with so many tattoos.

'Owing to my being tattooed from my neck to my heels, I was quite a lion in north-west black society,' Donald recalled.

When I would undress to have a swim, if a black camp was near, all its inhabitants would turn out to see "Him Plenty Picture Man". It was a large bit embarrassing sometimes, especially when the lady blacks would squat upon my scanty wardrobe so as to afford them the chance to closely examine my skin pictures, of which I have one hundred and fifty on my body and limbs. They fairly dazzled me with their modesty – my blushes were put down to sunburn. But in the north-west Territory the little matter of clothing is of no moment. Virtue is easy and attire is light. Air is the only costume worn. They wanted to add a few of their own tattoo marks, but as I was afraid that the wounds would not heal, I declined to have additions to my collection.

Leaving Auvergne Station on Monday, 20 November, Alex and Donald crossed the Baines River and rode through rugged sandstone ranges, reaching Newry Station, on the banks of the Keep River and close to the border with Western Australia, at midday on Wednesday, 22 November. The station was just a rough hut, most of it occupied by Aboriginal workers, who told the cyclists in broken English that 'Boss will soon come along'.

Reclining on greenhide stretchers on the verandah, Alex and Donald debated whether they should risk going on their worn-out tyres to Wyndham or not as Newry was the place to turn off. After inspecting the tyres they decided it would be 'madness' after all to visit Wyndham as it would increase the distance to Derby by 320 kilometres. Just as they were about to make a start, the manager, Mr Madden, rode up and assured them they were doing the right thing.

Mr Madden showed them a 'mud map', drawn in the dirt with a stick. It was pretty simple, but his local knowledge helped the cyclists to find the track across the Western Australian border.

The heat was intense as they travelled across loose country before striking a horse pad, which made riding easier. Crossing the Behn River, which rises on the Western Australian and Northern Territory border, they arrived at Argyle Downs, thirty-five kilometres west of Newry. The homestead, built by the pioneering Durack brothers, Patrick and Michael, in 1895, was renowned as one of the main social gathering places in the East Kimberley.

The arrival of the overlanders created a 'terrible commotion' among the Aboriginal workers, who mistook them for 'devil-devils' and urged the storekeeper to shoot them. They set up camp in a paddock just as a dust storm blew up and by the time they scrambled to the lee of the limestone homestead they were smothered in dirt and sand.

The next morning, having got provisions and directions, the overlanders headed to Ord River Station via Wild Dog Creek. After riding over a 'frightful track' they reached Ord River police station. The constable, named Freeman, was away, so the cyclists camped under a bough shed, but a windstorm unroofed it and they took shelter in a hut.

The duo had a swim in Wild Dog Creek the next morning before making a start, but the track across hilly and stony country was unrideable. Still trudging along in the dark, they happened upon Constable Freeman's camp. He was accompanied by a man named Muggleton, who was known as the 'Fire Fiend'. They were chasing an outlaw, Ben Bridge, who had escaped from gaol in New South Wales. Captured in Burketown, Bridge got away when the gaol there burned down. He fled to the Kimberley where he was engaged in cattle duffing, and soon would be pursued, at a gallop, across the homestead lawn of Argyle Station by the dogged Freeman.

The next morning, after receiving information about the stony track from Freeman, the overlanders pushed on, perhaps wondering if they would cross paths with the charismatic fugitive.

After a bad ride over black soil plains and a 'bath' from a thunderstorm, they arrived at Ord River Station on the bank of Forrest Creek on the afternoon of Sunday, 26 November. The manager, Mr Young, and his jackaroos were out driving cattle, but the book-keeper, Mr Larkin, made them welcome. Mr Young returned at six-thirty in the evening and told Alex and Donald that they must have been 'mad' to choose the 'worst season of the year' to cross the rough country of north-west Australia. The wet season was about to begin, which would almost certainly put an end to their ride. But having come this far, the cyclists were determined to persevere.

They stayed at Ord River the next day, patching up their tyres, and in the evening attended an Aboriginal corroboree, which included a demonstration of spear throwing. They had a go at throwing spears, but 'did not distinguish ourselves', which must have amused the Aboriginal audience.

On the morning of Tuesday, 28 November, they followed a track in a south-westerly direction up the Ord River valley. After riding across hard, ridgy country they stopped for lunch at the Nicholson River, a tributary of the Ord, in the shade of woodlands where they took potshots at some turkeys on the river bank.

After lunch a powerful headwind blew up which stopped them from riding. As they walked they were followed by a curious herd of cattle, which ringed around them, until they reached a river bank where they had tea under the shelter of pandanus and fig trees. A dust storm was approaching. At first the fiery sun shone through the dust, turning the landscape Martian red. The dust cloud then covered them and darkness fell across the landscape like an eclipse of the sun. Alex and Donald lay down under a sandbank until the eerie storm passed.

When they resumed their ride the duo followed several cattle pads in different directions, but they all petered out. At last they thought they had found the right track, following it for a considerable distance until it split into many faint paths. It was dark and they were thirsty so they decided to retrace their tracks to the river to camp for the night.

The overlanders ate the last of their tucker for breakfast before following the river until they came to a cattle pad on the open plain. The going was very rough with cracked black soil and long tussock grass to negotiate. On the horizon, about thirty kilometres away, the Hardman Range ran parallel with the river. A break in the range, the Hardman Gap, was the only way through towards Halls Creek and ultimately Derby.

The duo arrived at Hardman Gap around two o'clock. It was about three hundred metres wide with spinifex-covered hills rising on either side and was traversed by a level track, providing quite a different experience to the passage through Jasper Gorge. Leaving the gap, they struck hilly and rough limestone country. They had no food or water and the heat was unbearable. They gritted their teeth, determined to reach Bootie's Station that night, no matter what.

Instead, they camped among the steep and stony hills, listening to dingoes howling in the night. One dingo got within a few metres of them, but was sent away 'with a bullet in some part of his anatomy'. Unable to sleep, they sucked on stones to allay their thirst.

At daylight on Thursday, 30 November, the overlanders pushed on without saying a word, possibly because talking expended too much energy or their mouths were too dry. Seeing tall timber ahead, they hoped to find water, but the creek was dry. They dug a hole in the sand: nothing. Leaving their bikes, Alex and Donald went in opposite directions in the hope of one of them finding water. Fortunately, Alex stumbled upon the Elvire River, a deep channel of fine water named after the wife of Sir John Forrest.

Alex called out to Donald and slid down the bank to the water, his mate soon joining him in slurping big mouthfuls. Taking off their clothes, they lay in the water for an hour. Refreshed, they found a pad on the opposite bank which led to Bootie's Station. Mr Bootie was away chasing Aboriginal marauders who had speared his cattle, but a friend who was looking after the place for him made the cyclists welcome and the Aboriginal women who worked at the station prepared lunch for them.

The overlanders were exhausted, so after another swim in the river which ran near the house, they remained at the station for the night.

They departed after lunch the next day, Friday, 1 December, riding into a heavy headwind over rough spinifex country before striking open plains. At last they arrived at Flora Valley Station, 175 kilometres east of Halls Creek, where Nat Buchanan's son, Gordon, gave them a great welcome. In the evening they took part in a cricket match with the book-keeper and the Aboriginal workers.

While Alex and Donald were making fairly good progress, there was a potential problem which threatened to end their ride. Not surprisingly, after crossing such rugged country, their tyres were badly ripped up. They were scheduled to get new covers in Derby, but that town was hundreds of kilometres away and they had little chance of reaching there with their tyres in shreds. They had to find a way to patch up the tyres or the ride was over.

The overlanders stayed at Flora Valley an extra day to try to fix their frayed tyres. Improvising, they got the Aboriginal workers to scrape the hairs off a thin piece of greenhide and then put it in soap until midday. After lunch they cut strips from it and stretched them round the tyres, lacing them tightly. By evening they were firm and dry. The repairs may not have met Dunlop's standards, but they seemed to do the job.

Departing Flora Valley on Sunday, 3 December, Donald soon found that his back tyre was leaking despite his repairs, and he had to stop to pump it up. After another twenty kilometres they came to a spring where water flowed out of black mud at the foot of a hill, but it was full of snakes. Pushing on six kilometres they struck another waterhole and saw a water snake lying asleep in the water with its head on the bank. Alex shot it, and retrieving the body discovered it was 3.6 metres long with a girth of about three-quarters of a metre.

Continuing on a hard track, they crossed a dry creek and followed the track up a ravine fringed with cabbage and pandanus palms before striking a garden owned by 'a patriarchal-looking old man' named Mr Williams, but more commonly known as 'Greenhide Jack'. The old man conducted them through a grove of banana trees to his humpy where they sheltered under the verandah from the burning sun. The garden, with a stream running through it, lay between two rocky hills. There, Greenhide Jack grew vegetables to supply Brockman and Halls Creek.

When the overlanders were refreshed, two of Greenhide Jack's workers showed them a shortcut towards Halls Creek through slate hills covered with spinifex grass. The track was excellent and led them to the Brockman Hotel, the first pub they had seen since they left Katherine a month earlier.

The overlanders enjoyed a lunch of strong tea, damper and bottled beer, feeling 'in good heart' as they left the hotel. But riding on a hard, ridgy track, Donald could hear his back tyre leaking even faster as the greenhide softened and flattened out. Soon the pair had no choice but to get off their bikes and walk. It started raining, the first drops in the area in six months, and they were wet through when on Monday, 4 December, they reached the top of a quartz-capped ridge with Halls Creek below.

'Although not an imposing spectacle, scattered along the bank of a dry creek, the town was a welcome sight, for leading a bicycle over those slatey ridges in the wet had a most depressing effect,' Donald recalled.

In the only street in town the duo entered the Kimberley Hotel where they were given a hearty reception by the proprietor, Mr Kodell, and offered drinks and new pyjamas. News of the cyclists' arrival soon spread and by tea-time they had been introduced to most of the townsfolk – a total population of eight bushwhackers – who gave them a smoke social. What they lacked in numbers they made up for with enthusiasm. While Arthur had found Halls Creek dull, Alex and Donald did not get to bed until 1.00am, after having 'a good time with songs, recitations – also many speeches'.

Once more the overlanders were in telegraphic communication with civilisation. Assuming Frank's role as telegram writer, Alex sent a wire which was published in the *West Australian*. 'The Halls Creek boys tendered us a smoke social last night, and gave us a good time. We are not in the best form. The tropical climate, heavy damper and corned beef are not too good for the best cycling form. We can make heavy damper with any bushman now. We leave here today for Derby. The first stage is 170 miles long. We will wire from Derby.'

But Alex and Donald had to solve their tyre problem before they could push on. All the rubber was practically worn off the tyres and the canvas was nearly finished too. The only thing they could find was a few yards of water-bag canvas and they spent an evening sewing it around the tyres. The patched-up articles looked all right, but whether they would cope with the harsh country remained to be seen.

With the wet season upon them, Alex and Donald left Halls Creek without delay at nine o'clock in the morning on Tuesday, 5 December. Between Halls Creek and the Fitzroy Crossing, 289 kilometres away, were numerous creeks, and if they rose the overlanders would be stranded. They departed with a load of provisions for which Mr Kodell refused to take any payment. All eight inhabitants of the town assembled at the hotel to give them three cheers as they rode away.

Despite the threat of rain, water was scarce on this stage across rough country, and Alex and Donald would dig in sand for it until their fingers bled. After five days riding and walking they reached the Margaret River and camped in the soft sand in the centre of its dry bed.

No sooner had they got to sleep than they were awakened by thunder, lightning and gusts of wind that blew sand over them, forcing them to take cover under a sandbank. Heavy rain began to fall, but they managed to light a fire-stick. The skies cleared by 3.00am and they dug until they reached dry sand to make a bed, sleeping until daylight.

The next day they crossed Morgans Grave Creek, which was running strongly, about four times as they traversed swampy country. Coming to a dry creek, they camped for the night, having rice and a stale johnnycake for tea.

A light rain started to fall as they nodded off to sleep, but they were used to that. Then it became heavy and they were awakened by water rushing down the creek. With the water swirling around them, they grabbed their bikes and belongings and scrambled to the opposite bank, sitting up for the rest of the night, 'wet and miserable'.

At daylight the duo boiled rice for breakfast and then walked on, the wet ground being too soft to ride on. Crossing the Louisa River, they passed the Black Hills and came on good hard running in open country. At last they struck the Fitzroy River, arriving at the telegraph station 'dead beat'.

'We were well received and had the pleasure of seeing a white woman once more,' Donald recalled. 'Men were repairing the house, the white ants having practically eaten it down ... About the station we saw some very big blacks, one in particular being 6 feet 5 inches, and barring his legs being a bit fine, he was built in proportion.'

After crossing the Fitzroy River the overlanders passed the police station before stopping at a hotel for refreshments. The locals showed much interest in the duo and made an interesting comparison between Donald and Arthur. 'While partaking of the good things of the table, I was much amused to hear some of them criticising myself,' Donald recalled. 'On several occasions I had been told that Arthur Richardson and myself were the two hardest-faced individuals that ever crossed the Territory. (Although much bigger than Richardson, I had been several times mistaken for him.)'

It is telling that the outback bushmen saw the same 'hard-faced' character traits in Arthur and Donald and mistook them for each other. Iron-willed personalities, they shared an unyielding determination to accomplish an extraordinary feat.

At two o'clock an Aboriginal man informed the overlanders that the river was flooding. This was serious. If they did not cross it near Derby before the flood reached there they would have to try to get across in rafts, which would be a dangerous undertaking, especially as Alex could not swim. They decided to make a start at once, intending to reach Quanbun Downs Station, just off the Fitzroy River Road, that night, but their tyres were giving them trouble and they lost the track, ending up camping in swampy country. 'Getting onto a dry patch, we camped, but had anything but a jolly time, as we each got bitten by a centipede,' Donald recalled. 'Although we rubbed in nicotine, the burning pain did not let us sleep much.'

In the clear light of morning, Alex and Donald could see Quanbun Downs homestead about one and a half kilometres away. They arrived at the house just in time for breakfast, a Javanese cook making them a cup of coffee. After breakfast, Aboriginal women washed their clothes, and the manager, Mr Ferris, provided them with a 'sheep bazil' to patch up their tyres.

It rained again that night, but they left the station at dawn to beat the rising waters. The black soil plain was so sticky they could not even walk their bikes and had to carry them on their backs for half a kilometre before they struck firmer ground. They were back on the track after midday, but Donald soon got a puncture. Reaching Noonkanbah Station, they spent the wet and windy evening mending the tyre.

Anxious to push on, they left at nine the next morning. The track was only walkable and they had travelled just seventeen kilometres when they stopped for lunch at Mount Abbott, 103 kilometres from Fitzroy Crossing. In the evening they struck a good, hard track and after collecting water at Troys Lagoon they camped for the night in open country.

It was too muddy to ride in the morning so they walked for a while before camping, filling their time with revolver practice, until, at eleven o'clock, they made another start. After crossing Snake Creek they got onto the Fourteen-Mile Plain. In the distance they could see a homestead on a knoll. It was Liveringa Station, managed by the McLarty brothers, John and William.

The overlanders got a good reception, enjoying refreshments while lounging on the verandah with a view of a winding billabong on a branch of the Fitzroy River beneath them. The McLartys ran 60,000 sheep on the station, about one hundred kilometres south-west of Derby, but hearing the river was coming down they had shifted them off the river country, which was a dire warning to the cyclists.

After lunch they headed for Mount Anderson Station, arriving at the homestead, built at the foot of the mountain, at dusk. The manager was away, but an old cook named Tweed gave them tea before showing them some fine skins of carpet and water snakes, one measuring four metres. The reptiles were plentiful in the area: another potential danger to be wary of while wading through rivers.

The next day they put more 'sheep bazil' on the tyres and set off for Yeeda Station, sixty-four kilometres away. The road to Yeeda was splendid in dry weather, but now it was 'one big swamp'. After crossing a mud flat they arrived at Yeeda homestead at four o'clock on Friday, 15 December. The station manager, Mr Clifford, made the cyclists feel at home. After tea the overlanders joined the athletic Clifford in weight-lifting and pole-jumping, but they were in poor form.

When they arrived in Derby the next day the overlanders had finished the most arduous and dangerous part of their journey. They had travelled 1448 kilometres from Katherine in forty-nine days, averaging fewer than thirty-two kilometres a day. It would have been with an enormous sense of relief that Alex and Donald checked into a hotel near the jetty. After lunch they went to see the shipping agents to find out whether a shipment of tyres had arrived by steamer from Fremantle. They were disappointed to learn the tyres had been taken by the S.S. *Adelaide* to Wyndham, but were heartened when told that the steamer was due to return the next day. That evening they walked up and down the only street in the town, listening to some of the locals singing.

By nightfall the following day there was still no sign of the steamer. Then, at 11.30pm, the hotel proprietor called Alex and Donald to tell them the steamer was approaching. They took a horse-drawn tramcar to the jetty, arriving at the same time as the steamer, and picked up the parcel of new tyres, which they fitted in the morning.

The townsfolk in Derby warned them that the road to Broome, crossing the estuary of the Fitzroy River, was certain to be flooded and there was no point continuing. But they had come too far and overcome too much to abandon the ride. If they could avoid the flood waters, the worst of the ride was behind them, but if they thought the rest of the journey would be easy, they could think again.

Australian cycling champion Ben Goodson was among those who welcomed Arthur when he arrived in Rockhampton.

Stage Fifteen

A Travel-stained Phiz
and a Sun-browned Paw

Arthur
Townsville to Adelaide
12 November 1899 to 5 January 1900

WITH a light heart, Arthur embarked on the easiest stage of the ride down the east coast of Australia. Departing Townsville on Sunday, 12 November, he camped at Reid River and started for Charters Towers at 7.00am the next day, arriving at one o'clock in the afternoon. He was met by a number of the North Queensland League of Wheelmen and hosted in the evening at Earl's White Horse Hotel where 'a glass of wine was partaken of and his health toasted'. The president of the league, Mr J.J. Connolly, briefly welcomed Arthur in 'a few well-chosen words'.

Arthur left Charters Towers at 7.00am on Tuesday, 14 November, and rode in a south-easterly direction through Cardigan Station, Harvest Home, Mount McConnell, Hidden Valley, Conway, Mount Lookout and Lake Elphinstone, reaching the small town of Nebo, one hundred kilometres south-west of Mackay, on Monday, 20 November.

Nebo had been named by the explorer William Landsborough after Nabu, the Babylonian god of wisdom and writing. So it was an appropriate place for Arthur to pen one of his telegrams, which was published by the *Western Mail* on 25 November. It sounded like he had had as much fun in Charters Towers as the White brothers and Mackay.

Leaving Charters Towers I found it a worse place to get out of than Georgetown. I am keeping upon high country and dodging the storms, and have been fairly lucky so far, only getting into two. Armstrong and Craig [who had accompanied Armstrong on the Croydon to Sydney leg of his ride], the first Australian overlanders, also had a bad time of it through here. At Townsville and the Towers the local cyclists saw that I had a good time and plenty of fun ... From here I shall travel via St Lawrence. There are no straight roads about here. You have to go three hundred miles to get over one hundred.

Notwithstanding the winding roads, Arthur made 'rapid progress' down the Queensland coast. At St Lawrence he wired Mr E.W. Sheehy, the honorary secretary of the League of Queensland Wheelmen, stating that if not delayed by a strong headwind or by rain he expected to reach Rockhampton that evening: Thursday, 23 November.

A party of cyclists left Messrs J. Howard and Co cycle agency in Rockhampton at five o'clock in the late afternoon and rode along the Yaamba Road to meet Arthur, but they returned without him, having got their timing wrong. One of the local cyclists may have been Ben Goodson, who had represented

Australia at the 1899 cycling world titles in Montreal three months earlier. Arthur rode into town unescorted at ten minutes to seven, but was given a tremendous reception.

'Here Mr Howard, the Rover agent, is looking after me, and is finding me a bike to ride while here, thus avoiding the alteration of my own machine,' Arthur wrote in a telegram which was published in the *Western Mail* on 2 December. 'At a smoke concert tendered me by the local cyclists, I spent a most enjoyable evening, and I also had a very pleasant day out with the Rockhampton Touring Club to the caves, a distance of about seventeen miles out. Then I put in a day at Mount Morgan, getting a good look through the mine, reduction plants etc. The bike and tyres are still well, and everyone remarks upon the splendid condition of both. I am leaving for Brisbane tomorrow, via Gladstone.'

The *Goulburn Herald* described Arthur as being 'in the pink of condition' when recording his arrival in Rockhampton. Interestingly, Arthur told the *Herald* that he had met the White brothers and Mackay in Powell Creek and that they were 'looking well and in good spirits', omitting the fact they had nearly died in the desert and were exhausted. It was typical of Arthur to downplay the dangers and deprivations of the ride, not just for himself, but for his rivals.

About forty cyclists and supporters attended the smoke social tendered by the Amateur Cyclists Union in honour of the 'visiting cyclists' Arthur, Ben Goodson and Donald Fraser, who had won a number of intercolonial handicap races, at the Commercial Hotel on Saturday, 25 November. The chairman of the Rockhampton Gymnasium and Cycling Club, Mr W. Mennie, presided over the proceedings, which were recorded by the *Morning Bulletin*:

After the toast of the Queen had been duly honoured, the
company singing the national anthem and 'Rule Britannia', the
chairman said they had met that night to extend a welcome to
the well-known cyclists Messrs Goodson, Fraser and Richardson.
He thought the toast of the visitors should have been entrusted
to abler hands than his, as he had only been called on at the last
moment to undertake it. He could assure them, however, that as
one of the oldest cyclists in Rockhampton nothing could give him
greater pleasure than welcoming the visitors.

The *Morning Bulletin* described the two competing rides around
Australia as 'probably the greatest long-distance cycling feat
ever undertaken', but singled out Arthur for special praise.

Supposing that the attempt is successfully carried out by both
parties, the performance of Richardson will be much superior
to that of the White brothers and Mackay from the fact that he
is riding alone and was the pioneer of the more difficult portions
of the journey ... How likely he was to meet with accident or
illness one can easily imagine and therefore it is very gratifying to
know that his somewhat foolhardy feat is practically over so far as
personal danger is concerned.

After resting in Rockhampton for several days, Arthur expressed
a great desire to stay longer, but he reluctantly departed from
the post office at 9.30am on Tuesday, 28 November. A large
number of spectators who had gathered to witness his departure
loudly cheered him. He was accompanied out of town along the
Gladstone Road for about five kilometres by a prominent local
cyclist, J. Howard. Then, heading towards Brisbane, he was
alone again, which was probably just the way he liked it.

Arthur knew he had the White brothers and Mackay beaten as long as nothing went seriously wrong, and his confidence was reflected in an article in the *Gympie Times and Mary River Mining Gazette*. 'A cyclist named Richardson arrived at Gympie on Saturday on his tour round Australia, having started from Perth about five months ago,' the newspaper reported on 5 December. 'He has travelled via the Northern Territory and north Queensland, and proceeded south on his journey on Sunday. Other cyclists have started on the trip round Australia, but Richardson considers he will arrive at Perth before the others complete their journeys, and so be able to claim the honour of having been the first to ride round Australia on a bicycle.'

Arthur departed Gympie at 6.00am on Sunday, 3 December. He intended to arrive in Brisbane the following day, sending a wire from Landsborough, where he slept overnight, saying he would likely reach the city around 4.00pm.

The imminent arrival of the overlander 'excited an immense amount of interest' in Brisbane and a party of local cyclists set out 'in the face of threatening weather' to escort him into town. At Bald Hills, north of Brisbane, the cyclists noticed a lone rider, but dismissed him as being Arthur, because 'tidily attired and clean shaven' he did not look like someone who had 'faced the dangers of darkest Australia alone'. But as Arthur rode past the cyclists, there was something about him which 'impelled a query'. After discovering the rider was in fact Arthur, the local cyclists, perhaps a little embarrassed, accompanied him to Brisbane where he was 'put up' at O'Connor's Hotel in Fortitude Valley.

What was it about Arthur that 'impelled a query'? Was it his quiet determination? His indomitable will? A certain look in his eyes? Maybe it was charisma or aura. Whatever, it was almost instantly recognisable, the essence of Arthur.

The *Queenslander* published an article about Arthur in which he claimed the dangers of the ride had been exaggerated, perhaps withholding the most interesting detail for his own account to be published after the ride.

It was not long before a representative of this journal was on the scene and on entering the office of the Dunlop Tyre Company was introduced to a sunburned young man of wiry frame and light build, who turned from a basin in which he was washing himself and smiled a greeting from a halo of soap and water. Having completed his toilet, Arthur Richardson sat down in a resigned manner, showing that since he struck civilisation he has been thoroughly broken into the ways of the interviewer ...

Questioned about some of the reports which have been published of his adventures, Richardson denies their veracity. The country in the parts under notice was full of natives, who were usually to be found in camps not exceeding fifty. Many of these would follow him at a distance in the hopes of making a treacherous rush, but he relied upon a Colt's revolver which he carried and no actual brush ever took place. Speaking at this point of the sufferings endured by other overlanders, Richardson attributed much of it to their lack of bush knowledge, and with the air of one thoroughly familiar with the desert in all its phases, he declares that when they have thought themselves suffering most they have really not been so very bad off.

If Arthur was referring to the White brothers and Mackay, it is interesting that he was critical of his fellow overlanders, perhaps suggesting he never really considered the trio as serious competition.

Arthur had no intention of hurrying on the downward journey to Sydney, where he hoped to spend Christmas. From Brisbane he rode 125 kilometres west to Toowoomba, situated on the crest of the Great Dividing Range in the rich farming and grazing land of the Darling Downs. On Friday, 8 December, he was met at Helidon in the Lockyer Valley, twenty kilometres east of Toowoomba, by several members of the local branch of the League of Wheelmen and escorted into town.

The Toowoomba cyclists gave Arthur a smoke social that evening. 'There was in attendance of between fifty and sixty cyclists, which was indeed a splendid roll-up, considering the short notice given,' the *Darling Downs Gazette* reported on 11 December. 'The mayor took the chair at eight o'clock, and in proposing the health of Mr Richardson said it gave him great pleasure to be present there that evening as an old athlete to welcome a gentleman who was undertaking one of the most difficult rides ever attempted by a cyclist. He asked the company to drink to the health of the guest of the evening.'

In his toast, the mayor revealed that the around Australia ride had been suggested to the overlander by the Toowoomba bicycle manufacturer Mr Thomas Trevethan when they met on the Western Australian goldfields several years earlier, and that the overlander had considered riding one of his famous 'T' cycles.

According to the *Gazette*, 'Mr Richardson briefly replied and in doing so said that, with the exception of Rockhampton, he thought that Toowoomba had the most up-to-date cycle union of any place he had seen on his travels.' Arthur's characteristically brief response marked him as a man of few words. He was a doer, not a talker.

Leaving Toowoomba at seven o'clock on Sunday, 10 December, Arthur arrived in Warwick, situated on the banks of the Condamine River in the southern Darling Downs, at midday, after two Toowoomba cyclists had accompanied him for thirty-two kilometres as far as the rural town of Greenmount, where the author Steele Rudd had lived as a boy and attended the local Emu Creek school until the age of twelve. It was in 1899, while Arthur and the other overlanders were riding around Australia, that the *Bulletin* published an illustrated collection of Rudd's stories under the title *On Our Selection*, featuring the hilarious adventures of Dad and Dave from Snake Gully, which were also developed into an enormously popular radio show and became an icon of Australian culture.

For one of the only times on the ride, Arthur did not receive an escort into town by local cyclists when he arrived unannounced at Warwick. The oversight seemed to embarrass the local press. 'Richardson would no doubt have had a good reception from Warwick cyclists had they known when he was likely to arrive,' the *Warwick Examiner* reported on 13 December.

In Toowoomba the cyclists gave him a glorious time. He says they are building a track in Toowoomba which will be the best in Queensland and similar in every way to that on the Adelaide Oval. He expects to see Toowoomba the centre of Queensland bike racing. He speaks well of the roads in Queensland; those on the Downs he admires for they are lively and consequently no trouble to push a bike over.

The overlander was accompanied by W. Sterne out some miles onto the Stanthorpe road in order to clear the by-roads. Richardson expected to make Stanthorpe that evening. He is not bursting himself over the journey, and looks forward to some pleasant recreation in Sydney at Christmas and Melbourne at New Year.

The fact Arthur was not 'bursting himself' indicated he was growing ever more confident of completing his journey before the White brothers and Mackay and was not particularly concerned if they lowered his record or not. The only thing that mattered was finishing first. He may have also felt that the White party could not justifiably lay claim to his record because they did not ride alone. Or perhaps completing the ride in one piece had become his main priority.

From Stanthorpe, Arthur rode across the New England Tableland, the largest highland area in Australia, on his way to Armidale in New South Wales, arriving on Wednesday, 13 December, wet and weary after crossing the hilly country in driving rain. 'From Wallangarra to Deepwater it rained nearly all afternoon,' Arthur wrote in a telegram published in the *Western Mail* on 23 December.

> I arrived there very wet at 7.30 at night. I rode via Glen Innes to Guyra, the roads being soft and heavy and very hilly. It rained again all the afternoon, so I only did sixty miles, leaving at about 6.30 this morning and dodged the wet as far as Armidale. It is raining now and does not look too good. There are several very bad hills about here, having to walk both up and down. It was here that Denning had his smash. If the rain continues I do not think I shall be able to get to Melbourne for Christmas. The roads are getting heavy. The machine and tyres are all right.

The smash that Arthur referred to was an accident involving the overlander Jack Denning who had attempted to lower the Perth to Brisbane record in 1898, racing against Frank during Frank's epic ride from Perth to Rockhampton and back. Jack Denning had departed from Perth the day after Frank and the two passed and repassed each other en route to Brisbane. After leaving Armidale in the lead, Denning had gone several kilometres when he ran into an open drain which lay across the road at the bottom of a hill. He did not see it until it was too late. The front wheel, handles and fork of his bicycle were damaged, while Denning had a nasty fall, resulting in concussion. A passing farmer saw him lying unconscious in the drain, picked him up and brought him back to town. After remaining in medical care for four days while his bicycle was repaired, Denning resumed his ride, which he completed in fifty-eight days, two days inside William Virgin's time, but five days behind Frank's. Even though the remainder of Arthur's ride was meant to be relatively straightforward, the memory of Denning's mishap would have cautioned him against over-confidence.

On Saturday, 16 December, Arthur sent a wire from Wisemans Ferry, a small settlement on the Hawkesbury River, to Mr C.A. Grocott, the honorary secretary of the Sydney Bicycle Club, informing him that he would be arriving in the city the following day. Keen to recognise Arthur's 'sterling performance', Mr Grocott made arrangements for club members to meet him on the road and escort him into town.

Wearing a brown sweater, blue serge knickers and a soft white hat, Arthur got away at 6.30am and was met forty-eight kilometres from Sydney, near Windsor, by Mr Stan Lough of the Dunlop Tyre Company. As the pair neared Parramatta, the second oldest settlement in Australia, twenty-three kilometres west of Sydney, they were met by a large body of cyclists, representing the leading Sydney clubs.

The welcoming party included none other than a generous-hearted Frank, who, after breaking down at Pine Creek, rode a horse 225 kilometres to Port Darwin where he took the steamer *Guthrie* to Sydney. If Arthur was surprised to see Frank in Sydney, he did not mention it. Given that Percy Armstrong was keeping a close eye on the White party and the extensive press coverage of the rides, it is almost certain Arthur would have been aware that Frank had withdrawn from the journey. And it is also probable that Arthur knew Frank would be in Sydney when he arrived. No doubt Arthur offered Frank his commiserations for having to drop out of the ride. Perhaps the thought even crossed Arthur's mind that it was ironic that Frank, having tried to talk Arthur out of continuing from Powell Creek, was the one who was no longer in the race.

On his arrival in Sydney, Frank had reported to the Sydney Bicycle Club where he was again warmly welcomed and offered sympathy for his bad luck. As Donald was a member of the club, Frank had answered a 'fusillade' of questions about the welfare of Donald and Alex. Frank had assured the concerned club members that when he 'bade them adieu' they had been in 'splendid fettle'. As promised, Frank brought back trophies of his travels, including spears, boomerangs, waddies, stuffed crocodiles and even Aboriginal skulls, which were put on exhibition in the club's rooms. Souvenir collecting like this may seem a trifle eccentric and even disrespectful today, but it was not unusual in colonial times.

Arthur and his impressive escort stopped at the White Horse Hotel in Parramatta for lunch and at three o'clock made a start for the city. Near Clyde, a large number of League of Wheelmen riders joined in as did a second detachment of the Sydney Bicycle Club so that by the time they reached Homebush the party numbered about one hundred. At Homebush they stopped for refreshments and Arthur was formally welcomed to Sydney by the veteran rider Joe Pearson, who heartily complimented him on the success of his 'almost stupendous' undertaking.

Reaching the paddocks of Flemington, the order 'Two deep' was given and this formation was maintained right into the city. The procession of one hundred or so cyclists rode down George Street through Martin Place, reaching the landmark General Post Office, 'the finest example of the Victorian Italian Renaissance style in New South Wales', at about five o'clock. According to the *Sydney Morning Herald*, Arthur looked in good health. 'On Sunday afternoon Arthur Richardson, who is travelling around Australia, arrived in Sydney, looking none the worse for the hardships he has had to contend with during his long ride,' the newspaper reported on 21 December. 'Richardson, to look at, seems to be just the sort of man to successfully carry out such an undertaking as that of riding around Australia.'

After all the early doubts about Arthur's physique and stamina, people at last thought he looked the part, possibly because he was in such good condition after the relatively easy ride down the coast. 'I enjoyed fine weather, fairly good roads and magnificent scenery,' he recalled. 'Everywhere I met with a great reception and enjoyed myself immensely.'

Arthur was given three cheers before riding on to the Sydney Bicycle Club rooms in Elizabeth Street where he was feted after the 'stains of travel had been removed'. Mr William Rufus George, the club president and 'Father of Australian Cycling', proposed a toast to Arthur, admitting that when he had heard months earlier that a cyclist planned to ride alone around

Australia he was 'astounded at the apparent want of sense displayed'. But Mr George had changed his mind about Arthur. The dangers of the trip were many, but Arthur had got over the worst part of the journey. The remaining 3200 kilometres to Perth would be 'child's play' by comparison. Mr George also warmly welcomed Frank, saying it was unfortunate that through no fault of his own he had had to return to Sydney when he had half completed his journey.

Arthur briefly responded, saying he was a man of few words, but could not let the opportunity pass of stating that his reception in Sydney had been by far the warmest he had yet experienced. He thanked the club members for their welcome.

Frank also acknowledged the toast, saying that after some days with the Sydney club he had 'given up regretting breaking down on the road' and leaving Alex and Donald, who were now making their way along the Western Australian coast. He anticipated meeting them in Perth and on the way back to Melbourne would try to secure the record that was held by Jack Denning, boasting it would be 'easy to get'.

If Arthur had been as loquacious as Frank, he could have held the club's attention for hours, spinning yarns, but that was not him. A journalist covering the function for the *Australian Cyclist* observed that Arthur 'is a naturally retiring sort of man and is not inclined to talk much about his solitary ride. He states, however, that the difficulties of the undertaking are not nearly so great as would be imagined.

'The main disadvantage of the trip, he says, is lack of incident. There is nothing much to be seen of interest to the traveller, the succeeding day's travelling being only a repetition of the previous one ... Coming south he bitterly complained of being repeatedly put on the wrong road. On one occasion he had to cross a range of mountains on foot, dragging his bicycle with him, to reach the proper road.'

Arthur, like Frank, made the Sydney Bicycle Club his headquarters during his stay in Sydney. The two would have had much to talk about, perhaps over an oyster dinner. Frank would have been curious as to how Arthur managed to cross the Barkly Tableland on his own, while Arthur would have wanted to know how Frank felt about giving up his dream.

On Tuesday, 19 December, Arthur departed Sydney with Frank and two other Western Australian cyclists, Bert Brown and Wattie Green, a colourful trio to be sure, who rode with him to Melbourne where he now hoped to spend Christmas. Having covered this route three times already, Frank would have been in a position to offer Arthur valuable information about the track, although as Alex and Donald would later discover, Frank's intelligence was not always reliable.

Bushfires were raging in the ranges near Wooragee in north-east Victoria, burning three people to death and destroying thirty homes, but Arthur and his party managed to arrive in Melbourne on Christmas Eve, which was the best present Arthur could have wished for.

'We four did the tour together from Sydney via Mittagong, Goulburn, Albury and Euroa,' Arthur wrote in a telegram from Melbourne which was published in the *Sun* in Kalgoorlie on 31 December. 'From Albury to Melbourne it was very hot with north winds and bushfires, which were in places right across the road, making riding out of the question on Saturday and leaving one hundred miles with headwinds on Sunday to Melbourne. Mr Mather of the Dunlop Tyre Co. met me with a tandem about fifteen miles out. I am leaving this afternoon for Adelaide. The machine is all right.'

While in Melbourne, Arthur gave a newspaper interview in which he revealed he was thinking about fighting in the Boer War in South Africa when he completed his ride. The war between the British Empire and the Boer republics of the Orange Free State and the Transvaal had broken out in October 1899 after decades of simmering tension. The Australian colonies offered troops, and many men, including Arthur, were keen to do their bit for the Empire.

'Overlander A. Richardson, who is now speeding his way over the last section of his ride around Australia ... was interviewed in Melbourne, and in answer to the question as to his intentions after his ride had been accomplished, he said: "Well, you know what everybody is thinking about just now,"' the *Queenslander* reported on 20 January 1900.

'I've seen Australia, and I feel sure there's a good deal more to be seen in Africa, and something to be done too. What I mean is this: I can go anywhere a horse can go, and beat a horse on a week's journey – easily. I can do that and make a certainty of it, taking no risk at all. Now there must be a great call for express work in Africa at the present time, and it is in my mind that I could be of service there. And see a new phase of life – one which has attractions for every man whose blood runs red in his veins. So, though I've made no plans, I keep thinking about South Africa.'

Arthur enjoyed Christmas in Melbourne. 'The passing of Arthur Richardson around Australia is almost completed and just now the intrepid circumcontinenter is enjoying the Christmas festivities and warm welcome of marvellous Melbourne,' the *Quiz and Lantern* reported on 28 December.

'Pass on, Arthur, we are all anxious to see your travel-stained phiz and shake your sun-browned paw.'

After spending four days in Melbourne Arthur set off for Adelaide, but he was delayed in Kingston, 294 kilometres south-east of the South Australian capital, because he was unwell. Eventually he was met at Aldgate in the Adelaide Hills, twenty-one kilometres south-east of Adelaide, by members of the North Adelaide Bicycle Club and his brother Gus, who had come over from Western Australia. He rode into his boyhood home at 11.55am on Friday, 5 January.

South Australia adopted Arthur, who had been educated in Adelaide and was a member of the North Adelaide Cycling Club as well as the South Australian militia, as one of their own. It was in Adelaide that Arthur enjoyed his biggest public reception so far. Hearty cheers were given as he rode down King William Street to the General Post Office where a large crowd had assembled to welcome him 'home'.

'After some seven months of hard riding through and over almost inaccessible country, Arthur Richardson has at last reached Adelaide,' the *Quiz and Lantern* reported on 11 January. 'His sunburned features and spare, wiry frame speak for themselves, but unfortunately wheelmen on the other side of the world will hardly appreciate the stupendous nature of the ride, which can fairly be said to rank as one of the most famous rides in the world's history of cycling.'

Given a 'cordial reception' at the General Post Office, Arthur was immediately escorted to the South Australian Club Hotel where he was formally welcomed at a function arranged by the Dunlop Tyre Company and the cycle agency Messrs A.W. Dobbie & Co, which put his Beeston Humber on view at its warehouse in Gawler Place.

A large company, which included officials of the League of Wheelmen and the North Adelaide Bicycle Club as well as prominent citizens and enthusiasts, assembled to honour Arthur at the gathering, which was presided over by the South Australian premier Frederick Holder, soon to become the first speaker of the Australian House of Representatives when federation was achieved in 1901. As minister in charge of the Northern Territory, Holder had made an extensive journey by camel in 1895 beyond the MacDonnell Ranges, so he had some appreciation of the terrain Arthur had traversed.

Holder said he had been very pleased to accept an invitation to the reception to honour Arthur. The continent had been encircled by a wave of patriotism, he said, which showed that Australians were willing to share the responsibilities as well as the glories of Empire. According to the *Adelaide Observer*, Arthur had proved that he possessed all the 'pluck and endurance which characterised the British race. It required courage to face the Boers in battle, and it also required courage to carry out the remarkable journey of cycling round Australia. Hostile blacks, scarcity of water and many other dangers lurked in the path which Arthur had nearly completed, but he was pleased that he had gone through so far and hoped he would finish as well as he looked then.'

The premier's laudatory comments about Arthur were supported by the president of the North Adelaide Bicycle Club, Mr G.M. Evan, who suggested the cyclist's 'pluck and endurance' might be better used to fight the Boers in South Africa.

'The Duke of Wellington was reported to have said that the Battle of Waterloo had been won on the cricket fields of Eton and Harrow, and though he could not say that such a remark was really made, he knew that amongst those who were fighting in the Transvaal just now were many who would fight the better because they had been prominent in pastimes calling for pluck and endurance,' Mr Evan said. 'They fight the harder and are gamer for it.'

After the chairman of the League of Wheelmen, Mr J.R. Anderson, also congratulated Arthur upon his performance and the toast was enthusiastically drunk, the overlander, in characteristic fashion, responded briefly. He was glad to be back in Adelaide 'amongst his old club mates and pleasing associations'.

The North Adelaide Cycling Club put on a smoke social for their club mate Arthur, which was also attended by his brother Gus. The 'Green and Golds' assembled in their rooms in force to give Arthur a hearty welcome. 'This is the last part of the trip, and I am meeting old friends at every turn,' Arthur wrote in a telegram which was published in the *Western Mail* on 6 January.

With Arthur's strong personal connection to Adelaide, South Australians were naturally hopeful he would join one of their contingents if he decided to go to the Boer War, but he kept his options open. Nevertheless, his Adelaide friends were keen to assist him if and when he went to South Africa. A gentleman named Mr W.J. Powell, writing on an Advertiser, Chronicle and Express Offices letterhead, gave Arthur a letter of introduction to the war correspondent Mr W.J. Lambie, asking him to provide the overlander with any assistance.

Dear Lambie,

This will introduce to you Mr Arthur Richardson, a gentleman who has now nearly completed a bicycle tour right around Australia. The magnitude of this task you will understand as readily as I do. Utterly fearless, a thorough bushman — and all that that means, and a perfect gentleman withal, you will find him a most desirable friend and should you be able to render him any assistance by giving him any information you would be rendering me a great favour.

Mr Richardson has not joined himself to our second contingent for he prefers to have a free hand and if he does not do something startling with his bike before he leaves Africa I shall be surprised. Cecil Rhodes is not the only man who has vision. Kindly convey to our boys my appreciation of their effort and accept my best wishes for your personal safety.

Good luck.

W.J. Powell.

Unfortunately, Lambie never had an opportunity to provide Arthur with any assistance. He would be shot dead by Boers a month later.

After four days rest and recreation in Adelaide, Arthur intended to leave at eight o'clock in the morning of Tuesday, 9 January, but his departure was delayed until after three o'clock in the afternoon, following a lunch at the Globe Hotel where he was entertained by friends who 'wished him every success in his hot and weary journey over the big bight'.

Arthur's ride was being described as the 'climax of cycling journeys in Australia', but there were two cyclists pedalling down the north-west coast of Western Australia who were yet to concede that point.

A Group of Overlanders.

(SEE LETTERPRESS).

Mr. P. W. ARMSTRONG.   Mr. A. W. B. MATHER.
Mr. ARTHUR RICHARDSON.   Mr. FRANK WHITE.

This quartet of overlanders – Arthur Richardson, Percy Armstrong, Alfred Mather and Frank White – was photographed in Perth shortly before Arthur and Frank set off in different directions to become the first to ride around Australia.

Stage Sixteen

Miracles Do Happen

White brothers and Donald
Derby to New Norcia
19 December 1899 to 4 February 1900

STORM clouds darkened the sky as Alex and Donald prepared to leave Derby on Tuesday, 19 December. After a round of drinks and good wishes they set off at 2.30pm, doubling back down to Yeeda Station. The mud flat had dried considerably, but the road was still sticky. Alex's back tyre was leaking and he also had trouble with his chain, slowing them down. When they arrived at the homestead at eight o'clock the manager, Mr Clifford, told them he was leaving early in the morning to move some sheep because the Fitzroy River was about to flood. Mr Clifford doubted the overlanders would be able to cross the river, but he left instructions with the cook to provide them with provisions and to assist them across if the river was down.

Setting off again at nine-thirty the next morning, Alex and Donald passed hundreds of kangaroos and emus on their way to the river and were relieved to find they had arrived just in time.

The river was not yet flooded, but as they waded across they noticed big pools of water beginning to ripple, which signalled it was about to. Ascending the opposite bank, they followed the river downstream about half a kilometre until they struck the telegraph line and found the pad. By two o'clock, hot and thirsty, they reached the Logue River, a dry, sandy watercourse with stunted scrub and a couple of boab trees on its banks. On one of the boab trees, the last they saw on the ride, they noticed Arthur's initials, a reassuring signpost.

Unable to find water, they decided to push on to the next well, Nibubra, twenty-three kilometres ahead. At dusk, there was no sign of the well and the cyclists worried they had missed the turn-off. They were wondering what they should do when they saw an Aboriginal man in the distance. As he came towards them they gripped their revolvers in case he was hostile, but relaxed when they realised he had only peaceful intentions. The man led the overlanders to the well, and after quenching their thirst they gave him some tobacco and set up camp for the night.

Although feeling 'none too fresh', the overlanders made an early start the next morning, struggling through bluebush and high tussock grass. Arthur had told them that he had been able to ride most of the country between the Fitzroy River and Condon as the winter rain had set the sand, but now the sand was dry and powdery, known as 'powder and puff'. To make matters worse, a herd of horses had stirred up the pad, making it unrideable, which meant that Alex and Donald faced a long walk in intense heat, pushing their bikes through the sand.

If the heat and sand were not enough to contend with, the overlanders' clothes now started to chafe them, rubbing painfully against their skin, which made walking difficult.

Reaching a well, they drank a couple of quarts of 'clear, cool water' before finding shade under a huge creeper that had grown over two stunted trees.

At five o'clock the duo reluctantly left this 'haven of rest' and arrived at Taylors Lagoon, 125 kilometres east of Roebuck Plains Station, in a shower of rain at dusk. They camped for the night, Donald cooking the johnnycakes for tea as Alex had barcoo rot, an ulcerous skin condition, on his hands.

After a breakfast of rice and flapjacks, they pushed on, following the telegraph line along cattle tracks, of which only patches were rideable. As evening fell they came to a camp, where a party of well-sinkers made them feel welcome, and stayed the night.

The next morning they followed the well-sinkers' tracks and had an excellent run across a small plain to the Roebuck Plains Station, forty kilometres south of Broome. The manager, Mr Banks, provided them with new pyjamas and asked Aboriginal women to wash their clothes, while a playful parakeet kept them entertained. 'During meals I was much taken with a pet parakeet they had, with dark blue head and red and yellow body,' Donald recalled. 'He sat on the table and, if taken no notice of, helped himself from anyone's plate. When out on the verandah, he would come up and lie on his back to be tickled. When ordered to clear out, the parakeet flew into a tree close by, and next morning awoke me just at daybreak by pulling out a few stray hairs on the back of my neck.'

Alex and Donald departed the next morning at seven o'clock. The track to Broome was good, but when they reached the branch-line heading south, it all but disappeared. After about three kilometres Alex was feeling sick and had to lie down, ghostly white and drenched in sweat. There was nothing on the desolate plain but telegraph posts. Tying their mosquito nets together, Donald fixed them between a post and the bikes to shelter Alex from the burning sun. Alex dozed for an hour and then doggedly pushed on. At lunch-time they reached Thangoo Station, where the manager, Mr Roe, gave them a hearty welcome and refreshments.

Departing at nine in the morning, the overlanders rode across bumpy plains before striking heavy sand near the beach. After trudging through the sand for about a kilometre, Donald noticed he had lost his cyclometer, which had often helped them to find a turn-off pad to water. Alex suggested they push on, but Donald would not leave without it and retraced their steps. Inspecting every piece of scrub, he eventually found it in a stunted bush.

After reattaching the cyclometer, they headed off again, reaching Yardica Well, about sixty-four kilometres from Lagrange Bay, at sunset. Noticing smoke nearby, they went to inspect and came across three miners heading to Mount Broome in the King Leopold Ranges. The generous miners invited the duo to their camp to share their tucker and gave them an old tent to sleep on.

Well rested, the overlanders made an early start in the morning. It was 24 December, but they were feeling anything but festive. The heat was oppressive. Their leaky water cans were empty and they began a desperate search for water on the sandy track. Covered in sweat and sea salt, they followed some low cliffs overlooking the Indian Ocean, leading the bikes with difficulty through thick scrub. With no water in any of the rock holes or basins they passed, they eventually came to a white sand patch. Donald was exhausted and lay down under a small bush for half an hour, but eventually thirst drove them on.

After trudging through ankle-deep sand 'hot enough to shrivel up the soles of one's shoes' they arrived at Lora Well where they had a good drink and boiled some rice. Naturally, they were anxious to reach a homestead or a telegraph station to celebrate Christmas in some comfort. The miners they met the previous night had told them that after leaving Lora Well and crossing a sandhill they would strike a good run to Marshall's Station, fourteen kilometres ahead.

They pushed on, but at dusk they were still in the bush with no homestead in sight. So on Christmas Eve they camped on a sandhill about thirty kilometres north of Lagrange Bay and were so hungry and thirsty they could not sleep.

In the morning they dubiously wished each other a merry Christmas, 'or, more truly speaking, wishing ourselves back at home!' Donald added. They may even have felt like exclaiming 'Bah humbug!' as they continued along the sandy track, eventually coming to Marshall's Well, where they refreshed themselves with a drink of water and a cup of tea before heading off again. 'We had a drink and a wash, and seeing his house about a mile away, went across and found another Marshall, who was also having anything but a Happy Christmas ... he was nearly dead with one of the worst legs I have ever seen,' Donald recalled.

But at last things started looking up. Late in the morning Alex and Donald reached Lagrange Bay, 200 kilometres south of Broome. After a shower at the telegraph station, they joined the telegraph operator and some linesmen, who were 'good fellows', in their Christmas celebrations. 'They were much surprised, but seemed equally pleased to see us so we located for Christmas,' Donald recalled. 'Although most of our friends were down with influenza, we had a fine time. First a shower bath, grog ad lib; also eatables; and we finished up by having a musical evening, turning in at 1.00am.'

While Alex and Donald had expected to pass through Lagrange Bay two or three months earlier, at least they were now closing in on Perth, with the most dangerous part of their journey behind them. On Boxing Day morning they mended their leaky water cans, and after refreshments departed the telegraph station at 10.00am. After good riding on a big plain, they entered the pindan region, the red soil country of the south-western Kimberley.

The following day they came to Eighty Mile Beach, which actually extends along 220 kilometres of coastline between Port Hedland and Broome where the Great Sandy Desert meets the sea. 'The beach is a fine sight,' Donald recalled. 'The water must have been out fully two miles, the beach gradually sloping from the high sandhills to the water.'

The overlanders were told by a bushman they met approaching the beach that the sand on the track up ahead was terrible and they would be better off riding on the beach. Walking out about a kilometre, they struck a hard patch of sand and started to ride. But they were riding into a southerly wind, which turned into a gale, preventing them from advancing more than one hundred metres at a time.

Eventually, the wind forced them to dismount. Walking along the beach, Alex and Donald picked up many beautiful seashells, while thousands of seabirds flew above them. How they must have wished they could just spread their wings and fly over this harsh terrain.

After twenty-five kilometres the tide started to come in so they decided to cut across the sandhills and find the pad so they could locate a well to camp at that night. On a loamy 'powderpuff' plain, potted with 'millions' of de Rougemont's rat holes, they sank into the sand halfway up to their knees, struggling forward as best they could.

At dusk they struck a well and set up camp, using twigs from an Aboriginal mia-mia to light a fire. 'As soon as we lay down the rats came all round,' Donald recalled. 'By morning they had eaten our tucker bags, leaving us only the tea and one johnnycake.'

Alex and Donald headed off at six o'clock and arrived at Wallal telegraph station, about 380 kilometres south of Broome, after a 'hot and trying ride' over some big sandhills, in time for a late breakfast, refreshing themselves with watermelons from a garden.

Leaving Wallal at four-thirty in the afternoon, they rode on a good, level track for a few kilometres before ascending what was known as the Red Sandhill, which was a 'heavy trudge'. At dusk they reached Hall and Hesters Well and camped in a deserted bush shanty. During the night they were visited by a fox terrier, which must have reminded Donald of his own faithful dogs and maybe made him feel a little homesick. He gave the stray dog some bread, but it did not stay.

In the morning the duo ran into Mr Hall with a wagon two kilometres from the well. He told the cyclists that he and Mr Hester were building a new homestead about a kilometre ahead and had set up camp there. When they pulled up at the camp, Mr Hester ordered some Aboriginal women to cook the duo some meat and make damper for them. They pushed on after lunch, Mr Hall warning them to expect plenty of sand on the track to Condon.

The old bushman was not exaggerating. The following day the overlanders struck a thirty-kilometre 'solid patch of sand', which had seen a lot of recent traffic. 'It was about the hardest work we ever had,' Alex recalled. To add to their woes, they found their knickerbockers chafing to an 'unbearable' extent. Taking them off, they wrapped mosquito nets, which they had bought in Port Darwin, around themselves like kilts, which reduced their discomfort.

The overlanders spent New Year's Eve camping at a well on this deserted, sandy track, their New Year's resolution probably never to ride a bicycle around Australia again. It was 'hot and clear as usual' when they welcomed in the New Year in the morning and after having damper for breakfast they pushed on into the twentieth century. Leaving the main track, they followed a pad back to the coast and at dusk they arrived at Coolon Station where they were 'treated splendidly'.

The next day they reached Condon on the estuary of the De Grey River, 600 kilometres south of Derby, after travelling across heavy plain country. They felt 'a load off our minds' when they pulled up at Hadley's Hotel where they 'washed down the sand' with shandies.

'This run from Derby had proved a veritable hell on earth for bikes,' Donald recalled. 'Many days, from daylight to dark, we had only been able to do about twenty miles. Two miles an hour was excellent travelling. We had to drag the bikes through the sand in intense heat with no shade to rest under. The leaves of the most luxuriant tree could have been shot off with a pea rifle in ten minutes.'

After their refreshments Alex and Donald went to the store to do some shopping as their knickerbockers were practically worn out. All they could find were khaki pants, which they cut down, to go with new white shirts. After tea they rode to the post office, about a kilometre away, to have their books signed.

When they left at seven-thirty the next morning, Hadley, the hotel proprietor, refused to accept any payment for their board.

The overlanders were glad they had new clothes when they arrived at De Grey Station at the mouth of the De Grey River in the Pilbara, where Alexander Forrest had begun his historic 1879 expedition across the Kimberley to Port Darwin, for the station manager's wife was a 'most charming lady', who made them feel welcome. 'If only we had coats, we would have been contented to remain for all time!' Donald recalled. With the temperature soaring to 113 degrees, they greatly appreciated a cold beer on the shaded verandah of the brick homestead, 'one of the finest stations in the north-west'. At six o'clock they went down to the river for a swim. They were joined by several Aboriginal children, who, 'although only about two feet high', could give the overlanders a start and beat them.

They left early the next morning, Friday, 5 January, and the road improved until they reached the De Grey River, which they waded across while Aboriginal stockmen carried their bicycles. On the other side of the river the sand was worse than before. They were followed by a 'big mob of blacks' who were curious to see them ride their bikes.

Passing the branch track to Port Hedland, they arrived at Pippingarra Station, twenty-four kilometres away, at 12.15pm. The station manager, Mr Leach, was a former Perth cyclist and had met Alex before. He gave the overlanders a 'good time' and they soon felt recovered from their morning's toil.

Donald noticed that the Aboriginal workers looked 'very dejected' and Mr Leach explained they had just buried a young Aboriginal girl. 'The west coast blacks bury in the ground, sleep near the corpse, cover their heads with white feathers, cut their heads and bodies with glass, and become what is known as *tage*,' Donald recalled. 'They do not eat meat for six months.'

The duo departed at five o'clock, filling up their water cans at a well where the track crossed the Port Hedland–Marble Bar road. Crossing the wide, dry bed of the Yule River, the overlanders rode and walked over more sand and scrub, eventually reaching Mundabullangana homestead, built by stonemasons from Skye in Scotland and one of the 'best-equipped' they had seen on the ride. The owners, the Mackays (no relation to Donald), were escaping the summer heat in cooler southern climes, but the station manager, Mr Roberts, provided the overlanders with a shower bath, washed their clothes and laid on a 'sumptuous repast' before they pushed on again at four-thirty. With the ocean in view on their right they camped for the night on a soft patch of sand.

The next morning they rode along a sandy track to the port of Balla Balla, where they stopped for a bath and lunch, gazing across the mangroves to volcanic Depuch Island. After Balla Balla the road improved on the way to the Five-mile Well, but from there to Sherlock Station it became heavy again, although the duo still managed to do a lot of riding, the last ten kilometres in moonlight.

Making an early start in the morning, they had a good run through pretty, undulating country, reaching Roebourne at ten-thirty on Tuesday, 9 January. They spent the day in Roebourne having new shoes and water bags made. In the evening the locals gave them a smoke social and Donald made a speech. An hour later the government resident turned up and Donald had to give a second speech, which he found more tedious than pushing a bike through sand.

Donald's new shoes were not ready until lunch-time the next day, which delayed their departure. The overlanders were well and in good spirits, but they were weary and decided to 'take things easy' on the way to Perth.

'Until Alex White and his companion, Don Mackay, get through the Upper Murchison and Gascoyne country and come out at Mullewa, it is not likely that we shall hear anything further of them,' 'Pedal' wrote in the *West Australian* on 15 January. 'The belt of country they have entered from Roebourne is, perhaps, rougher than any they have yet traversed.'

After camping in the bed of a sandy creek that night, Alex and Donald reached Karratha Station early the next morning for breakfast. Making a start at nine o'clock, the duo filled their water bags at the creek, but it was full of tadpoles. Riding into a heavy headwind, they reached a well on Dry River for lunch. At dusk only a small stream of water was running as the duo crossed the Fortescue River, its banks lined with paperbark trees, before having tea at the Fortescue telegraph station. Pushing on a couple of hours later, they rode in the moonlight through rolling grasslands before camping at a well. In the morning they reached Mardie Station near the mouth of the Fortescue River.

Meanwhile, Frank had arrived in Perth, intending to meet up with Alex and Donald and ride with them to Melbourne. According to the *Morning Bulletin*, Frank had left Melbourne by the Adelaide Express train and picked up the mail boat from Adelaide to Perth. If Frank had managed to communicate with Alex and Donald by telegraph wire, he would no doubt have informed them that Arthur was well on his way to Perth and the completion of his ride. If so, Alex and Donald would have known that they had no chance of beating Arthur, but they may have wondered whether they could still lower his record, which would make their own journey worthwhile.

Rather than wait for Alex and Donald in Perth, Frank decided to ride northwards to meet them, but bad luck continued to plague him. On the way to New Norcia, the monastic town 144 kilometres north of Perth, he had a fall, taking the 'bark' off his kneecap, an injury that would bother him for the remainder of the ride.

Taking an inland route, Alex and Donald reached Boolaloo Station on the Ashburton River, 193 kilometres east of Exmouth, on Sunday, 14 January. 'Boolaloo' is an Aboriginal word meaning 'running water' and the Ashburton was never dry at this place. The duo got a good reception from the manager, Mr Young, who had worked on a station adjoining Donald's Wallendbeen before moving to Western Australia. After some refreshments, Alex and Donald had a bath in the river and mended eight punctures in their tyres, which were covered in bindi burrs, before departing at three o'clock.

After riding through an area known as the Gorge, a region of rough hills intersected by numerous creeks, the overlanders came to an unusually deep well, about twenty metres in depth. While Alex was pulling up a bucket of water, a strong wind blew his hat off. The hat seemed to hover above the well for a split second. Reaching for the hat, Alex caught it, but his foot slipped and he fell. Grabbing a leg of the windlass, he hung over the well. 'I rushed to try and rescue him, but being very strong, Alex was on terra firma before I could help,' Donald recalled.

Entering the Murchison–Gascoyne region, the overlanders took a shortcut towards Lyons River Station, located north of Gascoyne Junction. They had decided to drink only from Alex's water bag and conserve the water in Donald's. In the morning they woke up horrified to find that the wind had blown over

Donald's bicycle in the night and the contents of his water bag had spilt. They searched for water, but could not find any.

The situation looked grim until they came upon a 'well-defined road' that led them to Lyons River homestead, where they arrived at 2.00pm on Friday, 19 January. After plenty of eating and drinking, Alex and Donald departed at four o'clock for Bangemall, accompanied by the Lyons River manager, Mr William Hatch, for a few kilometres on his bicycle. Mr Hatch told the duo the country was 'splendid' for bicycles in winter, but the machines were never ridden at this time of year. 'Saying goodbye we felt relieved at leaving this stretch of country behind,' Donald recalled. 'It was going from Hatch's that Richardson, the other cyclist, got bushed.'

Crossing Dead Horse Creek, the overlanders rode over dusty red soil until they reached Bangemall at 9.15pm. They had something to eat and then got an early night, 'enjoying the luxury of a bed'. The duo was unimpressed with Bangemall, 'an apology for a street with six houses', but they stayed for a day, washing their pants and making themselves at home on the verandah, 'airing our legs while the pants dried'.

In the evening the overlanders saw some blond-haired Aboriginal people. 'I heard they came from a tribe living in the big desert,' Donald recalled. 'Their fair hair was a great contrast to their black faces.' The cause of the blond hair was a subject for debate. Was it due to mixing with Europeans during colonisation or was it a genetic mutation? Whatever the reason, these people made a favourable impression on the overlanders.

The duo intended to make an early start in the morning, but one of Alex's tyres burst and they were delayed until eight o'clock. After riding across a hilly and stony track they arrived at Morrissey Creek where they met some drovers taking a herd of sheep to the goldfields. The head drover, Mr Collins, gave the duo a hearty welcome and had lunch prepared for them.

After lunch Mr Collins sent an Aboriginal boy to fill the overlanders' water bags and they set off at four o'clock. Pulling up at nightfall to camp, they took a swig from their water bags and spat it out again. They guessed the Aboriginal boy must have filled the bags from a stagnant pool in which Mr Collins's camels had bathed. Still, they were thirsty and managed a few mouthfuls of the foul water to wash down their tinned meat. Camels provided the perfect solution for the problem of transport in the Australian outback. Between 1860 and 1910 an estimated 10,000 to 12,000 camels were imported, mostly from India and Palestine, while Australian cattle studs were also established. Driven mostly by camel drivers from Afghanistan, camels opened up the outback.

They celebrated 'Anniversary Day' at Mount Clere Station, 460 kilometres east of Carnarvon. Also known as Foundation Day, it was the colonial precursor to Australia Day, celebrating the landing of the First Fleet on 26 January 1788. Alex woke up in the middle of the night in great pain, suffering from the 'old complaint'. Donald started a fire and brewed some tea, which seemed to soothe Alex, who was feeling better when they pushed on at six o'clock in the morning. 'Alex was dead beat,' Donald recalled. 'Heavens knows how he had kept going so long!'

Crossing the Murchison River, a big sandy watercourse with a few stretches of salty water, the overlanders rode over mulga and saltbush country to Milly Milly Station, about 188 kilometres west of Meekatharra. After receiving 'splendid' hospitality from the station manager and his wife, Mrs Daly, the duo left Milly Milly at seven o'clock the next morning, riding on a sandy track against a heavy headwind.

They reached Manfred Station in time for lunch, but the station was short of food so they had to make do with a slice of bread and a cup of tea. Regretting not having resupplied at Milly Milly, they rode with empty tucker bags towards Boolardy Station, seventy kilometres away, camping near a well for the cold night.

Setting off at 5.30am, they reached Boolardy Station just after breakfast. After refreshing themselves with a shower and a square meal they felt 'fit for anything'. From Boolardy they struck a good road across granite hills, arriving at Murgoo Station at 5.30pm. The station manager, Mr H. Maloney, gave them a thoroughly enjoyable time with 'wines of many varieties, cigars and every luxury of the season'.

The overlanders learned that all the boundary riding on the property was done on bicycles. 'They kept a special room for the mounts,' Donald recalled. 'Among the number I saw a Dux machine. It was a very old warrior, and although in use for many years, it still did its daily rounds.'

Alex and Donald had a cup of tea and set off at six o'clock the next morning. At Murgoo they had sighted a railway line for the first time since leaving Pine Creek. Hearing that the track to Mullewa was nearly all sand, they tried riding along the line, but it proved the worst they had experienced. It was hard enough to walk along the line, let alone ride a bicycle. They decided to take the road and it was not as bad as they had expected.

The overlanders arrived at Mullewa on Wednesday, 31 January, in a dust storm. After some refreshments they headed to the Twelve-mile Well to camp and had an uncomfortable night in wind and rain. They made an early start in the morning, wanting to reach Mingenew, ninety-five kilometres ahead, so they could fix their tyres, which again had been punctured by bindi burrs. After lunching at Yarragadee Station, thirteen kilometres north of Mingenew, the duo struck hard, undulating country, with a heavy stretch of sand. Arriving at Mingenew at four o'clock, they fixed up their tyres and made an early start the following morning.

They got out of the Mid West just in the nick of time before major floods badly affected large parts of the Pilbara and Gascoyne regions, with the Gascoyne, Ashburton and Murchison rivers overflowing their banks for extraordinarily sustained periods. The rain was so heavy that the North West and Mid West regions were completely bogged. By Easter all the houses at Roebourne were surrounded by water, while buildings at Milly Milly Station were washed away.

After stopping at the Walebing telegraph station, in the Wheatbelt region, for morning refreshments on Sunday, 4 February, Alex and Donald ran into Frank and another cyclist just a few kilometres from the station. It is not known whether Frank surprised Alex and Donald or not, but it is more than likely he would have wired ahead to say he was heading that way.

How did Alex and Donald feel when they saw Frank, who had travelled all the way from Pine Creek to Perth to meet them? After what they had endured it would be understandable if they were happy to have his company again for the remainder of the ride, but Alex and Donald had formed a very close bond and may have wanted to finish the ride together, just the two of them. And how did Frank feel about watching his team-mates continuing the journey that he had planned and instigated? Was he frustrated or envious? Or was he simply glad to see them both alive, particularly his younger brother?

Frank was accompanied by the New Norcia postmaster, Mr L. White, who invited the three overlanders to stay with him for the night. With a lot of catching up to do, they had a 'most enjoyable evening' together.

The overlanders regretted they did not have enough time to inspect the Spanish Benedictine mission, dating back to 1846, that was located just a few hundred metres from the New Norcia post office. In an effort to convert the local Aboriginal people to Christianity, Bishop Salvado, the founder of the mission, had presented them with a painting of a Black Madonna and Child. 'Bishop Salvado had big numbers of blacks working on the place, also being taught, subsidised by the government,' Donald recalled. 'The blacks had strongly resented the Madonna and Child as whites and until a black representation was procured their religious training was a failure.'

The painting of the Black Madonna and Child was believed to have miraculous powers. Many years earlier a raging bushfire had threatened the mission. All attempts by the monks to stop the fire were in vain and the buildings were about to be engulfed in flames. A priest then hurried into the chapel and brought out the painting, propping it up in long grass in front of the mission, saying the Lord would protect it. The monks prayed as the fire burned to within twenty metres of the buildings and then, as if miraculously, the wind changed, blowing from the opposite direction.

If the painting of the Black Madonna and Child saving the mission from burning down was not a miracle, then the overlanders surviving their ride so far surely was.

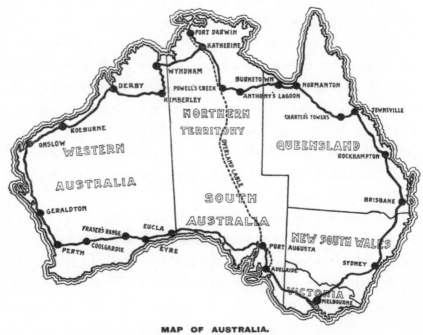

MAP OF AUSTRALIA.

Showing Richardson's Route—distance, 11,500 miles.

A map of Arthur Richardson's intended route was displayed at Percy Armstrong's Cycle Agency in Perth so the public could follow his progress, but he did not always stick to it.

Stage Seventeen

A Dream Come True

Arthur
Adelaide to Perth
9 January to 4 February 1900

REFRESHED after his stay in Adelaide, Arthur set off for Port Augusta on Tuesday, 9 January, accompanied by his brother Gus and, from Melrose, the oldest town in the Flinders Ranges at the foot of Mount Remarkable, by a female rider, Miss Haycraft of the North Adelaide Cycling Club. Riding at a fast pace, it took only two days to cross the gently rolling hills to Port Augusta.

Women's cycling in Australia was a controversial subject in the 1890s, but Arthur obviously had no objections to riding with a woman. Many men at the time believed cycling was 'unladylike' and made women manly. There were debates about whether women should be allowed to compete in races, what was appropriate clothing for them to wear, and what style of bikes they should ride. But as the popularity of cycling increased, more women became involved as spectators and participants. At first women wore everyday long skirts, but these often became tangled in the bike chains, leading to the more practical attire of the 'divided skirt' and 'bloomers costume'. American women's rights activist Susan B. Anthony stated in 1896 that cycling had 'done more to emancipate women than anything else in the world'. Two years later the 'petite and pretty' French cycliste Mademoiselle Serpolette, described as 'La Delicieux', visited Australia on a highly publicised tour to give demonstrations for the Gladiator cycling company. Drinking bumpers of champagne, Mademoiselle Serpolette was part of the gathering which gave Frank a farewell in Perth on his record-breaking ride to Rockhampton and back.

After having ridden 145 kilometres that day, Arthur and his companions were met at Stirling North, seven kilometres east of Port Augusta, by members of the South Australian Cycling Association and escorted into town. Arthur stayed the night at Mundalho Station, the residence of his brother-in-law, Mr W.G. Pryor. He left the next day, travelling alone after receiving a 'hearty send-off'.

'Up to the time that I left Port Augusta and entered into the desert country lying between there and our eastern goldfields I had spent a pleasant tour from Queensland,' Arthur recalled. 'Here, again, however, I had to face several hundred miles of heavy, dreary travelling.'

Crossing the Nullarbor, Arthur benefited from the experience of his 1896 journey. Remembering that the old track he had taken was terribly sandy, he took a different route this time, avoiding the dreadful Eyres Sand Patch, a stretch of fine white dunes acknowledged as the worst patch of sand in Australia. 'A day of sweating and swearing,' Arthur wrote of his trudge over the thirty-nine kilometres of sandhills in 52-degree heat after his first crossing. Although it meant riding

160 kilometres inland, the track he took this time was less sandy and he had a much easier ride.

'To Caloona Station, on the eastern edge of the Nullarbor Plain and near the coastline, I kept to the old route,' Arthur recalled. 'From there, however, I kept nearly a hundred miles inland and crossed the plains where there was a fairly good pad, and much less sand than on the old road. From Eucla I kept to the old road as far as Eyres Sand Patch, and then went along a totally new route for 140 miles to Ponton's. Then I crossed the sandy deserts to Fraser Range, and got to Norseman late in January.'

Norseman, the second-richest goldfield in Western Australia, was observing the 'Anniversary of Australia' when Arthur pedalled into the crossroads town, which had been named after an unwittingly helpful horse. In 1894, according to local lore, a horse named Hardy Norseman was tethered to a tree for the night by its owner, Laurie Sinclair. When Sinclair returned in the morning he was amazed to discover that his horse had kicked up a gold nugget, starting a gold rush. A bronze statue of Hardy Norseman was erected to commemorate the town's founding horse.

Arthur reached the familiar territory of Coolgardie, the third-biggest town in Western Australia at the time, at 6.30pm on Tuesday, 30 January, 'bronzed and hardy looking' after riding for twelve hours. The trip from Adelaide had taken twelve days fewer than his pioneering ride across the Nullarbor in 1896. A number of local cyclists rode out to meet him and accompanied him into town. He was taken to the Westral Hotel where a large crowd gathered for a reception that was accorded him by the Coolgardie Bicycle Club. A Mr A.T. Hore made a toast to Arthur's health, which was supported by several others, and characteristically the cyclist responded briefly.

Later on, Richardson was waited upon by a representative of
the *Miner* and in answer to a few questions he stated he felt in
the best of health, although he appeared to be a trifle thin. The
latter circumstance was, however, only to be expected after
the heavy, gruelling work that he had undergone during the last
seven months. His fine appearance was not, though, as might be
expected, any indication of want of powers of endurance, a proof
of which was the ride that he had done that day. Not having his
papers with him he could not go into any details of the ride that he
had accomplished, and, in fact, he modestly hinted that he had not
done a great deal. The facts, though, speak for themselves on this
point.

In the matter of clothing the intrepid rider accomplished
something which will take a great deal of beating, for he was clad
only in long woollen stockings, cycling pants, a white woollen
sweater and a soft felt hat, and he carried not another stitch of
clothing of any kind with him.

'Didn't you find the nights cold at times?' said the interviewer.

'Well, yes,' replied the rider. 'I did, but I had to get
accustomed to that kind of thing.'

Continuing, Richardson said that neither he nor his machine
needed to lay up for alterations or repairs during the trip. He
had now and again felt somewhat off colour, but he was never
compelled to seek medical attention, although on a couple of
occasions he took a day's spell to recuperate after particularly
trying experiences ... He expected to reach Perth any time
between Saturday evening next and the following Monday
morning.

For an experienced overlander such as Arthur, the last
560 kilometres from Coolgardie to Perth were expected to be

covered easily and newspapers around the country were already lauding his achievement. 'The feat is certainly one of the most remarkable yet accomplished by Australian wheelmen,' the *Healesville Guardian and Yarra Glen Guardian* reported.

> When this ride was first mooted it was set down as a mad freak and one fraught with the greatest danger, but the cool-headed, plucky Western Australian ex-cycling-dispatch-rider quietly took on all risks and the ride is now a fait accompli.
>
> When he left, on June 5 last, he expected to make a circuit of the continent in six months time. Though he has taken a month longer there cannot be any doubt that his ride is one of, if not the most meritorious, ever accomplished.

But Arthur's final stage was not as straightforward as observers might have imagined. Normally, he was unflappable, but he came close to chucking it all in just as the prize was within his grasp. He departed Coolgardie at one o'clock and was accompanied for about four kilometres on the road by a few of the town's leading cyclists, but he was bitterly disappointed not to have company all the way to Perth. Arthur usually enjoyed his own company, but with the finish line in sight, he was keen to complete the ride. He had telegraphed that he could reach Perth by four o'clock on Saturday afternoon, 3 February, if pace (a rider who sets the pace in front and acts as a windbreak for the cyclist following) was provided, but for whatever reason his request was ignored.

Frustrated by this lack of support, Arthur's progress from the goldfields was further retarded by the poor condition of the road. In previous years miners had travelled this road to make their fortunes on the goldfields, but now it was practically abandoned, and Arthur had difficulty obtaining food on the lonely track.

Arthur was particularly disgusted with the advice he received upon leaving Southern Cross, the site of the first major gold discovery in the eastern goldfields in 1888, inspiring one of the last great rushes in the world. He had been told incorrectly that he would strike settlements on the road west, so did not carry any provisions with him. In one instance he only had half a loaf of bread and water to last him two days. Suffering from hunger that could have been easily avoided, Arthur felt so angry that he was tempted to throw his bicycle into the bush and finish the journey by train, but he continued in his weakened state towards York in the picturesque Avon Valley, just under one hundred kilometres east of Perth.

At dusk on Friday, 2 February, Arthur camped in the open fifty-five kilometres from York. He set off again at six o'clock the next morning, stopping at a waterhole for a breakfast of bread and water and a nap. Pushing on again at eleven, he reached York at three o'clock on Saturday afternoon.

Arthur was met in York by Mr Clem Salkilld of the Rover Cycle Agency, who provided him with a fortifying meal. Thanking Mr Salkilld for his kindness, which evidently restored his faith in humanity, Arthur left York at 4.30pm and proceeded on his journey, reaching the bustling railway junction of Chidlows Well, forty-five kilometres east of Perth, the same night.

Percy Armstrong and many others rode out a considerable distance to meet Arthur and escort him on his final triumphal stage into Perth. After stopping for lunch at Midland Junction, seventeen kilometres east of Perth, Arthur arrived in the city at 3.30pm on Sunday afternoon, 4 February, and was greeted by an enthusiastic crowd of about two thousand people, who frantically cheered him as he rode through the streets to the General Post Office. The crowd would have been even bigger, if not for some confusion about the time of Arthur's arrival.

It had been generally expected that Arthur would arrive the previous afternoon and a large crowd had congregated near the General Post Office. When it became clear that he would not be coming that day the crowd gradually dispersed. It was then announced that he would reach Perth at eleven o'clock on Sunday morning. A couple of thousand people lined St Georges Terrace and waited patiently for nearly two hours for his arrival. Suddenly a party of wheelmen swept from Adelaide Terrace into St Georges Terrace. Hundreds of people seated on the kerbstones and lounging about in groups rushed into the roadway while a couple of troopers galloped in and forced a line through the throng. The cyclists rode through the avenue so formed with a grimy-looking rider in their centre. 'Richardson!' the crowd cried. But it was just a hoax to relieve the boredom.

The crowd was then told that Arthur would arrive at three o'clock and the same number of people gathered again to cheer him. Excited onlookers rushed the roadway as Arthur, followed by several dozen cyclists, rode into the terrace. What was going through his mind? A sense of satisfaction or relief? Perhaps both. And though, no doubt, Percy Armstrong would have informed him of the whereabouts of the White brothers and Mackay, would Arthur have scanned the faces in the street, just to confirm they had not yet arrived in Perth?

Cheers resounded as Arthur, bemused as always by all the attention, alighted at the General Post Office and there was a mad scramble to shake hands with him and slap his back. After signing his time-book, he then took his final ride, just around the corner to Armstrong's Cycle Agency, and the crowd ran after him, colliding with each other in the rush. Hundreds of people scurried into Hay Street and in less than two minutes the front of the agency was packed with a jubilant crowd. Like a modern-day rock star, Arthur was hurried into a cab and driven away amid wild cheering. His trusty bicycle was put on display at Armstrong's before being sent to England for exhibition.

Winning the race around Australia, Arthur had realised the dream of the overlander. It had taken him almost eight months (or 243 days and four hours) to ride around the continent. 'Pedal' claimed Arthur had ridden 11,500 miles (18,507 kilometres), but his cyclometer registered only 11,150 miles (17,944 kilometres). Nevertheless, it was still a world long-distance record for a continuous ride.

According to one observer, Arthur looked as 'brown as a berry and as hard as nails'. While Arthur admitted he'd had 'rather a bad time of it' from Coolgardie to Perth, he was 'full of go' and could do it again straightaway if necessary. But he also conceded that had he pushed himself with the intention of putting up a fast time he would have 'collapsed altogether'.

The ride around Australia was a tour de force. While Arthur never claimed to be an explorer or journeyed into regions previously untravelled by Europeans, he was still a pioneer of the wheel, accomplishing an epic feat which required extraordinary courage, skill and ingenuity. He had created history, but he had also enabled Australians to view the continent with a whole new perspective.

And he succeeded at a time when riding around Australia was deemed all but impossible. Unlike modern around Australia rides, there were no paved highways, mobile phones or roadhouses in the outback. From the cold and wet start of his journey to the blazing hot sun of northern Australia and temperatures that had to be experienced to be believed, Arthur had shown extraordinary persistence and endurance to complete the ride. Nothing could better demonstrate the capabilities of the bicycle as a means of locomotion in inhospitable country than Arthur following rough bush tracks, cattle and horse pads and even crossing pathless terrain. And then there were the seemingly interminable sandhills, lonely deserts, the stony and mountainous country, the endless black soil plains and the crocodile-infested rivers that at times made cycling almost an impossibility. Even if occasionally he had to walk and carry his bike, he still crossed the country faster than any horseman would have been able to. And he did it all with a quiet, unassuming nature, which belied his great strength of character.

'Pedal' claimed that Arthur's ride around Australia surpassed the deeds of all other overlanders. 'To Richardson is due the credit of first accomplishing a ride which outshines the deeds of these overlanders in every respect,' 'Pedal' wrote.

While Australia can compare favourably with other parts in all branches of athletics, it is generally admitted that we have produced men who excel in those aspects of wheeling life which call for a display of endurance, daring, pluck, hardihood and resource.

They have come from among the men who, in the earlier history of the goldfields of this colony, demonstrated the utility of the cycle in pioneering work, and in opening up country previously a blank on Australia's map, but now teeming with a civilised population. To the bicycle is to be attributed much of the advanced state of the treasure-producing areas of the vast colony. One of the men who first gained experience with the cycle on the goldfields was Richardson, and he has put the means to a greater test than any other man by his completion of the journey round Australia.

Even in his moment of triumph, Arthur was characteristically modest about his achievement, claiming he had suffered no more hardship than the pioneering prospectors in Western Australia's goldfields. 'Many people warn me that I shall feel the effects of the ride later on,' Arthur said. 'How that can be I am at a loss to understand. The trials were no greater than hundreds of our prospectors have had to withstand, and many of them are undergoing similar trials today in the search for gold out back.'

This was typical Arthur self-effacement, but he had a genuine respect for the prospectors who had 'opened up' the country and the dispatch riders who raced across the goldfields. This was where Arthur had served his apprenticeship as an overlander and he regarded conveying messages across the desert at breakneck speed as being just as dangerous as riding around Australia.

A formal reception for Arthur was held at the Esplanade Hotel. The 'pleasant little gathering' was attended by several prominent citizens, including the premier of Western Australia, Sir John Forrest; the minister for Crown Lands and a future premier, Mr George Throssell; Alexander Forrest, the mayor of Perth; and the overlanders Percy Armstrong and Alfred Mather. The premier gave the loyal toasts and then praised Arthur, expressing doubt that any journey had been accomplished that was as 'difficult and diversified' as Arthur's.

He spoke highly of the intrepidity, energy, pluck and endurance which Arthur had demonstrated. Over twenty years earlier the premier and his brother had gone over some of the country which Arthur had traversed and they had looked upon that as a tremendous feat. But there were no bicycles in those days and they had to be content with shanks's pony, or a not too well fed horse, he joked.

Again, Arthur was typically modest in reply, simply thanking those present for their kind treatment of him. He did not regard public speaking as one of his accomplishments, but he intended to publish a record of his experiences and proposed to take his bicycle to South Africa and endeavour to 'give Kruger some trouble'.

While Arthur had ruminated about South Africa during his ride, and there had been speculation that he would enlist, this was the first time he confirmed his intention to fight in the Boer War. Like many a red-blooded Australian male, Arthur was keen to answer the call to arms. But after demonstrating the utility of the bicycle in outback Australia, he was also anxious to prove the machine had a role to play in warfare. It seems clear he had decided some time earlier to join a Western Australian contingent and had waited to arrive in Perth before making an announcement.

Arthur also received a civic welcome in the mayor's parlour, which was attended by thirty 'leading citizens', including the attorney-general, Mr Richard Pennefather, and several of the city councillors. The mayor gave 'the health of Mr Richardson', cordially welcoming to the city the cyclist who had accomplished the 'wonderful ride' round Australia. He was glad to take the opportunity of welcoming Arthur on behalf of the city of Perth. He did not think a better man could be selected for South Africa, because if he saw a Boer he could leave him behind in no time. More seriously, he wished Arthur every prosperity, and if he went to South Africa he hoped he would return to Western Australia again safe and sound.

Arthur had achieved something that no one thought was possible, but he was about to embark on a new quest even more dangerous. Whatever he might accomplish in the future, nothing could ever diminish what he had just done. It was so much more than a pioneering bicycle ride around the continent. On the eve of federation, Arthur had given people from Brisbane to Broome something to cheer about, a sense of pride in a new country.

Stage Eighteen

A State of Excitement

White brothers and Donald
New Norcia to Harrow
5 February to 12 March 1900

THE reunited trio left New Norcia at nine o'clock in the morning of Monday, 5 February, with 144 kilometres to ride over a hilly road to reach Perth. They wired ahead to say they expected to arrive at six o'clock in the evening. At five o'clock they arrived at Midland Junction, doing the last kilometre against a strong headwind in a shower of rain, making it difficult to see the track. They were met by a party of Perth cyclists and after a refreshing drink were escorted into town, the welcoming party riding in front to create a windbreak. 'We found the road exceptionally rough, the metal being very bare – hardly the thing expected when entering a capital!' Donald recalled.

On schedule, the overlanders arrived in Perth at six o'clock, a day after Arthur finished his ride and exactly seven months after the White brothers' departure from Melbourne. Given they had been in telegraphic communication while in New

Norcia, it is almost certain they would have been aware that Arthur had arrived in Perth the previous day. He had completed his ride, but Alex and Donald still had a long, long way to go. They certainly would have been relieved to reach civilisation where they could recuperate before heading east on the final stages of their harrowing journey.

A party of fifty to seventy cyclists escorted them up St Georges Terrace to the General Post Office where they were given three cheers by a crowd of a couple of hundred onlookers, including family and friends of the White brothers. Whether Arthur was in the crowd is unknown, but it would not have taken long before the overlanders caught up with each other. After Alex and Donald had their books signed the trio rode to Armstrong's Cycle Agency where they left their machines. Alex went home with some friends, while Donald checked into the De Boos Hotel. After tea Alex turned up at the hotel and he and Donald went to the theatre. It said a lot about the bond that had developed between the two that after so much time away from home Alex chose to spend the evening in his mate's company. Maybe Frank had an oyster dinner with Arthur.

Perth was in a state of excitement to have all of the overlanders in the city at the same time. 'During the past week the local cycling world has been stirred to enthusiasm by the arrival in Perth of three daring wheelmen engaged in riding round our island continent,' the *Western Mail* reported on 10 February.

Whether Frank was offended by his omission we do not know, but he was feted along with the other overlanders while in Perth. Alex's rugby club, the Perth Pirates, together with the Metropolitan Cycling Club, organised a reception for all four of the riders at Jacoby's Bohemia Hall on the evening of Tuesday, 6 February.

Percy Armstrong presided over the function which was attended by an enthusiastic crowd of around one hundred cyclists. A proud and no doubt delighted Armstrong stated that though many overland rides had been accomplished, crossing Australia from north to south and east to west, there had never been a journey like circling the continent. It had been the 'dream of the overland cyclist', but the journey was now a reality. He extended hearty congratulations to Arthur on completing a journey that had established a world record and eclipsed any ride yet attempted by overlanders of other countries.

In other parts of the world, Armstrong said, long and adventurous journeys had been completed, but never since the introduction of the modern cycle had there been such a demonstration of its utility or such a practical example given of the pluck, stamina and endurance for which the Australian cyclist was famous.

Armstrong said that when danger loomed, cyclists in foreign countries were escorted by mounted guardians and when in tight places they did not hesitate to travel by other means than the bicycle. In Australia such a thing was not tolerated, and if the overlander did not stick to his wheel he was not regarded as an overlander at all.

The rides of the Australian overlanders were examples of what could be done on the wheel, and though many people were sceptical about the value to the community of these adventurous journeyings, there were none who did not admit that they showed that Australians possessed that pluck and dogged perseverance which had made the British nation what it was.

A 'Brit', Robert Louis Jefferson, had shown that the bicycle could be a means of rapid locomotion in different countries, but it had remained for the sons of Greater Britain to show that in desolate lands, and under disadvantageous conditions, the bicycle provided a means of transport that was previously unknown.

Armstrong concluded by congratulating the overlanders on an achievement which was of 'marked interest and value to the whole cycling world'.

After the toast was drunk with 'considerable enthusiasm', Arthur rose to respond and was greeted with prolonged cheering. As always, Arthur was brief. He was glad to be back in Perth. During his long ride he had seen and crossed by diverse means many fine rivers, but he had never been so pleased as when he crossed the Swan because he knew he only had a few more miles to travel. He wished the other overlanders luck and was certain that they would succeed.

Alex was also greeted with enthusiastic applause when he rose to respond. He said that he and Donald had had some 'rough and trying' experiences, but the worst was over. He drew more applause when he acknowledged that all credit was due to Arthur for engaging in such a 'terrible ride' unaccompanied, and declared that all other rides 'paled into insignificance'.

Donald was prevented for a considerable time from speaking by the reception he got when he rose to respond. He did not think he had done anything to warrant such a reception as he was only halfway round yet, while Arthur had finished and Alex had only a couple of thousand miles to go. Alex had been a 'splendid mate' and he could not have wished for a better. Arthur's lonely ride had been one of 'marvellous pluck and endurance'. Only those who had traversed the country could appreciate the magnitude of the ride. Donald said he was riding round Australia to establish an amateur record and found himself a 'bobtail third'.

In response to repeated calls, Frank also spoke briefly. He would have come through with Alex and Donald if his machine had 'stood him in good stead', but he would accompany the others as far as Melbourne.

While Donald had self-effacingly referred to himself as a 'bobtail third', he still had his eyes on Arthur's record. This race was not over yet.

With pencil and paper, Donald calculated he needed to ride 3747 miles (6030 kilometres) in fifty days to break Arthur's record. The press gave him little chance and even Donald acknowledged the odds were against him. He knew the record from Perth to Brisbane of fifty-three days and seven hours had been set by Frank when he was fresh, during cool spring weather after winter rains had set the sandy track. Now it was extremely hot and the tracks would be soft and loose. And Donald had had a 'skinful' of overlanding. He was leg-weary after seven months on a rough track and his ankles were swollen 'in a most unpleasant way'. Nevertheless, he had a sporting chance and was determined to give it a go.

Alex would have realised he had little hope of lowering Arthur's time, but he was doggedly determined to complete the course if only to fulfil his contract, but he was also harbouring another ambition, which was to set a world record for the longest continuous ride.

Whether Arthur believed Donald and Alex could break his records is not known, but he supplied his rivals with rough plans and directions as to the best route to follow, including how to avoid the awful Eyres Sand Patch.

Arthur's generosity in sharing his knowledge demonstrated the camaraderie of the overlanders, who were competitors but still 'comrades of the wheel'. Arthur, it seemed, was

Frank White, in light clothes in the centre, is given a send-off by members of the
Metropolitan Cycling Club in Perth as he departs on his record-breaking ride to
Rockhampton and back in 1898.

satisfied with the distinction of being the first to ride around
Australia. No matter how many times his record might be
broken, this was something that could never be taken away
from him.

A crowd of about one hundred assembled in front of the
General Post Office in Perth to witness the departure of Alex
and Donald at one o'clock on Wednesday, 7 February. Their
machines had been completely overhauled and after the short
rest they claimed to be in fine form. Wiping the sweat from
their brows in the afternoon heat, the riders mounted their
bicycles and were heartily cheered as they were escorted a
short distance by a number of local cyclists, including Frank,
who was detained by business in Perth and intended to catch
up with them by taking the goldfield's mail train to Tammin, a
station 180 kilometres north-east of Perth.

Alex and Donald reached Chidlows Well in the evening and stayed the night. They had a good run to York the following day where they were welcomed by the secretary of the local bicycle club, Mr J. Ross, as well as several members before resuming their journey on the old teamsters' road to the goldfields. Riding through a bushfire on tracks that were cut up, they picked up Frank in Tammin before pushing on to Hines Hill on the edge of Lake Baandee, 240 kilometres east of Perth.

Even though Frank was no longer officially part of the ride around Australia, he resumed the role of writing telegrams, including one from Hines Hill, which was published in the *Western Mail*.

Hines Hill, 9 February, 8.40pm. Picked up the boys at Tammin midday. They had had a rough time, fifty miles of bushfires to come through. My injured knee is very troublesome, but I will battle through. The track is very heavy. Had a good time in Mr Leak's fruit garden. Was caught in a thunderstorm at three o'clock this afternoon. Expect to reach Southern Cross tomorrow. Have not done any perishes [to die or come near to dying of thirst or starvation] for tucker yet. Frank White.

The overlanders departed Hines Hill on Saturday morning, 10 February, and after riding on a sandy road arrived in Carrabin, a small town on the railway line between Merredin and Southern Cross, in time for lunch. They reached Southern Cross that evening and made an early start the next day, arriving in Boorabbin for lunch and Bullabulling, eighty kilometres further on, for tea.

The trio reached Coolgardie at 12.15pm the next day, Monday, 12 February. The weather was the hottest it had been in four years, the thermometer registering 114 in the shade. But the cyclists were overwhelmed with hospitality. They were entertained by Mr W.B. McKee, host of the Denver City Hotel, at a reception which was presided over by a big, genial Irishman named John Finnerty, Coolgardie's first resident magistrate and mining warden, and attended by the popular Italian cyclist Massimiliano Porta, who visited Australia several times in the mid to late 1890s to race before settling in Western Australia where he worked as a sharebroker, bookmaker, miner and cycle agent.

Warden Finnerty proposed the toast of 'success to the two cyclists' with bumpers of champagne which were drunk with enthusiasm. Whether Frank was offended by being omitted from the toast is hard to know, but he probably still felt he had something to offer Alex and Donald on their ride. He had ridden twice over the difficult track between Coolgardie and Port Augusta and would have felt able to guide his companions safely and swiftly across it.

In a hurry to get away, the overlanders departed Coolgardie at four o'clock, following a camel pad towards Norseman. Just out of town they came across a train of 200 fully loaded camels, which were frightened by the sight of the bicycles. 'Coming alongside of them, they did not seem to admire us,' Donald recalled. 'Several commenced to roar and buck, one especially; as I passed him he broke away his nose line and sent his load (boxes of kerosene) high and dry in all directions. The excitement and language of the drivers was something one would not forget in a hurry. In a body they made for us. Putting on a spurt, we soon were out of range of their curses.'

The overlanders were held up when Frank broke the front fork of his bicycle at Horse Rocks, about thirty-three kilometres out on the road to Widgiemooltha, where the biggest nugget in the history of the Western Australian goldfields, the Golden Eagle (1136 ounces or 32.2 kilograms), would be discovered in 1931. Frank returned to Coolgardie to repair his bike and then set off again to catch up to Alex and Donald, who intended to ride through Norseman and on to Fraser Range Station to wait for him.

Frank had caught up to them by the time they reached Widgiemooltha for an early lunch the next day. While they were eating, Frank recommended a shortcut across Fraser Range, an area of granite hills covered with dense eucalyptus forest, which would allow the cyclists to avoid Norseman and save riding around eighty kilometres. The locals told the trio the track was sandy and waterless and strongly advised them not to risk it. 'Don't be foolish,' one told them. 'Stick to the Norseman track. There may be no water in the Binyarinyah [sic] rock holes.' They ignored the warning.

Alex and Donald departed without Frank, who remained behind, recovering from a bout of gastroenteritis, but he had given them directions. When at dusk they reached the immense Binyarinyinna Rock, nine metres high and covering a few hectares, rain had started to fall, and while they were soaked, at least water was plentiful.

After lighting a fire and wringing out their wet clothes, they tried to find the track to Fraser Range Station, and discovered not one track, but two. They felt the track that Frank had indicated veered away too much to the north, while the other track seemed like the right one. Against their better judgement, they trusted Frank, believing 'the man who had been here before should know best'.

Setting off at daylight on St Valentine's Day, Alex and Donald expected to reach Fraser Range Station by the afternoon so took only enough food for breakfast and a light lunch. The track was loose, but rideable. They came to a big patch of granite rocks, but they held no water. According to Frank, they would strike more rock holes soon so they were not too concerned. Instead, they struck a patch of sand and then salt lakes, no doubt starting to question Frank's directions.

The track then turned north-west, which meant they were going in the wrong direction. By 2.30pm they were nearly sixty-four kilometres from their last camp and their food and water had just about run out. They decided to camp and wait for Frank. If he did not arrive by 4.30pm, they would go back. At 5.00pm they drank the last half pint of water between them and with 'heavy hearts' started back with a howling wind blowing sand into their eyes. It was just as well they decided to retrace their tracks because they later found out there was no water for 160 kilometres in the direction they had been heading.

The ride back to the patch of granite rocks was a 'heart-breaker'. At midnight, 'half dead' from thirst, they searched for water, but could not find a drop, the heat of the day and the wind drying up any rain that might have fallen. The night was cold and they lay down behind some rocks and fell asleep.

At four in the morning they made a start and after a few kilometres captured a goanna, which was either 'drowsy or in bad health'. Donald strapped the reptile behind his saddle and they pushed on, returning to Binyarinyinna Rock at 7.30pm.

'At last we got our thirst quenched, and while Alex made a fire, I disembowelled the iguana,' Donald recalled. 'He was about three feet long. Leaving the skin on, and unfortunately the fat inside him, I placed him on the coals, and holding him by the tail worked him about until cooked. He smelled anything but good, but tasted A1. By the time we picked all the bones we only wished we had a dozen or more.'

Alex and Donald filled their water bags and started back to Widgiemooltha. Along the way they met Frank, who expressed surprise at the track being wrong, claiming there was only one track when he went through previously. Frank had three sandwiches with him and while they ate them they decided to re-tackle the Fraser Range hills, now 144 kilometres ahead. Frank was confident of finding the right track and they did not want to go back to Widgiemooltha, forty-eight kilometres behind them, if they could help it.

Arriving once more at Binyarinyinna Rock, they took the other track, which had appeared to Alex and Donald to be the correct one, but it soon delivered them to a series of salt lakes. Leaving the lakes they ascended a sandhill and then rode through timbered scrub, but could not find any water. Eventually, Frank admitted he was 'bushed' and they had no choice but to go back to Widgiemooltha, now around ninety kilometres distant. Frank, being comparatively fresh, pushed on ahead of the others. If Alex and Donald did not turn up at Widgiemooltha the next day, he would send out a relief party.

Alex and Donald were very weak, but preferred to keep moving in the cold of the night, eventually stopping after midnight to camp behind a granite boulder. They started a fire and had a smoke before sleeping until daylight. At 10.00am they made a start and were met a kilometre out of town by a camel driver whom Frank, who had reached Widgiemooltha at 2.30am, had sent out with food for them. Arriving at Evans Hotel in Widgiemooltha 'more dead than alive', they were treated well by the proprietors, Mr and Mrs Evans, who gave them a plate of cornflour, which revived them. 'Throughout this perish I had a craving for cornflour,' Donald recalled. 'Do what I would, I could not get it out of my mind.'

While Frank had saved Alex and Donald near Powell Creek, this time he had nearly killed them. And the so-called 'shortcut' had cost them three precious days and sent them 300 kilometres for nothing. 'We are now all very weak, but we will push on to the finish,' Frank wrote in a telegram from Widgiemooltha.

Donald grew despondent about his chances of lowering Arthur's record, while Alex questioned whether he had enough strength left to complete the ride, contract or no contract. 'Dead beat', the two of them slept for the rest of the morning until they were woken up for lunch. At three o'clock the trio took the regular route to Norseman, a camel pad running alongside the East–West Telegraph Line, and found it good riding. Mr Evans had given them a bottle of champagne, which they drank, 'considering this the easiest way of carrying it'.

The overlanders spent a comfortable night at the Pioneer Hotel and arrived in Norseman the next day, Saturday, 17 February, in time for a 'square meal' for lunch. Leaving in the afternoon they were escorted by a local cycling champion, Gus Ambrosius, who put them on the road to Fraser Range Station, one hundred kilometres further on.

The next day they saw Aboriginal people from Norseman travelling to a corroboree, before stopping at a homestead on Fraser Range Station where they met the 'celebrated' drover Tom Knowles, who had shot some Afghan camel-drivers at Boomer Rocks some years earlier, following a dispute over a waterhole.

Frank cajoled Alex and Donald into staying at the homestead for a day because he had sprained his foot when he hit a stump. 'I did not appreciate the delay, but decided not to be disagreeable,' Donald recalled. They left at eight o'clock the next morning, and after crossing sandhills and limestone ridges, all the while troubled by headwinds, they camped at a rock hole sixty kilometres from Fraser Range Station.

The trio arrived at the Balladonia telegraph station the following evening. The telegraph master, Mr Ponton, provided them with tea and they had a good night's sleep in comfortable beds.

After breakfast, the overlanders, who were intending to follow Arthur's directions and avoid Eyres Sand Patch, packed a big supply of food, had their time-books signed by Mr Ponton, and departed at nine o'clock. The pad was good at first, but then they hit sand, riding into strong headwinds. Leaving the main track which went by the beach, they took a left-hand pad and struck inland, coming back to the telegraph line in eleven kilometres. The pad along the line was good and after a few more kilometres they stopped to camp, erecting a windbreak from wood to shelter them during the cold night.

The trio made a start at daylight on a heavy track, finding plenty of water at the No 2 tank, twenty-seven kilometres further on, where they had a wash and a 'substantial' breakfast. Riding through limestone country, they saw several blowholes. 'Holding my hat over one, I let it go, and the force of air carried it fully 12 feet into the air,' Donald recalled. Walking most of the afternoon, they 'battled on' until ten o'clock before camping for the night.

Early the next morning, Thursday, 22 February, the trio set off, carrying very little water because their aim was to reach Graham's Water Tank, forty-eight kilometres ahead, and about five kilometres past the loop-line leading to Eyres Sand Patch.

After just one and a half kilometres of good track, they struck sand, dragging their bikes over sandhills for the next twenty or so kilometres, before camping under a few bushes to escape the extreme heat of the middle of the day.

Drinking the last of their water, they pushed on. In the distance they could see heavy smoke rising from a bushfire ahead, which made them uneasy. A kilometre and a half after passing the loop-line to Eyres Sand Patch, they were confronted by a ring of fire right across the track, which made it impossible to go any further. Unbelievably, Eyres Sand Patch seemed to be their only hope. Returning to the loop-line, they found a clearing in the scrub where they left their bicycles in order to walk to the Eyre telegraph station to investigate, hoping they would not have to drag them across the worst sandhills in Australia. The telegraph station, on the coast, was close to Eyres Sand Patch, and is now the site of the Eyre Bird Observatory.

As they trudged through the sand towards the telegraph station, it was perhaps not surprising that tension began to surface between the overlanders. His own man, Donald was clearly wearying of Frank's sense of seniority.

'Frank White was very grumpy,' Donald recalled.

Not waiting for us, he started for the Patch. When we were ready we followed ... The first sandhill to be tackled must have been about half a mile up and steep, with the sand loose, going over one's shoe tops every step ... Gaining the top, right on to the horizon was nothing but big white sandhills. Coming to the next, I had to take many spells. My legs were going back on me.

Descending it, we came unexpectedly on Frank, lying under a bush, apparently asleep. Rousing him, I told him to come on.

He reckoned he was dying, and implored me to stay with him. Feeling fair done, I told Alex, who seemed the strongest, to go on. I would follow when I had a spell, and, if possible, bring Frank along. I watched Alex stagger up the next sandhill and disappear. I was too thirsty to stay longer and felt frightened to lie too long on the hot sand. Frank would not move; he persisted in wishing me to stay with him; but I could do him no good, and Alex might fail to reach the telegraph station. So, promising to send Frank out water and a horse if I got through, I made a start.

How many spells I took, or how I staggered over those sandhills, heaven only knows. At last I sighted the houses. Getting to the linesmen's quarters, I found a tank, and started to empty it. Looking round, I saw a horseman starting from the main buildings, two hundred yards away. A few minutes later, young Mr Graham, seeing me, came over. Alex had arrived twenty minutes before me and had got them to send out the horse to our assistance.

Going over to the main building, Mr and Mrs Graham gave a splendid welcome. While talking, I had a look at the thermometer, which even now was still over 100 degrees. Tea being now ready we ate; and when half through Frank arrived.

Whether Frank was upset with Donald for leaving him we do not know, but there appears to have been a coolness between them from this point on, with Donald showing increasing irritation with Frank for consistently putting them on the wrong track.

Before going to bed, the cyclists had a long yarn with Mr Graham who had been the telegraph master at the station for more than twenty years. Just in front of where the station stood was the site where John Eyre had found water and killed a sick pack horse for food while resting for three weeks during his journey across the Great Australian Bight in 1841. Mr Graham had kept some of the horse's bones, discovered years later, as curiosities.

After a good night's sleep the overlanders felt refreshed in the morning, but they had no desire to trudge back across the wretched sandhills to where they had left their bicycles, so Mr Graham arranged for a camel to take them. 'The three of us on board could not have looked picturesque and we felt anything but comfortable,' Donald recalled.

Locating their bikes, the trio fell off the camel in 'a heap' and set off again for Graham's Tank. The track was covered with embers from the bushfire. When they reached the tank they found it was half full, but it had been fouled by a dead animal so they boiled the stinking water and made tea.

The overlanders made a start on a loose track that followed the coast to Eucla, 240 kilometres ahead. They stayed overnight at Madura, a deserted sheep station on the Roe Plains, which had been originally set up in 1876 to breed cavalry horses for the British Indian army. There was a tank full of water under the house and the trio had a bath on the verandah before leaving in the afternoon.

After staying the night at the White Tank, where the owner, Mr Scott, provided the overlanders with a 'pick-me-up' of tinned peaches, they reached Kennedy and McGill's station, Mundrabilla, the first sheep station in the Nullarbor region, the next day for breakfast. They were so well treated there they almost forgot thoughts of around Australia records. 'The owners were typical Scotsmen [Stuart McGill was Scottish, but William Kennedy was Irish] and to get away before lunch was out of the question,' Donald recalled. 'Though this was a loss of time, their genial society made ample compensation. I felt much inclined to risk records and stay a few days.'

When the overlanders pushed on towards Eucla, sixty-seven kilometres east, after lunch, Mr McGill, an enthusiastic cyclist, accompanied them until they reached a windmill where 'the best of friends must part'. The trio camped for the night in a patch of scrub and when it started to rain they gathered wood to make a windbreak and light a fire, but they still spent a 'cold, miserable night'. They had not carried coats since leaving Camooweal, and now, close to the ocean, the summer nights were cool. 'With only knickers and guernsey, it made me feel as though I had struck Klondyke,' Donald recalled.

Making an early start on Monday, 26 February, the overlanders rode on a level limestone track and could see the iron roof of the Eucla telegraph station, in the easternmost locality in Western Australia, by eight o'clock. An hour later they arrived. There were twenty operators at the station, half of them Western Australians and the other half South Australians, operating different codes. The operators proudly presented each of the overlanders with a copy of the local newspaper, the *Eucla Record*, telling them that Eucla was the smallest community in the world with its own newspaper. 'They seemed a jolly lot and spared no trouble to give us a good time,' Donald recalled.

The weather was '120 degrees in the shade' but the overlanders were feeling strong and well again. Leaving Eucla after lunch, they ascended a limestone range 121 metres high. At the top they were afforded a spectacular view of the telegraph station, white sandhills and the sea. In front of them were endless, treeless plains. They rode with caution through sand and mallee scrub, stumps lying all over the track, reaching the Thirty-Mile tanks by dusk, where they camped, but they were unable to sleep in the bitter cold.

The overlanders took as much water as possible from the tanks, for the ride to Nullarbor pastoral station was a 144-kilometre dry stage. Although the track was good, they rode into a fierce headwind and did not reach the station until nine o'clock at night.

Rain delayed them at Nullarbor for a day, and they left at seven o'clock the following morning. Passing the head of the Great Australian Bight they encountered heavy sand on the way to Nanwarra Station, where the country improved a little with a 'thin coating' of grass.

From the small coastal town of Fowlers Bay (formerly Yalata), they struck sandy mallee scrub for most of the 130-kilometre ride to Denial Bay, which had been so named in 1802 by the explorer Matthew Flinders because of 'the deceptive hope we had formed of penetrating by it some distance into the interior of the country'.

The overlanders arrived at Denial Bay at dusk on Saturday, 3 March. Now in fertile farming country, they stayed the night at McKenzie's boarding house, leaving at seven o'clock the next morning. During the day they took the wrong track three times. 'Frank White, who ought to have known the road, got us out of our course,' Donald tersely recalled. 'But a trusty farmer on two occasions got us back to the right road by a shortcut which saved several miles.' From here they followed the telegraph line along the shore to Smoky Bay, named by Matthew Flinders for the smoke from fires lit by Aboriginal people, then continued across the base of the Eyre Peninsula.

Crossing the Gawler Ranges, the overlanders made good progress on a hard track, reaching Yardea telegraph station for breakfast on Monday, 5 March. Frank sent a telegram from Yardea, which prompted the *Weekly Times* to claim that Alex and Donald had no chance of beating Arthur's record. 'The chance of breaking Richardson's record has now gone absolutely for to accomplish that feat they should have been in Melbourne last Sunday.' The newspaper's calculation applied to Alex, but not Donald. He still had a chance, but he only had three and a half weeks to reach Brisbane.

The overlanders rode on a hard but stony track until they stopped at Thuriga Station for lunch. Passing through saltbush country, the road branched. 'As usual, Frank got us on the wrong track,' Donald recalled. Pulling up at a deserted station they found a track that joined the telegraph line leading to Nonning sheep station at the eastern end of the Gawler Ranges, arriving there at 8.15pm. Frank's consistently wrong directions were becoming a real source of friction with Donald. A conspiracy theorist might be tempted to think Frank was consciously or unconsciously trying to sabotage Alex and Donald, perhaps out of jealousy, but it is unlikely he deliberately misled them and instead just made mistakes. It would have been interesting to know Alex's reaction, but he was silent on the subject.

They had a 'good feed', but not a good night's sleep. 'The sheepskins we were given to sleep on smelled bad enough to give a blowfly typhoid fever,' Donald recalled. 'In the middle of the night I awoke. Was I dreaming, or were there myriads of insects crawling over my body? Striking a match, I found the latter. The heat of my body had livened up a nest of maggots. Getting up, I took off my clothes, and turning them inside out soon shook out the invaders. Rousing our host, he gave us some chaff bags, so we got a few hours sleep before daylight.'

Waking up at six o'clock, the overlanders were itchy, the chaff off the bags 'irritating every inch of our bodies', and spent the morning scratching themselves. Setting off, they crossed a big saltbush plain and stopped at Wartaka Station, about thirty kilometres from Port Augusta, for lunch.

At four o'clock they could see the Tabletop Mountains that circle Port Augusta, and arrived in the town four hours later. Pulling up at Britten's Hotel they had a 'square' meal and went into town for a shave. Then they put bigger gears and new tyres on their bicycles before turning in for the night.

With the last stretch of desolate country behind them, the worst of their journey was over. The remainder of the ride would be made on relatively good roads. 'We retired feeling at last that all troubles and risks had been left behind, and that, with ordinary luck, my exertions would at least be repaid by lowering a few records,' Donald recalled.

Leaving at eight the next morning, Wednesday, 7 March, the trio ascended the steep Horrocks Pass in the Flinders Ranges, named after the English pastoralist and explorer John Horrocks, who was accidentally killed in 1846 when his camel caused his gun to discharge while he was leading an expedition to find grazing land. After reaching the summit, an elevation of 462 metres, they had a good downhill run to Wilmington, forty-three kilometres south-east of Port Augusta, stopping there just twenty-five minutes for lunch.

Departing Wilmington at midday, the overlanders travelled 196 kilometres to Clare, the best day's ride of the tour, arriving at eight o'clock. After another early start the next morning, they arrived in Gawler, the first country town to be established in South Australia, at 11.30am. After lunch they rode south on a rough road the forty kilometres to Adelaide, and were escorted into town by local cyclists, arriving at the General Post Office at 1.55pm on Friday, 9 March. Dressed in khaki, the overlanders presented a 'travel-stained and sun-browned appearance'.

Unlike Arthur, the trio did not stay in Adelaide. With Arthur's record within reach, they stopped for just two hours at the Globe Hotel in Port Adelaide and at 4.30pm resumed their ride to Melbourne where Alex, at least, would complete his circling of the continent.

The White brothers and Mackay must have run over a black cat somewhere along the way because their journey continued to be plagued by misfortune; this time, they suffered a bout of food-poisoning. On Sunday, 11 March, they arrived at Edenhope on the shores of Lake Wallace in the Western District of Victoria, in 'good nick', but after eating tinned fish for tea they fell ill on the road to Harrow the following day, particularly Alex, who was soon bedridden. Alex had just 402 kilometres to go to complete his journey around Australia, but he could not pedal another metre. The White brothers persuaded Donald, who was not feeling too well himself, not to wait for them and to push on and try to beat Arthur's record. Frank remained with Alex to help him recover and try to complete the ride. It would be tragic for Alex to withdraw so close and yet so far from the finish.

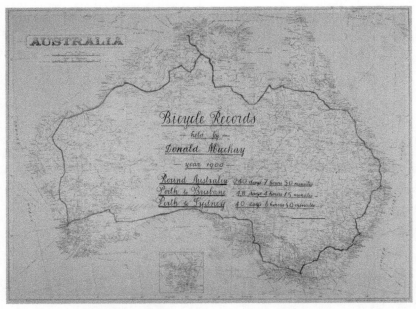

An amateur cyclist, Donald Mackay broke several long-distance records on his ride around Australia, including lowering Arthur Richardson's time by three days.

Stage Nineteen

Not Bad For an Amateur!

White brothers and Donald
Harrow to Brisbane
12 March to 27 March 1900

D ONALD did not want to leave Alex. They had become such great mates on this adventure of a lifetime that it felt wrong to leave him behind. But Donald also knew his chances of lowering Arthur's record would be ruined if he waited for him to recuperate. So on Monday, 12 March, Donald reluctantly set off to complete his ride alone. 'At Harrow, a town close to the Victorian border, I said goodbye to my mate Alex,' Donald recalled. 'He was laid up with dysentery. Seeing it would be a couple of days before he could ride again, and as I could do him no good by staying, but my chance of the records would be lost, I reluctantly said goodbye.' Donald made no mention of Frank, whom, one suspects, he was not sorry to be parting with.

With Arthur's record in his sights Donald clapped on the pace, travelling over familiar territory, which he had covered while returning from his search for gold in north-west New South Wales five years earlier. His last day's run into Melbourne was the longest of the trip — 246 kilometres — and he arrived late on Tuesday night, 13 March, looking 'gaunt and hollow', having lost 8 kilograms in weight since the ride began. Donald had covered 1255 kilometres from Port Augusta to Melbourne in six days, his best performance so far.

While in Melbourne, Donald gave the *Australian Cyclist* magazine an interview in which he was brutally honest in his opinions, saying he would not do a round Australia ride again for 'all the gold in the Indies'.

'I know I am old enough to have had more sense than try it,' Donald said.

> I think I must have been mad — my friends let me down lightly
> and say 'eccentric'. All I know is that main strength and stupidity
> pulled me through. When I got in a tangle, or was lost, I just went
> bull-headed whatever way seemed the easiest. Life is too short
> for such a trip, and I would not do it again for all the gold in the
> Indies. I tell you what, when I was about six weeks out, if I had
> had the pluck to chuck it up I would have done so; however, as
> I never funked before, and I have been in some rough adventures,
> I forced myself through a journey which I can only describe as
> a touch of pure Hades. Blazing sun, bad water, want of food,
> dangers from crocodiles and blacks, and, oh! those bubonic
> mosquitoes.

Asked what advice he would give a cyclist who had ambitions of circling Australia, Donald said he would strongly advise against it.

> I would counsel him, on the Bible if he wanted it, that the trip
> is not worth the candle. The privations endured are worse
> than the trip from Earth to the Hellespont. The first thing

to contend with is ordinary sickness; next, malarial fever or dysentery; last, but not least, your bicycle smashing up, plus the awful perishes for want of food and water. Mosquitoes, ants, flies, heat, dirt and other entrees are included without charge. These tell upon you, and I can assure you that although I was never ill in my life, this trip has told upon my constitution. I am weaker in every way. My side aches, and my limbs are weary from the continuous riding and plugging over the weary, monotonous wastes of scrub, rock and swamp. There is, with one exception, nothing really worth seeing. The exception being near the Katherine, at a place called the Jump Up, a hill which rises from the tableland. The view is magnificent. No: there are plenty of other places where the cyclist can enjoy life without regretting every day that he was ever born to be such a fool as to tempt his Creator.

Donald was clearly over the ride, but the ride was not yet over. Not wasting any time, he departed Melbourne at 2.55pm on 14 March, but got no further than Kilmore, sixty kilometres north of Melbourne, after riding into a strong headwind and light rain. But he made up for it the next day, riding 219 kilometres on a bad road to Chiltern, where he stayed the night.

Two days after Donald left Melbourne the White brothers arrived in the Victorian capital, bringing to an end Alex's long and painful ride around Australia, one that he had never intended to undertake, but one he would not give up, no matter the obstacles placed in his way.

Alex had spent two days in bed in Harrow and was treated by a doctor before resuming his ride, determined to fulfil his contract. He was so weak that he and Frank only rode sixty-five kilometres the first day, forty-eight of which were in the rain, and they were 'wet through' when they reached the township of Cavendish on the Wannon River. But he was almost recovered by the next day and they had a good run to the gold-rush town of Ballarat, 105 kilometres north-west of Melbourne.

Leaving Ballarat early in the morning, they rode into a heavy headwind on their way to Keilor, eighteen kilometres north-west of Melbourne, where they arrived at four o'clock in the afternoon. They were met there by an old Perth friend, Jack White, and were escorted into the city by a big group of cyclists, although Frank noticed, perhaps downheartedly, that there were not nearly as many to meet them as there had been in Perth.

It had taken Alex eight months and eleven days, or twelve days longer than Arthur, to circle the continent. Given the ill health he had endured for much of the journey, it was a wonderful achievement. Like Donald, Alex, sick and exhausted, vowed he would not do it again 'at any price'.

But Alex was not finished yet. Having failed to beat Arthur around Australia or to lower his record, Alex was determined to distinguish himself in another way. Despite still being weak, on Wednesday, 21 March, he left Melbourne for Albury and rode there and back, adding 400 miles (643 kilometres) to his 11,000 miles (17,702 kilometres), which set a new record for the world's longest continuous ride. He may have felt some satisfaction, but his triumph would be short-lived.

Unfortunately for Alex, Donald not only had Arthur's record in his sights, but his as well, which showed that mateship did not matter when it came to overlanding records. Two days after leaving Melbourne, Donald arrived in Albury in time for breakfast at the Albury Hotel. He was enjoying a grilled steak when a reporter from the *Albury Banner and Wodonga Express* introduced himself. Donald told the reporter he was leg-weary from the long ride and would be 'quite full of it' by the time he finished. He did not have much time to spare to beat Arthur's record, but he was not going to 'break things' in the attempt. He reiterated that he would not do it again because life was too short.

After consulting a local cycling identity, Fred Blacklock, about the roads, Donald left Albury at ten o'clock, accompanied by Mr J. Fuller of the Blacklock and Fuller Cycle Agency as far as Gerogery, about thirty kilometres away.

Donald had decided to ride to Sydney via Wagga Wagga, the town straddling the Murrumbidgee River in the Riverina region, so he could visit Wallendbeen and catch up with family and friends after being away for so long. This route was forty-eight kilometres longer than the more direct route via Gundagai, which seemed like an unnecessary detour for someone intent on breaking a world record, but he was familiar with the track, which was advantageous.

There were several heavy rainstorms between Wagga Wagga and Sydney, but the wet weather did not prevent Donald's club-mates from the Sydney Bicycle Club escorting him into the city. He reached the General Post Office at 7.50pm on Monday, 19 March, and was greeted by a big crowd of excited local cyclists. He spent a couple of enjoyable hours at the Sydney Bicycle Club's rooms where he had 'the pleasure' of meeting the Canadian cyclist Karl Creelman, who was touring the world by bicycle. Whether Creelman gave Donald any ideas, he did not say.

Even though Donald had a lot of friends and acquaintances in Sydney, he did not stay long. He could hear the ticking of the clock. Anxious to get away, he left the General Post Office at 7.45am the next day, Tuesday, 20 March, once again escorted by hundreds of cyclists. He had ten days to reach Brisbane and beat Arthur's record. Unless something went badly wrong, his goal was well within his grasp.

Frustratingly, the record of the final stage of Donald's ride is almost blank. Unlike Arthur and the White brothers, he was not contractually obliged to promote the ride. He did not write any telegrams to newspapers to keep the public informed of his progress. A self-promoter would have taken the opportunity to create publicity for himself, but he was not a fame-seeker.

It would have been a fairly straightforward trip, following in reverse the same inland route that Arthur had taken along the Great Northern Road on the way down. At the start of the ride Donald was overweight and struggled to keep up with the White brothers, but he ended up breaking a number of records, including lowering Arthur's time. Taking a week to ride from Sydney to Brisbane, Donald arrived at the Brisbane General Post Office at 5.15pm on Tuesday, 27 March, amid resounding cheers. It had taken him forty-eight days and four hours to ride to Brisbane from Perth, lowering Arthur's around Australia record from 243 days and four hours to 240 days, seven hours and thirty minutes. He had also lowered the record from Perth to Sydney, held by Jack Denning, from forty-four days to forty days, six hours and fifty minutes and the record from Perth to Brisbane, held by Frank, from fifty-three days, seven hours to forty-eight days, four hours and fifteen minutes. Not bad for an amateur!

A report of Donald's ride and arrival was published in the *Queenslander* on 7 April:

At 5.15pm on 27 March there rode up to the Brisbane General
Post Office a tall, spare young man, dusty and tired-looking,
attired in brown knickers, sweater and cork hat, and mounted on
a bike which bore unmistakeable signs of a long journey. To those
who had seen Donald Mackay on his departure from Brisbane
on the 30th of last July when he weighed about fourteen and a
half stone [92 kilograms], it was somewhat hard to realise that
this was the same man now reduced to a little over twelve stone
[77 kilograms], but Donald Mackay it was without doubt and
there was no change noticeable in the cheeriness of his voice as he
heartily grasped the hand of the representative of this paper, who
was on hand to meet him.

Later in the evening, after Donald had checked into the
Hotel Cecil, he spoke with the *Queenslander* journalist. If the
bicycle and tyre manufacturers had been hoping for a glowing
report on the ride, they would have been disappointed. While
he expressed satisfaction at lowering Arthur's record, this
achievement did not change Donald's view that the ride was a
complete waste of time.

'Now that his ride is over he is inclined to look upon it as so
much lost time from which there can be absolutely no beneficial
results,' the *Queenslander* reported. 'It was undertaken, as far
as Mackay was concerned, solely in a spirit of adventure and
with a desire to see the country, but it has proved a hard task,
entirely without result.'

Donald was disgusted with the trip, claiming the overlanders
did not traverse any country which had not already been explored
and that the wilderness of northern Australia would have been
better travelled on horseback than bicycle. Furthermore, he
questioned whether the ride could be accurately described as

'around Australia' because they had cut so many corners and walked about 3000 kilometres of the route. The cyclist, he said, could not appreciate the scenery because 'plugging along over rough country on the machine, there was little chance to look about, and when walking and pushing the bike there was less inclination'. The only satisfaction Donald had was lowering the records.

But the *Queenslander* suggested that Donald may have benefited from the ride in one way at least. 'Though depleted in pocket and flesh, Mackay still looks well, and, providing there are no ill results from the exposure he has suffered, he may yet benefit by his travels, if only in the way of a curb to his eccentricity.'

While Donald had lowered the record, Arthur's ride was viewed by purists as the more meritorious because he was the first around Australia and had done so alone. 'Without wishing to detract in any way from Mackay's record, it should be remarked that Richardson did not set out with the intention of establishing a time record, his motives being simply love of adventure and a wish to see the country, and, furthermore, whilst Richardson accomplished his ride alone, a far more dangerous undertaking, Mackay had company,' the *Northern Argus* reported on 6 April.

Not surprisingly, Arthur's great supporter 'Pedal' was dismissive of Donald's record-breaking ride. 'It is claimed for Don Mackay, who recently concluded a journey round Australia in company with Alex White, that he completed the circuit of the continent in two days less time than Richardson occupied in his memorable ride,' 'Pedal' wrote on 21 April.

Seeing that Richardson was not on record-breaking bent this is of little moment. Of the relative merits of the riders there cannot be any doubt, and Mackay, with much good grace, looks upon Richardson's performance as much superior to his own. It seems to me, however, that the majority of Australian wheelmen and of those who take an interest in wheeling matters look upon the accomplishment of all journeys in as short a period of time as possible as the first essential. The hardships endured, the difficulties surmounted, the trying experiences and the display of pluck, endurance and intrepidity, unfortunately are, as a rule, regarded as a secondary consideration. When the racing instinct is lessened in the Australian youth, he will regard such journeys as those recently concluded by the overlanders in their proper light.

After a few days rest in Brisbane, Donald mounted his reliable Dux again. He had lowered Arthur's record and now he aimed to beat Alex's record for the world's longest continuous ride. 'As I have proved myself to hold the record as the greatest fool in the country by making such a journey, I am going the whole hog, and will get the record for the longest continuous ride,' Donald said.

He intended to ride to Sydney or Melbourne, but pressing business commitments prevented him. Instead, he rode to Newcastle, which was far enough to claim the record. Perhaps for a change of scenery, he rode south to Newcastle by the coast roads, which he regarded as the best track 'if one can take time and hit the night tides'. Riding in the rain from Brisbane to Lismore, he made a slow time. The track from Tweed Heads to Lismore was 'a bit rough' and he had a bad fall riding down a hill, but the rest was 'A1'. He arrived in Newcastle on Monday, 9 April, having covered 11,600 miles (18,668 kilometres) and, in his own words, 'completing one of the most dreary and uninteresting rides that a man has ever undertaken!'

Donald's view of the ride would change dramatically with the passage of time, when thirst, hunger and aching muscles were but a distant memory.

Maybe he and the other overlanders had been foolhardy and mad, as Donald seemed to think in 1900, for undertaking such a hazardous, seemingly impossible, journey. But he, Arthur, Frank and Alex all had a dream, the dream of the overlander, that of becoming the first to ride around Australia on a bicycle. With courage, determination and a love of adventure, these free-spirited pioneers on wheels raced each other around this vast island continent, facing the kind of dangers that most people today could never even imagine.

The overlanders deserve to be remembered as heroes. Popular opinion tells us that Australia became a nation on the bloody beaches of Gallipoli, but national consciousness was not born when those first ANZAC troops landed. There was already a sense of Australia well before federation. It was evident in the poetry of Banjo Paterson and Henry Lawson, in the singing of Nellie Melba, in pioneering work in the outback, and in four overlanders riding around the continent on bicycles. Fearless Arthur, laconic Donald, fun-loving Frank and stoic Alex helped to define the character of an aspiring nation.

Epilogue

The Last Great Adventure

TWO months after Arthur rode around Australia, Dunlop published *The Story of a Remarkable Ride*, which was the overlander's account of the journey as told to 'Pedal'. The *West Australian* had already serialised the story in three instalments, but Dunlop reproduced it as a booklet to maximise publicity.

The cover was real Boy's Own Adventure stuff, typical of the manly and exciting fiction that Arthur enjoyed, promising a ripping yarn. The inspiration for the illustration on the cover was Arthur's unhappy experience with his Aboriginal guide on the way from Wave Hill to Victoria Downs. The artwork depicted a camp site in the outback with Arthur, clad in a long-sleeved shirt, trousers and a tam-o'-shanter cap, aiming his revolver at an Aboriginal man who is about to disappear with his tucker bags into long grass on the other side of a creek.

The Story of a Remarkable Ride was very well received by the press and the public. The booklet, which was distributed gratis by Dunlop, was so popular that by May 1900 it was already in its third edition of 10,000 copies. Arthur's story captured the imagination not only of the Australian public: several English newspapers and magazines also published detailed serial accounts of his ride.

While readers in both hemispheres were enjoying the story of Arthur's ride, the overlander was fighting the Boers in South Africa. After riding a bicycle around Australia, he would have been entitled to a well-earned rest, enjoying his triumph and perhaps capitalising on his fame. But Arthur immediately volunteered for the Western Australian Bushmen's Contingent for service in the Boer War.

Arthur's return to Perth had come soon after the 'Black Week' of 10 to 17 December 1899, which had seen British forces decisively defeated at Colenso, Stormberg and Magersfontein, suffering 2776 men killed, wounded and captured. The towns of Mafeking, Ladysmith and Kimberley were besieged by the Boers and the Empire was in crisis. In this climate, young Australians, who regarded themselves as British, rushed to join in the fighting. In the list of the Third Bushmen's Contingent, Arthur was enrolled as:

```
64. Arthur Richardson, 28, South America,
prospector. Three years South Australian
Militia.
```

It was ironic that having ridden around Australia on his bicycle without sustaining an injury, Arthur broke his arm soon after joining the Bushmen's Contingent, putting his service in South Africa in doubt. On the afternoon of Wednesday, 28 February, Arthur, an acting corporal, was dispatched on horseback from Perth's Karrakatta military training camp to carry a message to Claremont on the north bank of the Swan River. As Arthur was leaving the precincts of the camp a dog ran in front of him, causing his horse to swerve suddenly, throwing him violently to the ground.

Arthur sustained a fracture of the upper bone of his right arm. He was attended to by Dr Ingoldby in the hospital tent before being removed to his lodgings in Perth that evening to receive additional treatment. He was regarded as an excellent soldier and great regret was expressed at his misfortune. His commanding officer, Major Vialls, was determined that Arthur should go to South Africa if there was even the slightest chance of him being of service. He could rest his arm on the voyage to Cape Town on the S.S. *Maplemore* and hopefully it would be mended by the time the contingent was in the field.

In recognition of his cycling feats, Arthur was allowed to take a bicycle to South Africa. Before boarding the S.S. *Maplemore* on Wednesday, 14 March, the day that Donald left Melbourne for Brisbane, Arthur was presented with a handsome pair of field glasses by Percy Armstrong, never one to miss an opportunity, and a Beeston Humber path-racer by the Humber Cycle Company.

'He has had the bright parts bronzed, in order to prevent the glint of the sun's rays on the nickelling attracting attention if he is engaged in scouting or dispatch work,' 'Pedal' wrote in the *West Australian* on 15 March.

In the event of Arthur surviving the conflict in South Africa unscathed, the Beeston Humber Company made him an offer to ride from Cape Town to Cairo. According to the *Critic* in Adelaide, Arthur considered it: 'Arthur Richardson, who went to the front with the Western Australian Bushmen's Contingent, broken arm and all, meditates cycling from the Cape to Cairo. Australians forever!' It is not known why Arthur did not accept the offer. Maybe the contract was not worth the risk or perhaps he thought the ride impractical. It certainly would have been an amazing sequel to his around Australia ride.

Promoted to sergeant-major, Arthur was appointed to the headquarters staff of the Rhodesian Field Force under Major General Sir Frederick Carrington, who had famously crushed the 1896 Matabele rebellion. Arthur served as a special dispatch rider – by bicycle, horse or boot – between Bamboo Creek and Umtali. He again broke his arm in a fall, whether from a horse or his bicycle is not known, and was left to recuperate at the field hospital at Marandellas in Rhodesia.

Arthur had earlier fought at Elands River when Carrington's forces attempted to relieve troops besieged at a depot there in August 1900. On the first day of fighting he got close to the enemy lines on his bicycle with a party of about twenty skirmishers and scouts, with the main body of the field force, mostly Bushmen, three to five kilometres in the rear. The Boers did not fire a shot until the scouts got within 700 metres of them and then they all started blasting away at once.

The whole party dismounted and crawled away from their horses, eight of which were shot within eighty metres of Arthur, who got off his bike and hid like the rest in high grass, behind ant hills and rocks, in ruts or anywhere they could find. 'For about an hour we had a very warm time of it,' Arthur wrote in a letter to his mother. 'If anyone moved to try and get a shot he got shot at.'

After a while some of the Bushmen from Carrington's main force scaled a *kopje*, or small hill, behind the scouts and started firing away, but they too had to make for shelter as the Boers began shelling them with two guns from a ridge. The first two shells (15-pounders) dropped short and the Bushmen felt the full effect. Not only did they make an 'infernal screeching' noise, but burst when they landed, throwing stones, dust and lumps of iron everywhere.

The Bushmen, however, soon hunted the Boers into the open and got some shots at them with their rifles, giving them 'a bad few minutes' as they crossed the ridge. It was then quiet for a time, which gave the Bushmen a chance to count the casualties. There were three wounded and Arthur rode back to camp and got an ambulance for them.

About midday the Boers started shelling the Bushmen again with 15-pounders and quick-firing infantry guns. 'I was a little in the rear, and one could not help laughing to see the horses (which are held in groups of four, one man to each four),' Arthur wrote to his mother. 'They were just making for shelter when the shells came flying right into them, and they scampered in all directions, the shells knocking up a dust all amongst them. None of them seemed to get hit, however.'

It was good that Arthur could keep his sense of humour in such a dangerous situation, but he was not laughing for long. His party, watching the others from a gutter about a metre deep, was not being shot at much, but all of a sudden a huge shell burst just behind them. 'It was the enemy's 94-pounder trying to pick up the range of our guns on the ridge and for about five minutes it was a good place not to be in,' Arthur wrote.

The shelling continued until three o'clock when the Bushmen started a steady retreat, their force of about 600 not being strong enough to challenge the Boer pounding. They retreated until dark, arriving about ten o'clock at the river where they had left their transport and several guns.

During the next two days the Bushmen were engaged in more fighting as the Boers tried to cut their column off. Altogether twenty men were wounded, eleven were missing and a lot of horses and mules were shot. As they continued their retreat towards Mafeking, they burned stores along the road to prevent them from falling into Boer hands. 'The retreat put us in mind of a new rush on the goldfields,' Arthur wrote. 'The night before we got in here there was a good deal of excitement, people clearing away as they thought there was going to be another siege.'

Arthur stated that his was the only bicycle to come through all the Bushmen's recent actions, the other machines belonging to his forces having been abandoned while in action. 'During the first day's fighting, the other cyclist, who was out along with the scouts, abandoned the bike, and crawled into shelter in the grass, but his was a government bike, and mine was my own,' Arthur explained.

A letter Arthur wrote to Messrs A.W. Dobbie & Co. from Mafeking would have made a wonderful advertisement for Humber bicycles and Dunlop tyres:

> Since writing you from here ... we have been getting more or less fighting every week, and as I have been dispatch riding on nearly every column round here, I have had the Humber bike under fire in some pretty warm places. It is the same in every particular as the bike I rode around Australia, and is standing the rough country splendidly. The tyres, which are Dunlop roadsters, made in Western Australia, are the envy of all the other cyclists about here. If I return with the contingents, you may expect to see this bike at many a North Adelaide cycle club run.

Arthur's military career in South Africa came to an end on 15 May 1901, when he was invalided to England with pneumonia. He stayed in Middlesex with the diamond merchant Alfred

Mosely, the father of Rita, who would become Arthur's second wife, and of Dr Frederick Mosely, Arthur's friend. Writing to a friend in Perth, Arthur stated that he intended to tour England, Scotland and Ireland before returning to Australia. While in England, Arthur was one of the few Australians to receive his Boer War service medal from the hand of King Edward VII at a ceremony at Marlborough House, London, on 29 July 1901.

King Edward and Queen Alexandra were both keen cyclists. While the royal couple did not ride in public, they often cycled around the royal Sandringham estate. Given the publicity Arthur's ride had received in Britain, it is likely the king would have been aware of his historic circuit of Australia. Perhaps the king and the overlander had an opportunity to have a polite conversation about Arthur's journey. The king, no doubt, would have been curious about the amazing feat, and Arthur, true to his modest character, would have downplayed the dangers. Arthur would never big-note himself, even if a king commanded him to do so.

Arthur returned to Australia from England in December 1901, 'completely restored to health'. His desire for travel and adventure carried him to many more countries. Between the Boer War and World War I, Arthur had a variety of occupations in Africa and South America. He was the leader of an expedition on the disease-ridden west coast of Africa, known as the 'White Man's Grave', for two years; a miner in Patagonia until he became ill with fever; the manager of a gold mine in Peru; and a dispatch rider in North Africa. He was clearly drawn to wild and remote places, free from the cloistered restrictions of civilisation.

Stopping in Australia in 1907 on the way from England to Chile, Arthur's arrival in Fremantle was recorded by the local

A serious-looking gathering celebrate Arthur Richardson's marriage to his first wife, Gwen, in Valparaiso, Chile, in 1913. The occasion may have seemed glum, but it was unfashionable to smile in photographs in that era.

press, which remembered his epic ride. It was while Arthur was in Chile that he met his first wife, Ruth Gwendolin Bedwell Stedman, known as Gwen, whom he married at the British consulate at Valparaiso in 1913. They had one son named Herbert James Arthur Richardson, who was born in Valparaiso in 1914. Arthur and Gwen were later divorced.

In July 1916, Arthur sailed on the passenger ship *Oransa* from Coquimbo in Chile to England to enlist in the British army for the war with Germany. After landing at Liverpool he was commissioned as a temporary second lieutenant in the Royal Engineers on 10 September. A month later, on 10 October, he arrived in France and was posted to the 176th Tunnelling Company, based near Vimy Ridge. During Arthur's time the company supported the attack made by the 4th Canadian

Division on 9 April 1917. The company dug and maintained the Coburg and Gobron subway tunnels which assisted the ultimately successful Canadian assault, during which more than 10,000 Canadian servicemen died.

Living and fighting in a dark, cavernous, subterranean world would have been alien for most soldiers, but was especially so for Arthur, who was accustomed to the wide open spaces of the road as an overlander and dispatch rider. Many soldiers were blown to pieces or buried alive beneath the battlefields in this new, terrifying form of warfare.

An underground soldier's worst nightmare was the deafening noise of an explosion and the damage it could cause. In a shell explosion on 10 April 1917, Arthur was severely wounded, breaking his ribs and sustaining internal injuries. The army medical board found that Arthur was:

> struck by a piece of H.E. shell ... which fractured the tenth
> and eleventh ribs on the right side and at the same time causing
> internal injuries in the abdomen. This would subsequently set up
> symptoms of neurasthenia, and intestinal pain. He has recovered
> from the neurasthenia, but still complains of intermittent
> abdominal pain on his right hypochondriac region. The board
> think that this abdominal pain is caused by the presence of
> adhesions, the extent of which is very doubtful, but which
> undoubtedly involves the hepatic flexure and probably part of the
> ascending and transverse colon as evidenced by the localisation of
> the pain set up by constipation or the administration of aperients.

While it was not mentioned in the board's assessment, it seems certain that Arthur suffered from shell shock, or post-traumatic stress disorder as it is known today. The board determined that

Arthur was not medically fit to return to active service and he was evacuated to England on 4 May 1917, where, after many months in hospital, he contributed once more to the war effort, but never returned to overseas duty. He filled various domestic appointments in the Royal Engineers and was promoted to acting captain on 28 April 1918. He ended the war as a captain at the Royal Engineers Signals at Wareham in Dorset. Relinquishing his commission on 30 August 1921, Arthur returned to Chile aboard the R.M.S. *Orita* on 21 December 1922.

As time passed Arthur continued to have trouble with his abdomen, while he also became partially deaf and his eyesight deteriorated. Most importantly, he suffered from a nervous condition resulting from the shell explosion, which would have tragic consequences.

On 26 July 1934, Arthur married Rita 'Betsy' Elliot-Druiff (née Mosely), the widow of John Elliot-Druiff, in Kensington, London. He was sixty-two years old and she was forty-nine. The couple lived at Troutsdale Lodge, adjacent to Rock Farm, near Hackness, Yorkshire. Rita owned the farm and some others in the district.

An English relative of Arthur's on the Merrifield side of the family, John Walker, remembered Arthur coming to his family home when he was a young boy. He said Arthur told wonderful stories of his adventures all over the world. He once told John that when he returned from the war he was sitting on a train on the London Underground, feeling terrible, when a cranky woman ticked him off for not giving her his seat. He said, 'That's right, ma'am, the next station is Baker Street.' This defused the situation and the woman went off with a puzzled look. John Walker always loved Arthur's visits.

The war had left Arthur with mental as well as physical scars, which resulted in a tragic murder–suicide. The bodies of Arthur and Rita were found at their home on 3 April 1939. Arthur had died of a self-inflicted gunshot wound after shooting his wife. At the inquest at Snainton, near Scarborough, Arthur's brother-in-law Dr Frederick Mosely gave evidence that Arthur had been seriously wounded in the war and suffered 'brainstorms', blowing small things out of proportion. The Richardsons' chauffeur–gardener said that Arthur sometimes had a bad temper for very little reason, but at other times you could not meet a nicer man. Arthur's will was written on 10 March 1939. He left all his money and goods to his son.

A verdict that Arthur had murdered his wife and then committed suicide was recorded at the inquest. There was insufficient evidence to show the state of Arthur's mind at the time. But some of Arthur's descendants have a theory to explain the motivation behind the tragedy, which they believe may have been a kind of mercy killing. Rita's family was Jewish and it was well documented in the newspapers of the time that Adolf Hitler was persecuting Jews in Germany. The Germans were massing troops on the Polish border. If Hitler invaded Poland, Britain would be at war with Germany. Given Arthur's fragile state of mind, and his tendency to blow things out of proportion, it is conceivable that he imagined a Nazi invasion of Britain would be a fate worse than death for British Jews, including Rita. Arthur's final act may have been a courageous, if misguided, attempt to protect his wife. While there is no hard evidence to support this theory, it reflects the family's admiration for Arthur and their belief he would not have committed such a violent act without a reason.

It was a tragic end for such a brave and adventurous man, the most unassuming of heroes.

* * *

In contrast, Donald lived a long and happy life, but he never quenched his thirst for adventure. He returned to Wallendbeen to recuperate from his record-breaking bike ride and attend to work on the station, but continued to indulge his passion for travel. In 1901 he spent six months travelling in Europe and America. Then, the following year, at the age of thirty-two, he decided to settle down and marry. After all of Donald's travels around the world he married a local beauty who lived just across the road from Wallendbeen. Amy Isabel Little was born in Newtown, Sydney, in 1880, but later lived at Wahgunyah, opposite the Presbyterian church on the Wallendbeen property. Donald and Amy were married at the Congregational church at Homebush, Sydney, on 16 April 1902. From all accounts their long marriage was a very happy one.

'I did one of the most sensible things a man can do,' Donald recalled. 'I got married! They say marriage is a lottery, with more blanks than prizes. Well, in my case, my luck was in; I got a real good sport for a life-mate. After nearly forty years of married life, I can honestly say that getting married was the most sensible thing I ever did in my life!'

Donald and Amy went to live at Turriell Point on the water at Port Hacking, south of Sydney, where he built a federation-style house (now heritage-listed) of brick and sandstone, on what is now known as Wallendbeen Avenue, and named it Wallendbeen Lodge. The house had a superb view of Burraneer

Bay. The couple enjoyed an idyllic life of sailing and fishing, but Donald soon became restless again.

In 1906, Donald's brother, Kenneth, was appointed chairman of a royal commission to enquire into conditions in British New Guinea, or Papua, which was formally transferred to the control of the Australian government that year. Kenneth jokingly suggested that Donald should explore Papua, which was inhabited by 'cannibals and headhunters'. Donald's curiosity was piqued and so began his career as an explorer.

In July 1908 Donald led and financed an expedition to Papua to investigate the headwaters of the Purari River. The purpose of the expedition was to discover minerals and land suitable for European habitation. Donald contracted malaria, but he was determined to push on. On 18 October he noted in his diary:

> Terrific rain. I feel a compound wreck, very depressed. Hitherto, without boasting, I thought I could hold my own with any man at hard work, or putting up with rough going. But now this fever is getting me down. I guess if I have to swing over the Edge, I won't have such a rough spin when I put out on the last Great Adventure. Strange that, at last, every man, whether he wants to or not, has to explore the Unknown ...

Donald recovered and the expedition discovered extensive deposits of coal on the banks of Thukuri Creek, but the area was unsuitable for European settlement. Donald had hoped to reach the Fly River, but impassable mountains forced him to abandon the exploration after six months of suffering from fever, sores, poor food, exposure and native arrows. 'There is nothing left to do except turn back,' Donald wrote in his diary. 'After all this beastliness, worry and expense, my hopes have been dashed to the ground, and the satisfaction of traversing the country from here to the Fly River is still left to someone else, whom Fortune may treat more leniently.'

Donald's next big adventure was sailing the South Pacific in search of buried treasure. Early in 1911, Donald and a yachtsman friend, Mr C.H. Relph, purchased a 50-foot yacht, *Alfreda II*, and sailed for the island of Tanna in the New Hebrides (Vanuatu) with two Americans who owned treasure maps allegedly drawn by the pirate Benito Bonito. Arriving at the island they found the grassy knoll where the treasure was supposed to be buried, but the knoll was four to five acres in size. Realising it would take forever to dig up the whole area, they returned to Sydney empty-handed.

At the outbreak of World War I, Donald, aged forty-four, immediately tried to enlist for military service, but to his surprise he was declared medically unfit owing to a minor complaint caused by his 'strenuous life'. A minor complaint would not have held Donald back, but regulations were regulations. He made considerable contributions to patriotic funds and war loans to assist the war effort and at the end of the war paid for a memorial to the ninety men of the Wallendbeen district who had served overseas.

Brigadier General David Miller unveiled the Soldiers Memorial Obelisk in front of a large crowd in the centre of Wallendbeen township on Wednesday, 13 October 1920. A magnificent monument, the obelisk stands more than ten metres high and is composed of polished granite with a trachyte base. On the base of the spire is a design in metal of crossed flags and a rising sun. A metal plaque bears the names of the men who served.

Although Donald had travelled the world, central and northern Australia had a greater attraction for him than any other country, having a 'unique appeal'. Ever since he met Mr Chambers, the surveyor, at Newcastle Waters during his record-breaking ride, Donald had dreamed of exploring Central Australia to fill in the blanks on the map at the red heart of the continent. In 1926, Donald, at an age when most men were starting to think about retirement, financed and led an expedition to the Northern Territory, where, with the anthropologist Dr Herbert Basedow and relying on a team of camels rather than one trusty bicycle, he became the first European to cross the mysterious Petermann Ranges.

Two years later Donald led another expedition, this time with pack horses, through Arnhem Land, gleaning valuable information about the region, and bringing back memories of his ride through Darwin and Katherine twenty-nine years earlier.

The climax of Donald's career as an explorer was a series of aerial surveys of Central Australia which he conducted in 1930, 1933, 1935 and 1937, covering a total of 1,857,021 square kilometres, more than one-quarter of the whole of Australia. On 23 May 1930, the prime minister, James Scullin, farewelled Donald and five other members of the first aerial expedition at a banquet at Parliament House in Canberra, but the explorer undertook the surveys at his own expense without any government support, chartering the planes and paying the pilots and crew.

A month before the first survey began Donald received a letter from Harold Lasseter, the now legendary gold-seeker, asking Donald to drop him off and keep him supplied while he pegged his claims on a still-sought-for gold reef that he claimed was 'three times as big and rich as Kalgoorlie'. There was no room in the survey planes for him so Lasseter went off with another party and became lost. The bushman Bob Buck, a member of Donald's aerial expeditions, found his body in the Petermann Ranges in 1931.

Some of Donald's descendants are convinced he was searching for Lasseter's Reef during his inland explorations. 'There's no doubt he was looking for Lasseter's Reef,' Donald's great-great-nephew Mike Baldry told me over dinner at Wallendbeen. 'There was a connection between Mackay and Lasseter. All I can say is I remember Dad saying there was some crossover of them.'

The aerial surveys produced far more useful maps than had previously existed and greatly increased the knowledge of remote areas, but there was a sense that Donald's efforts were unappreciated.

'Many of Australia's early explorers — men whose names are held in grateful remembrance today as the trailblazers of this vast continent — opened up new frontiers in the face of official apathy and discouragement,' Arnold G. Hudson wrote in *The Land, Farm and Station Annual* on 27 July 1938.

> But poor though it was in many instances, the official support and recognition accorded those early explorers was considerably more than the present Commonwealth government has given to the man who, in this twentieth century, has traversed and charted more of unknown Australia than any other explorer in our history. That man is Donald Mackay, a member of a pioneer pastoral family, and leader of the Mackay Aerial Expeditions to Central and North-Western Australia. Wholly financed from his own private purse, these expeditions have surveyed and mapped for the first time an area equal to one-quarter of the continent, a vast territory in most of which no white man had ever set foot.

Yet this great national work has received no recognition of any kind – not even an official thank you. Even when, late last year, he presented to the Commonwealth government large-scale maps incorporating every detail charted by his four separate expeditions to Central Australia, months went by before their receipt was even formally acknowledged.

Australia's response to Donald Mackay's great public-spirited exploration work has been silence – cruel and unaccountable silence.

Donald's achievements, however, were recognised by one of Australia's greatest explorers, Sir Edgeworth David, whose journeys to the Antarctic made him a hero. Professor David wrote a letter to Donald after he returned from the 1933 survey, congratulating him.

I have seen your beautiful map. Please accept my heartiest congratulations to you for having produced such a monumental piece of work. Surely all patriotic Australians should be grateful to you for all time for having lightened so much of the darkness in what before was so little known, or even entirely unknown, in our great island continent. The map is a beautiful piece of draftsmanship and surveying. I shall always value it highly, for the very important additions it makes to our knowledge of Australian geography.

It is not accurate to say that Donald's achievements went completely unrecognised by officialdom. In 1934 a large ephemeral salt lake, which covers both Western Australia and the Northern Territory, was named Lake Mackay after Donald, who was the first European to document it in 1930. He was appointed OBE (Officer of the Most Excellent Order of the

British Empire) in 1934 and CBE (Commander of the Most Excellent Order of the British Empire) in 1937, but many of his supporters believed he deserved a knighthood.

Perhaps Donald cruelled his chances of that higher honour when he created international headlines by criticising the treatment of Aboriginal people in Central Australia. On 18 July 1933, the *Brisbane Courier* reported that in an address at a reception for members of the Mackay aerial expedition the previous day:

> the leader of the expedition (Mr Donald Mackay) expressed the hope that the Aborigines would not be molested. Central Australia is the last place, said Mr Mackay, where the Australian blacks are making a last stand against the white civilisation. We have heard of the German atrocities, but they are nothing to the Australian atrocities. Blacks have been shot down and poisoned by water. They are inoffensive men as a rule and in most instances the trouble was the fault of the white man. I hope that for the present white men will not settle the country. We have large Aboriginal reserves there and let us keep them.

When Donald's criticism was reported in the British press, the Australian prime minister, Joseph Lyons, expressed concern that the nation's 'good name' would be damaged. 'We do not object to the publication of statements which are founded on facts and can be substantiated,' Lyons was quoted as saying in the *Telegraph* in Brisbane on 21 July. 'We are extremely desirous of securing information which will help us faithfully to carry out our duties in the Northern Territory, but we deprecate unsupported statements based on incidents alleged to have occurred many years ago.'

But Donald would not back down. He offered to withdraw his criticism only if Lyons could prove that the treatment of Aboriginal people had been humane.

On his return from his second aerial survey in 1933, Donald was quoted as saying: 'I think in my life-time I have seen as much of Australia as most people, and the more I see of it the better I like it. I've had a rough spin at times, but, all said and done, I've had a lot of satisfaction out of it. I was never intended for the city. I can't act the part.' Donald's comment contrasted starkly with his earlier unfavourable remarks about his ride around Australia. Perhaps the comment only related to his explorations, or maybe he was starting to look back on the ride more fondly.

In his retirement Donald continued to be a philanthropist, giving generously to worthy causes. One of his most significant gifts was the land on which the Caringbah RSL was built on the corner of Banksia Road and Cawarra Road, which was renamed Mackay Street in 1970. Although in ill health, Donald laid the foundation stone on 12 October 1957, but sadly did not live long enough to see the building completed. For many years after Donald's death, members of the club gathered at the entrance for a few moments to honour his memory.

Donald died on 17 September 1958, aged eighty-eight, at Sutherland Hospital, and was cremated after a Presbyterian service. Amy had passed away two years before. A report on Donald's death in the Sydney *Daily Telegraph* described him as a 'noble old gentleman' and 'the last of Australia's colourful band of early explorers'. According to the *Telegraph*, 'adventure was in his blood. He would finish one dangerous journey only to look forward to something more arduous – and more dangerous.'

Gordon Buchanan, the son of the pioneer pastoralist Nat Buchanan, described Donald in his book *Packhorse and Waterhole*:

Spare and muscular, Donald Mackay stands well over six feet,
with that slightly forward inclination of the head peculiar to some
investigating men of action. His steadfast eyes, accustomed to scan
the fiery far horizons, have the penetrating gaze of the bushman
wont to study the ways of nature rather than the moods of man.
Not much of a talker, but a dinkum doer, this great-hearted
Australian deserves well of his country.

Donald had been extremely negative about his ride around Australia immediately after he completed it, saying it was a waste of time and he would never do it again for anything. But for all his outstanding achievements in exploration he came in the end to regard the ride as his greatest accomplishment. 'Donald Mackay, extraordinary explorer and adventurer, listed his greatest triumph as the circumnavigation of Australia by bicycle in 1899–1900,' Marcia Thorburn wrote in her local history, *The Wallendbeen Story*.

As Donald and Amy did not have any children, there was a question mark over what would be done with Wallendbeen. According to the family, Donald had intended to leave the property to the Inland Mission of Australia, which underlined his empathy for Aboriginal people. Instead, it was put on the market and bought by members of the Baldry family, who were great-grandchildren of Alexander Mackay. The family has set up a trust fund generated from the sale of Donald and Kenneth's archives, and it is planned that some of that money will go towards honouring Donald's original intention and benefiting Aboriginal people.

* * *

Details of the lives of the White brothers after the ride around Australia are sketchy. In 1902 Frank moved to Northam, a town situated at the confluence of the Avon and Mortlock rivers, about ninety-seven kilometres north-east of Perth. The White brothers' father, Jesse William, was living in Northam, but he was ill. Frank's sister Kate came across from New Zealand to nurse him, but she died before he did. Frank set up a building business in Northam in 1903 and the following year he married Lillian Weir in Perth. They had a daughter, Avice Kate, who was born the same year.

Unfortunately, Frank's business failed and he ended up in the bankruptcy court. He returned to Melbourne and lived in Hawthorn where his second daughter, Thelma, was born in 1907 and his son, Kenneth Francis, was born in 1910, but by 1954 he was living in Hampton, then a place of market gardens and now a wealthy bayside area. Frank continued to work as a builder and probably span yarns about his cycling adventures to anyone who would listen. He died in 1969 of a chest infection, aged ninety-eight, which supports the theory that cycling contributes to longevity.

Family lore suggests a scandal led to Alex moving to South Africa. Alex married Elizabeth Pegg (née Brown) in Durban on 11 August 1904. The family believes Elizabeth may have come from Tasmania. Elizabeth was forty-four and Alex only twenty-six, the big age difference possibly causing shame in that conservative era.

Alex and Elizabeth divorced in 1915 and he married Sophia Wilhelmina Bryson in June 1917. Sophia was believed to have been born in Northumberland, England, in 1869, which would have made her nine years older than Alex, who seemed to have a preference for older women.

When Alex arrived in South Africa he listed his occupation as carpenter, but he later owned and operated a hotel in Pietersburg (now Polokwane) in the Northern Province halfway between Pretoria and the Rhodesian (now Zimbabwean) border. Two of Alex's brothers, George and Arthur, also moved to South Africa, and he remained in contact with his family in Australia. The family has kept a Christmas card which Alex sent to his younger brother Fred in 1909.

On the left-hand side of the card is a printed message, which reads:

Since hearts of friends,
Who seldom meet,
Are linked by memory's golden chain,
This little card
Is sent to greet you,
As a Christmas dawns again.

There was a personal note on the opposite page, but it was also printed rather than hand written.

Christmas 1909
To wish you every Christmas happiness,
With the hope that the
New Year may prove another link to bind us closer still
From Mr & Mrs A.H. White
Johannesburg

Alex, who never complained and never gave up, died in Pietersburg in 1941, aged sixty-three.

The White brothers' tradition of overlanding was kept alive by their younger brother Fred, who, in 1911, reclaimed for the family Frank's Fremantle to Sydney record, which had been lowered by the famous Australian adventurer and long-distance cyclist Francis Birtles. Fred beat Birtles's record by just two hours, which the *Melbourne Punch* reported was 'not much of a beating, but still enough to swear by'.

* * *

Sadly, the memory of the overlanders soon faded into obscurity. Within a decade of the completion of the historic rides around Australia the cycle craze which had swept the world gave way to a new fad, the car craze. The speed and comfort of the car soon superseded the bicycle. Never one to be left behind, Percy Armstrong evolved his cycle agency into the Armstrong Cycle and Motor Agency.

It was not long before adventurous motorists were setting out to establish long-distance records in the same way the overlanders had done. In the first crossing of Australia by car in 1908, Henry H. Dutton and Murray Aunger drove a Talbot from Adelaide to Darwin. But the transition from the bicycle to the car was personified by Francis Birtles, who cycled around Australia twice and crossed the continent several times before completing more than seventy crossings of Australia by car. In 1927–28, Birtles even became the first person to drive a car from England to Australia.

That is not to say that the tradition of long-distance cycling ceased. In 1914, Eddie 'Ryko' Reichenbach, the son of

German immigrants, broke Albert MacDonald's sixteen-year-old record from Darwin to Adelaide, riding in the opposite direction in twenty-eight days and seven minutes. Sir Hubert Opperman's endurance cycling feats in the 1920s and 1930s earned him both national and international acclaim. Foreign and Australian cyclists such as Arthur Wakeling (1931), Joan Joesting-Mahoney, 'the Perimeter Queen' (1991), Perry Stone (2003), Eugene Schilter (2004) and Erik Straarup (2008) have continued to ride around Australia, setting new benchmarks. Their record-breaking rides have not received the same fanfare that surrounded Arthur, Donald and the White brothers, but it is a little bit like climbing Mount Everest. Everyone celebrated Sir Edmund Hillary and Sherpa Tenzing Norgay reaching the summit in 1953, but not necessarily those who came after them.

The current unsupported around Australia record-holder is Peter Heal, a retired public servant. He was fifty-two and a risk manager with the ACT government when he undertook his ride in 2010 on a recumbent bicycle, which places the rider in a reclining position. It took Peter just under forty-nine days to ride around Australia. Of medium height and with a wiry frame, Peter's physical appearance elicits much the same sort of reaction as Arthur's 116 years earlier.

'Somebody said I thought you'd be taller, bigger,' Peter told me as we sat in the courtyard of his home in the Canberra suburb of Duffy on a hot January afternoon. 'You've got to have the DNA to put up with being dehydrated, low on food, that sort of thing. Some people just fall apart when it gets to that.'

It was as if Peter, independent-minded and quietly adventurous, was a lineal descendant of the overlanders. Born in Melbourne, he started cycling while he was living in Adelaide as a young man. After moving to Canberra with its network of bike paths, he began to commute to work by bicycle. In 2004 he joined Audax, a long-distance cycling club which honoured Arthur and Frank by naming awards after them, and the idea of riding around Australia started 'brewing'. Like the overlanders of yesteryear, Peter crossed Australia before he circled the continent. In 2009 he rode from Perth to Sydney in just under twelve days, lowering the previous record by two days.

'I did my across Australia, thinking maybe sometime I'll do something else,' he said.

I didn't tell anybody about that. About twelve months later I thought I might do that. Because it was there. I can't think of much other reason I did it. It was there and I thought I could do it after my across Australia.

It was an adventure. It was amazing. When you think about it now. Phew! I was very lucky. I had the right weather. No disasters or anything like that that could blow you out of the water. I didn't feel threatened or anything other than by those big trucks. The Bruce Highway. There's no shoulder. It's just nuts.

I didn't think I was at risk or isolated. You knew you had to do either 150 [kilometres] between a roadhouse or 300 to get to the next roadhouse. I wasn't in desperation. It gets pretty remote up towards Fitzroy Crossing and those sort of places. But there's always cars going past. Grey nomads out there. If you ran out of water, you would only have to stand in the road and they would stop.

Peter is full of admiration for the overlanders, particularly Arthur for riding around Australia alone. 'It was amazing,' he said.

And the other thing is how would you know what was ahead of you. You might have a mud map which says here is Kimberley Station, but it wouldn't be very accurate. You're here, mate, and that's where you've got to get to. He probably had a compass, but golly, it would have been tough navigating because there wouldn't have been other people or vehicles out there.

It would be great to make a bike like theirs and go and do it like that and not use any bridges or modern roads. It would be amazing if you could. It would be good to go out there with my moustache and pistol.

The dream of the overlander is a recurring dream. But whatever long-distance rides are accomplished in the future, no one can ever repeat what Arthur Richardson, Donald Mackay and the White brothers achieved more than a century ago. As Peter Heal testified, it would be impossible to replicate the conditions of late nineteenth century Australia and re-create the danger and adventure of riding around the lonesome continent on a bicycle. The overlanders were the pioneers, blazing the trail, and their feat cannot be equalled let alone surpassed.

As we sit on our comfortable lounges and watch the highly paid and pampered riders of the Tour de France on our wide-screens, the original long-distance riders of a more innocent age deserve to be remembered and honoured for accomplishing what was truly one of the last great adventures.

The Story of a Remarkable Ride

BY A. RICHARDSON.
PERTH

PRESENTED WITH THE COMPLIMENTS OF .
THE DUNLOP PNEUMATIC TYRE CO. of Aust. Ltd.,
Melbourne, Sydney, Adelaide, Perth, Brisbane, and Christchurch (N.Z.)

ILLUSTRATION CREDITS

National Library of Australia: Arthur Richardson, *The Story of a Remarkable Ride*, The Dunlop Pneumatic Tyre Co. of Australasia, Melbourne, 1900: 126, 250, 321

Courtesy of Bruce Cameron: 10, 17, 22, 302

Courtesy of Jim Fitzpatrick: 34, 87

Museum of Applied Arts and Sciences: 70, 284 (00x05363, Photo: Marinco Kojdanovski)

Museums Victoria: 13

Noel Butlin Archives Centre / Australian National University Archives: 190

Roey Fitzpatrick: xii-xiii

State Library of New South Wales: 97 (*The N.S.W. Cyclist*, 10 May 1900, M796.505/3), 108 (*The Australian Cyclist*, 10 August 1899, Q796.505/3), 112 (*The N.S.W. Cyclist*, 31 August 1899, M796.505/3, 132 (*The Australian Cyclist*, 20 July 1899, Q796.505/3), 146 (*The Austral Wheel*, March 1898, MJ4T4), 153 (*The N.S.W. Cyclist*, 27 October 1898, M796.505/3), 178 (*The Australian Cyclist*, 30 August 1899, Q796.505/3), 212 (*Australian Cycling Annual*, 1897, M796/A)

State Library of Western Australia: 58 (Arthur Richardson on a bicycle, 1897, 000739D), 189 (*The Western Mail*, 20 May 1898), 232 (*WA Cyclist*, 9 June 1899), 268 (*The Western Mail*, 20 May 1898)